ORCHID FLOWERS / THEIR POLLINATION AND EVOLUTION

By L. VAN DER PIJL and CALAWAY H. DODSON

ORCHID FLOWERS

Their Pollination and Evolution

by

L. VAN DER PIJL

and

CALAWAY H. DODSON

Published jointly by The Fairchild Tropical Garden and the

UNIVERSITY OF MIAMI PRESS

Coral Gables, Florida

Copyright © 1966 by C. H. Dodson
Library of Congress Catalog Card Number 66-28521

Manufactured in the United States of America
Printed by Atlantic Printers and Lithographers, Inc.

PREFACE

In 1862 Charles Darwin published his book entitled "The Various Contrivances by which British and Foreign Orchids are Fertilised by Insects." It was a remarkable little book describing his personal observations on the pollination of British orchids and containing a discussion of the probable pollination mechanisms of a number of the strange and fascinating tropical orchids. The latter discussion was based upon the study of tropical orchid flowers produced in greenhouses in Europe. Darwin, unfortunately, had no way of knowing the nature of the actual pollinators of these tropical orchids and therefore extrapolated from the information available on the pollination of local wild orchids. In 1877 he published a second edition of the book and considerably augmented the portion on tropical orchids. He was able to take advantage of observations on the pollination of several tropical orchids made by Dr. Crüger of Trinidad and by Fritz Müller.

Darwin's "Origin of Species" published in 1859 overthrew the idea of independent creation of species prevalent before that time. One of his important points in that book was that "no organic being fertilises itself for a perpetuity of generations, but a cross with another individual is occasionally—perhaps at very long intervals—indispensable." In attempting to weather the storm of criticism which resulted from the publication of this unpopular viewpoint and to prove his point, Darwin undertook several lines of research. One of these involved the study of the remarkable adaptations found in the orchids which help to ensure cross-pollination. As he himself indicated, there are exceptions, but in the vast majority of instances cross-pollination was the favored system and was the rule in most of the higher orchids. He proved his point.

In 1909 a Darwin Centenary was celebrated in Cambridge. This prompted Rolfe (1909-1912) to prepare a long series of articles on the evolution of the orchids. Rolfe, however, was interested only in the morphological similarities between plants, completely neglecting the importance of floral ecology.

Several books have appeared recently celebrating the Centenary of the publication of Darwin's "Origin of Species." Most of the books briefly cite Darwin's pollination work, with R. Bell's (Editor) "Darwin's Biological Work" (1960) devoting a chapter (by H. L. K. Whitehouse) to a discussion of the general matter of cross-pollination from two other books by Darwin (1876 and 1877). His book on orchids, however, is referred to in the general preface only, though with praise as never being superseded.

With this book we intend to honor the Centenary of the publication of Darwin's important book which was an inspiration to floral ecologists of his and later times. We feel that a comprehensive account of later developments is due and appropriate after a century. The information which has become available in the past hundred years concerning the pollination of orchids is not great but in many instances enough basic observations on tropical orchids have been accomplished to make a sizeable contribution to the understanding of the reproductive dynamics of the family. By outlining and illustrating the general principles and reviewing basic trends of pollination in the Orchidaceae, including our own observations and those of other recent workers, we hope that a useful contribution can be made.

ACKNOWLEDGMENTS

We wish to express our appreciation for encouragement and constructive criticism provided by Dr. Robert Dressler of the Smithsonian Institution, Dr. Verne Grant and Dr. Lee Lenz of the Rancho Santa Ana Botanic Garden, Dr. G. Ledyard Stebbins of the University of California, Dr. Charles Michener of the University of Kansas, Dr. J. van der Vecht and Dr. D. J. Kuenen of Leiden, and Dr. B. J. D. Meeuse of the University of Washington. Much of the pollination observation and the preparation of the manuscript and illustrations was supported by the National Science Foundation. For identification of pollinators we thank the staff of the Smithsonian Institution and Dr. Karl Krombein in particular. Many identifications were kindly supplied by Padre J. S. Moure of the University of Paraná, Brazil, Dr. Paul Hurd of the University of California, and Dr. Michener. We also wish to thank the numerous persons who have forwarded information, gathered through personal observations, regarding orchid pollination. Their observations are cited in the text. All photographs were supplied by the authors unless otherwise noted.

Special thanks are due to Dr. Aaron Goldberg of the Smithsonian Institution for his advice and comment on the manuscript.

Finally it is with pleasure that we acknowledge the contribution made by Mr. G. P. Frymire to the early work in tropical America. His enthusiasm and clear insight of the significance of the phenomena observed made this work possible.

CONTENTS

CHAPTER	PAGE
1. INTRODUCTION—THE ORCHID FLOWER	1
2. THE FUNCTION AND POSITIONS OF THE LABELLUM	7
3. THE FUNCTION OF THE COLUMN	15
4. ATTRACTION IN THE FLOWER	21
5. THE POLLINATORS	27
6. ORCHIDS AND BEES	33
7. ORCHIDS AND LEPIDOPTERA	83
8. ORCHIDS AND BIRDS	91
9. ORCHIDS AND FLIES	101
10. OTHER POLLINATORS AND AUTOGAMY	123
11. MIMICRY AND DECEPTION	129
12. THE ORCHID FLOWER AS A LIVING WHOLE	143
13. SPECIATION AND NATURAL HYBRIDIZATION	163

APPENDIX

SYNOPSIS OF TAXONOMIC RELATIONS IN THE ORCHIDS . 175

LIST OF ORCHIDS AND THEIR KNOWN POLLINATORS . . 181

LITERATURE CITED 193

GLOSSARY 199

INDEX 205

"I carefully described to Huxley the shooting out of the pollinia in Catasetum, and received for an answer, 'Do you really think I can believe all that?'"

Unpublished Letter, May 17, 1868
Darwin Papers, Cambridge University Library

CHAPTER 1

Introduction—The Orchid Flower

To most persons an orchid is a colorful flower, with a large lip, surrounded by ribbons and worn as a corsage. However, the orchid enthusiast learns early in his experience that most orchids are not of that nature. The majority of the species produce small flowers which are not necessarily colorful. These orchids, sometimes called "botanicals"—often with scorn by the grower of hybrid orchids, are eagerly sought after by the true orchid enthusiast. The family is noted for an abundance of kinds with a seemingly unending array of strange and often grotesque variations. Perhaps this explains why the enthusiasm of the orchid collector does not become satiated. The collector of other groups of plants sooner or later acquires the majority of the different kinds in the group of his choice and then finds his interest lagging for lack of something new. This "early decline" does not affect the orchid enthusiast for there are probably more than 20,000 species in the family and he can collect to his heart's desire. The orchid family is one of the largest, and we estimate that it comprises nearly 7% of all species of flowering plants.

The strange and complex flowers of a *Stanhopea* or *Coryanthes* nearly defy description. The sensitivity of the lip of *Pterostylis* and other orchids causing the lip to clasp tightly against the column when irritated mechanically seems incredible.

NOTE—Many generic names probably unfamiliar to the reader will be encountered in later pages. In order to introduce some clarity we have included a scheme of classification of the orchid genera and figures comparing higher categories of the system proposed here with those of previous authors. This information is found in the Appendix on pages 176-180. Since the time of Darwin several nomenclatorial changes on the generic level have been made in the orchids. Names as Darwin knew them often have been included in parentheses in the list of orchids and their pollinators which is also contained in the Appendix.

A formidable number of author citations would be required to cover all of the notes and brief comments on pollination of European orchids which have been published in European journals in the past hundred and fifty years. Therefore, unless they are of specific importance in the text, we have tended to omit them and refer to Darwin's book, Knuth-Loew (1898-1905), or Ziegenspeck (1928).

The mechanical pollen-throwing mechanism based on leverage-tension in *Catasetum* is remarkably precise and complex. Is it possible that all of the extraordinary characteristics of these and other orchid flowers have a function in the reproductive biology of their particular group? What is the reason for the evolution of so many strikingly different floral forms within a single family? If such diversity and extremity are advantageous in the evolution of an obviously successful family why haven't other families followed the same pattern? What made all this possible?

We don't pretend to have all the answers to those questions but we do believe that the pollinators of the orchids have played a major role in their evolution. To us, it seems only logical that a family which was probably already highly "pollinator oriented" at its inception should develop characteristics which would augment evolution based on complex pollination mechanisms, thereby effectively reducing hybridization and consequent reblending of differentiating populations in early stages of the development of the species. However, other families which were just as "pollinator oriented" as the orchids have not developed extremes. Perhaps this is why they tend to remain small in numbers. It seems possible that the particular specializations of the orchid flower have lent impetus to rapid evolution based on pollinators after achieving some sort of "breakthrough." In the following pages we will analyze the characters of the orchid flower and compare them with an uncomplicated flower such as might be encountered in the lower monocots or dicots. We will postulate what a primitive orchid flower must have been like (no verifiable fossils exist). In later chapters we will discuss a considerable series of observations of pollination of orchids by natural agents. In this manner we hope to demonstrate the reasons for our conclusions.

THE ORCHID FLOWER AS COMPARED WITH OTHER FLOWERS

The primary characters which distinguish the orchids as a group are found in the flower. In Figure 1 we compare an uncomplicated flower with a generalized orchid flower. Starting from the bottom of the illustration of the "ordinary" flower we encounter the stem which supports it called the pedicel. Directly above, and at the base of the flower itself, is a whorl of green, leaf-like organs called sepals. Above and inside the sepals is a whorl of colored petals. These are the asexual parts and are developed to protect the flower or to attract a pollinator. Inside (also arranged in whorls) are the sexual portions of the flower. First are the stamens, which consist of a filament (the slender stalk which supports the anther) and the anther (usually containing four sacs filled with loose pollen grains). There may be several whorls of stamens. In the center of the flower is the pistil, which is composed of an enlarged portion called the ovary topped by a stalk-like style with the stigma at its apex.

The pollen in the anther is powdery and is usually carried from the anther of one flower to the stigma of another by a pollinating agent. Once on the stigma of another flower the pollen grains germinate and produce pollen tubes which grow down through the style into the ovary. The ovary contains a series of small structures called ovules. When a pollen tube reaches an ovule it enters and two male gametes pass into the ovule. There one unites with the egg cell and produces a zygote. This cell divides in a preordained manner and develops into an embryo. The other parts of the ovule develop into the accessory portions and the whole is called a seed. If conditions are favorable the seed will germinate and develop into a mature plant.

The "uncomplicated" flower just discussed would be typical of the primary division of flowering plants called dicotyledons in which the sepals are usually green and number from two to many, the petals likewise number from one to many, and the stamens can be very abundant. Other characters separate them from the monocotyledons, to which the orchids belong. The monocots, as they are commonly called, usually have the flower parts either in three or multiples of three, i.e., three sepals, three petals, six stamens, three carpels, etc. The lily and amaryllis families are associated with the orchids and in some respects are comparable.

The description is of a generalized flower and it must be kept in mind that all manner of variations may be found. Often the variations are such that the families may be characterized by them. Our generalized flower is not to be considered as a primitive flower. It is simply a flower composed of the sepals, petals and essential parts found in most flowers. Primitive angiosperm flowers were apparently similar in many respects and will be discussed more extensively in Chapter 12.

The flower shown in Figure 1 is a generalized orchid flower, being neither primitive nor advanced. Starting at the bottom is the pedicel which supports the flower. Here the ovary, with its ovules, seems an integral part of the pedicel. The orchid flower (and many others) has an inferior ovary. The sepals and petals are similar, often highly colored and in sets of three. One petal is developed as a

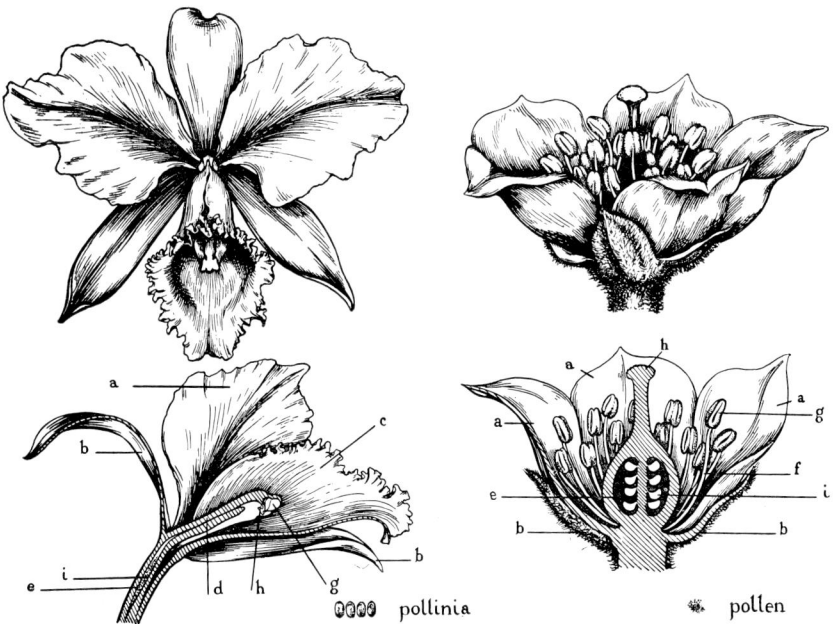

FIG. 1. Comparison of a generalized orchid flower with an uncomplicated flower. a. Petal. b. Sepal. c. Petal transformed into a landing platform and called a lip. d. Column composed of united pistil and stamens. e. Ovary. f. Filament of a stamen. g. Anther. h. Stigma. i. Ovule. (Drawing by P. Fawcett.)

landing platform for the pollinator and is called a labellum or lip. The sexual portions of the orchid flower are quite different from our "ordinary" flower and tend to characterize the family. The filaments, anthers, style and stigma are reduced in number and fused into a single structure called the column. In one relatively small group (the lady-slipper orchids) two anthers are present, one on each side of the column (members of one primitive subfamily, the Apostasioidae, have three anthers). The majority of the orchids retain only a single anther at the apex of the column.

THE PARTS OF THE ORCHID FLOWER

1. *The ovary*

In the orchid the ovary is composed of three carpels. The carpels have fused so that the only outward evidence of their existence is the three ridges on the outside of the seed pods. The mature seed pod does not open along the lines of juncture but rather down the middle between them. The ovules, which are arranged along three ridges (the placentae) inside the ovary, do not develop until some time after the flower has been pollinated, thereby contributing to the long delay between pollination and opening of a ripened pod.

The lip is oriented upward in the bud but as it later develops twisting takes place in the pedicel or ovary so that the lip is usually oriented downward by the time the flower opens. This process is called resupination and will be discussed at length in Chapter 2.

2. *Sepals and petals*

In most of the monocots the sepals and petals are so similar that they are not distinguished and fall under the collective term, perianth (or may be called tepals). In the orchids, however, they are usually quite distinct and are therefore termed sepals and petals. The petal opposite the fertile stamen is called the lip, as we mentioned above. Often two or even all three of the sepals are joined and the lip, other petals or the sepals may be attached to the column for some distance. One of the characteristic differences between the orchid family and other advanced monocots is that the fertile stamen or stamens, that is, the one or more which are not reduced, are all on one side of the flower, opposite the lip. This makes the flower bilaterally symmetrical. It can be cut down the middle on one line so as to present mirror images.

3. *Nectaries*

There are several types of nectaries in the orchids, including extra-floral types which secrete nectar on the outside of the buds or inflorescence while the flowers are developing. These often have functional significance and will be discussed on page 22. Shallow cup-like nectaries at the base of the lip are common. Some nectaries are in long spurs produced either from the joined sepals or from the base of the lip. Members of the *Epidendrum* complex have long tubular nectaries embedded in the base of the flower alongside the ovary. Nectaries on the side-lobes of the lip are known and general nectar secretion along the central groove of the lip is common.

4. *The column*

In most of the orchids the stamens and style are completely joined into a single organ, the column. However, in *Cypripedium, Apostasia* and some higher orchids such as *Spiranthes* they are only partially united. In some cases an extension of the base of the column with the lip attached at its apex forms the column foot. In many instances this structure exudes nectar.

5. *The anther*

In most of the orchids the anther is a cap-like structure located at the apex of the column. In some of the more primitive orchids the anther is superficially similar to that of a lily or amaryllis. In *Habenaria* and its allies the anther projects beyond the apex of the column but is thoroughly attached. Sometimes the two halves of the anther are widely separated and have led some botanists to believe that they represent two anthers. In one subfamily, Cypripedioideae, two anthers do occur and are placed on each side of the column. These are usually considered as primitive.

6. *Pollinia*

In most orchids the pollen grains are bound together by viscin threads in masses, or pollinia. Two basic kinds exist: one has soft, mealy packets bound together to a viscin core by viscin threads, and is called sectile; the other kind forms a series from soft mealy pollinia, through more compact masses, to hard wax-like pollinia. *Goodyera, Habenaria* and *Spiranthes* have the former and the latter are found in *Sobralia, Phajus, Cattleya,* and *Oncidium* and become harder in that order. The hard, waxy pollinia usually have a small amount of mealy pollen with viscin strands which attach the pollinia to each other or to a "viscidium." This portion of the pollinium is termed the caudicle.

7. *The stigma*

The stigma is usually a shallow depression on the inner side of the column. It is composed of the three stigmatic lobes found in the typical monocot flower; however, they are thoroughly grown together. Faint lines can often be seen on the surface of the stigma, dividing it into three parts. The stigma produces a sticky, sugary solution in which the pollinia are deposited. The pollen grains germinate in that solution and grow into the column. Lobes of the column often close around the stigma shortly after pollination.

In the majority of the orchids a portion of one of the three lobes of the stigma is specialized and forms a structure called the rostellum. Some primitive species have no rostellum and the pollinia simply stick to stigmatic liquid, which is first smeared on the back of the insect. In many orchids the rostellum sticks down between the stigma and the anther in the form of a flap. As the visiting insect begins to back out of the flower it brushes the rostellum, which is covered with a sticky liquid. The pollinia are then picked up from the anther and stick to the insect's body. A further specialization occurs in more advanced orchids where the caudicles of the pollinia are already attached to the rostellum and a portion of it comes off as a sticky pad called a viscidium. In the most advanced genera a strap of non-sticky tissue from the column connects the pollinia to the viscidium. This band of tissue is called the stipe and should not be confused with the caudicles which are derived from the anther. Orchids which have a stipe also have caudicles which connect the pollinia to the apex of the stipe.

The presence of the labellum as a landing platform for insect pollinators and the reduction of the stamens and pistil of the flower to a single structure, the column, is certainly the apex of floral adaptation to insects as pollinating agents. Once achieved, this combination provides a foundation for all manner of specializations for attraction of specific pollinators. The development of the strange and complex reorganizations which are found in the flowers of many orchid genera are directly attributable to evolutionary forces interplaying on the basis of such a preexisting foundation.

CHAPTER 2

The Function and Positions of the Labellum

In our discussion of the flower in Chapter 1 we pointed out that the labellum is initially the adaxial, median, inner petal. The labellum originally occupied the upperside of the flower in the primordial orchid—and still does so in buds. The great majority of orchid species, however, have the labellum—through one process or another—turned downward during the development of the flower into what is called a resupinate position. The labellum offers a landing place or provides other advantages, such as positioning the insect for the deposition of pollen on its dorsal surface (termed nototriby). Nototriby is commonly associated with hymenopteran pollinators (with the exception of certain bees, e.g. Megachilidae). The derived position may be genetically fixed in the species so that the flowers are resupinate in relation to the axis of the inflorescence. The resupination may also be influenced by the weight of the flowers on a slender inflorescence, causing it to nod or be pendant so that the effect of the resupination may disappear with respect to the total aspect of the inflorescence. In other cases the flower achieves the reverse position physiologically (actively) by itself, responding negatively to gravitation, so that the resupination disappears when gravitational forces are excluded, as in Goebel's (1920) experiments. In addition, resupination may be considered primarily from the standpoint of the column (i.e., twisting of the column in *Mormodes* and *Satyrium*).

A scheme of the ways in which resupination and its opposite, non-resupination, can occur is presented below:

I. THE RESUPINATE POSITION (Labellum below).

    a. Nodding; the bending over of the top of the inflorescence so that the labellum turns down (Cypripedioideae, Fig. 2,Ia). (*Apostasia*, *Ophrys* and *Serapias* bend back alongside the rachis.)

FIG. 2. The resupinate position of the orchid flower. Ia. Nodding over at top of the inflorescence (*Cypripedium*). Ib. Hanging inflorescence (*Cymbidium*). Ic. Torsion of the pedicel (normal type, *Cattleya*). Id. Torsion in the inflorescence rachis (*Lycaste*). Ie. Bends in flower parts (*Satyrium*). (Drawing by P. Fawcett.)

FIG. 3. The non-resupinate position of the orchid flower. IIa. Absence of torsion in erect flowers (*Satyrium*). IIb. Reverse torsion in upper and lower parts of the gynaecium (*Ceratandra*). IIc. Torsion of 360° in the pedicel (*Angraecum eburneum*). IId. Torsion of 180° in hanging flowers (*Cycnoches*). IIe. Lack of torsion in hanging flowers with a 180° bend in the pedicel (*Gongora*). (Drawing by P. Fawcett.)

b. Hanging inflorescences (*Cymbidium*, Fig. 2, Ib).

c. In erect flowers through torsion, primarily of the pedicel, but also of the gynaecium (normal type, Fig. 2, Ic).

d. In other erect flowers through torsion in or underneath the inflorescence rachis (*Lycaste aromatica*, Fig. 2, Id).

e. Partial resupination by bends in flower parts (*Satyrium*, Fig. 2, Ie).

II. THE NON-RESUPINATE POSITION (Labellum above).

a. In erect flowers by absence of torsion (*Satyrium*, Fig. 3, IIa) or reverse torsion in upper and lower parts of gynaecium (*Ceratandra*, Fig. 3, IIb)

b. In erect flowers by torsion in the pedicel or gynaecium of 360° (*Angraecum eburneum*, *Malaxis* spp., Fig. 3, IIc).

c. In hanging or nodding flowers, 180° torsion (*Cycnoches* and *Cirrhaea*, Fig. 3, IId).

d. In hanging or nodding flowers, 180° bend without torsion in the pedicel (*Gongora*, Fig. 3, IIe).

III. A certain transverse symmetry can be reached by torsion of parts (column and lip) to opposite sides (*Haemaria*, *Macodes* and *Mormodes*). The ecological reasons for this in the first two genera are discussed on p. 89 and the third, *Mormodes* will be discussed on p. 66 (Fig. 4).

Let us now discuss the importance of these phenomena—and labellum formation in general. We will begin with the original position (refer to the diagram of the hypothetical flower in Fig. 5) and discuss the morpho-physiological aspect.

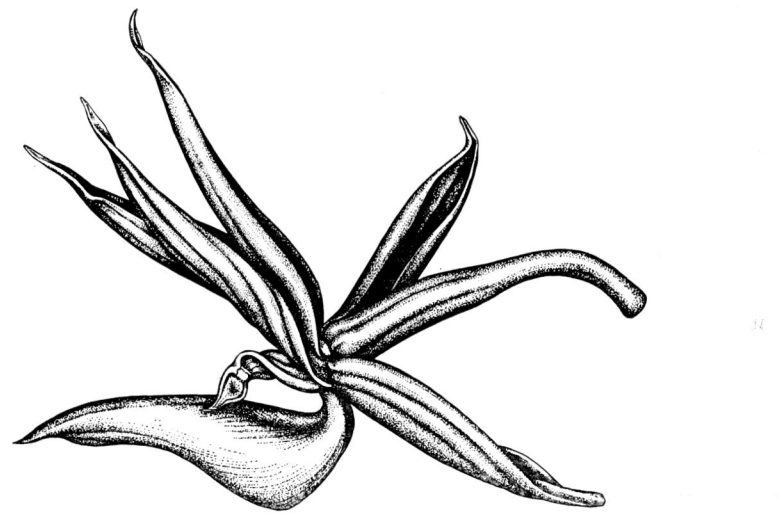

FIG. 4. Transverse symmetry in the flower by torsion of flower parts to opposite sides in *Mormodes*. (Drawing by P. Fawcett.)

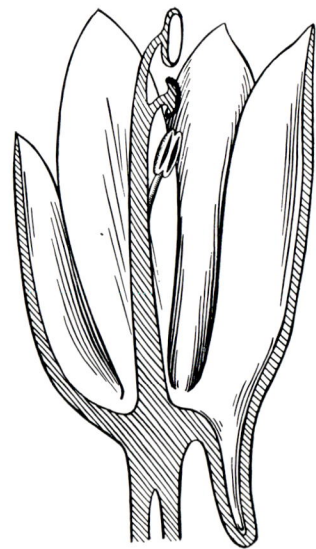

FIG. 5. Diagram of a hypothetical, primitive orchid flower. (Drawing by P. Fawcett.)

MORPHO-PHYSIOLOGICAL ASPECT

As the inner whorl of the perianth tended to become corolla-like, one of the inner tepals expanded to form a landing platform. It was natural that it should be one of the median tepals. This alone might indicate which became the actual labellum-tepal. In order that insects could fit between them, the large labellum-tepal needed to be placed in juxtaposition to the adaxial stamens (these were already dominant in the ancestral stock and even now are so in the Apostasioideae) and finally to the single stamen remaining after the process of centralization. That stamen was, of necessity, the one on the far side of the style so that the style might also stand in juxtaposition to the prospective labellum (we may already accept a connection between this stamen and the style at this point). In *Neuwiedia*, of the Apostasioideae, all three stamens on the far side of the style are still fertile (Fig. 6). In addition, the stamen should preferably be a median one, therefore the median, outer and lowermost stamen was naturally indicated. The combination of the tepal and stamen mentioned is perfect in providing a precision mechanism for bees which have exacting space requirements. It still suffers, however, in regard to higher bees (with nototribic tendencies) by the wrong position of the whole due to the inherent drawback of the trimerous condition. This could be remedied by resupination.

If two stamens remain in a flower with two exits from a trap-labellum (already inverted by a bend as in I-a of the resupination scheme above), the two lower ones of the inner whorl would be better oriented—as was realized in the Cypripedioideae. It is curious that in a much later phase, *Satyrium* (see discussion below) developed two entrances to the flower. This resulted in the placement of the two portions of the anther so far apart on the sides that some authors (cf. Garay, 1960) considered them as separate stamens.

The Zingiberaceae, in a parallel zygomorphic development based on the same principle, averted the difficulty of trimery in a different manner, viz., by developing a "labellum" out of two or three lower stamens and sparing the median one of the inner circle. This at once resulted in nototriby.

ECOLOGICAL ASPECTS

Now, let us discuss the ecological aspects of the function of the labellum. Were the first orchids of the flag-type, with the labellum erect as a showpiece, as in the present day Papilionaceae, with sternotribic (deposition of pollen on the ventral surface) pollen presentation on bees? Grant (1950) suggested that orchids are derived from bird-pollinated ancestors. The inferior ovary and the superior position of the labellum therefore might be considered as remnants. That is, the inferior ovary serves as protection against the hard bill, and the superior position of the labellum is indicative of the flag-type. The indications for early pollination by birds in the family are weak, however, and the basic zygomorphy and reductions in the flower parts do not plead for it.

Were these characteristics derived from moth pollination? One is tempted to think of the prevalence of sphingophilous flowers in the lower habenarias in connection with this possibility. The labellum in those plants is generally resupinate, however, and when non-resupinate, rarely so by primitive absence of torsion (mechanism II-a).

In the primitive genus *Thelymitra* (the sun-orchids of Australia), which has little differentiation in the perianth, two upturned tepals have colored dots and are the showy parts. The labellum, however, is already resupinate and—though details about pollination, torsion and the value of the curious columnar callus are lacking—it must result in nototriby. In the ancestors of higher orchids, the Apostasioideae, the labellum is little differentiated, but the deficient ecological literature on them gives the impression that (at least in *Neuwiedia*) visitors land on the downturned labellum. This also requires investigation.

Or were the first orchids provided with pendant inflorescences (mechanism I-b), so that the labellum could function as it was? In some epiphytes, such as

FIG. 6. Somewhat diagrammatic sketch of the flower of *Neuwiedia*. (Drawing by P. Fawcett.)

certain species of *Cymbidium*, this provides a simple solution. For the original, terrestrial plants, however, only mechanism I-a (nodding), as in the Cypripedioideae, is suitable. Was resupination then made necessary by the change to an erect position, viz., from flag-type to gullet-type? A change from sternotribic to nototribic bees may have been a strong influence here.

In the Zingiberaceae we find a reverse change. The gullet-type of flowers, e.g., those of *Alpinia*, *Curcuma* and *Roscoea*, have nototribic pollination even to the extent of having Salvia-like anthers without need of torsion. From these the sphingophilous flag-type, e.g., *Hedychium* and *Globba*, apparently developed secondarily.

Since most of the torsion in resupinate flowers occurs in the pedicel, rather than in the gynoecium, little danger of interference with dehiscence of the fruit occurs. In some cases the gynoecium unwinds slightly to provide a straight fruit.

As the mechanisms in the scheme demonstrate, and as was said before, the non-resupinate position is not just primitive but can be clearly adaptive. For older discussions of this point see Ames (1938) and Goebel (1920) who mention species of *Arpophyllum*, *Disa*, *Epipogium*, *Nephelophyllum*, *Nigritella*, *Oberonia*, *Satyrium*, *Angraecum*, *Malaxis*, *Spiranthes* and *Epidendrum*. Goebel—who is otherwise averse to ecological explanations—points out that in some species of the sphingophilous genus *Angraecum* (e.g., *A. eburneum*, Fig. 3, IIc the non-resupinate position, mechanism II-c) may result in taking away an obstacle to the hovering visitor and in providing a visual aid of the flag-type.

In *Disa*, e.g., *D. uniflora*, function and importance of the labellum have been changed by adaptation to visits by butterflies (confirmed by observations). No wonder it is small and often upturned. In some species the flower is entirely reorganized (see Vogel, 1954: 117-120; 1959: Fig. 63).

Vogel (1959) gave a fine analysis of the flowers of *Satyrium*. The upturned labellum with a double spur has the function of an upper lip. The side of the column nearest the lower lip is now out of reach. Nototribic pollination is nevertheless obtained by resupination of the column only, with a curve bringing anther and stigma to the side of the new lower lip. This solution, together with the presence of two spurs, if applied to many different visitors, might mean the start of a new development in the family.

In some species of *Cryptostylis* the non-resupination is a special adaption in connection with pseudocopulation. *Epipogium aphyllum* seems simply to make things difficult for its bumblebee pollinators, according to Rohrbach (1886). In the *Stanhopea* alliance and the Catasetinae non-resupination (by the detour of mechanism II-d) is clearly functional in making inverted, intoxicated bees slide or fall downward, as described on p. 70. The genus *Catasetum* and its allies usually have resupinate male flowers, with the anther above, throwing the pollinaria downwards, and non-resupinate female flowers with the receptive column below (Pl. IIIb-d). In the latter situation the position of the labellum seems merely a consequence of the floral mechanism.

After this ecological analysis of resupination it is easy to deal with Nelsson's (1954, p. 209) all too simple "anti-teleological," "causal" explanation. This explanation neglects the functions of the flower and also regards resupination as just a consequence of physiological processes (which is in itself a useful approach for treatment of certain aspects of the question). He ascribed the resupination of the labellum to pure physiology and believed that the equilibrium of food supplies was disturbed by the labellum in its original position. That is, the antagonism of a genotypical strong force toward higher parts favored by the organization-type of the family to the physiological, geotropically induced, stronger development of auxins and the greater food claim of the lower part. The resupination would bring the labellum down so that the two forces could now work together.

We would like to point out that this is not a causal explanation, but is also "teleology" of a physiological kind. Such a special physiological sensitivity is not an explanation, as it simply returns to the question of how this special property is to be explained. Nelsson himself admits that his physiological explanation is insufficient when a large labellum is not resupinate and when a labellum turns 360°. We feel that the position of labellum and column are of manifold origin and clearly directed or "aimed" at special functions, overriding ordinary physiology. The resupination in parts of organs (*Satyrium*) and the difference between resupination of male and female flowers (*Catasetum*) also prove the inadequacy of "just physiology."

The lip is not only the bearer of the functions of landing, of providing a general showpiece and of determination of dimensions, but also of guidance toward the center. The guidance is clear from its special form, color, dots, and stripes, etc. More important, the labellum, with spurs and callus, is almost the only source of food (cf. p. 22). The discussion of such secondary structures and appendages, however, — as the variety in form of all sepals, the motility and sensitivity of the labellum, and its subdivision into a basal hypochile and a terminal epichile—falls within later chapters.

CHAPTER 3
The Function of the Column

In discussing the function of the column we must again turn to the diagram of the hypothetical flower in Figure 5. The function of pollen deposition became as we saw, centralized in one anther in one precise place, in the median plane opposite the labellum. Being introrse, this anther deposits pollen on the most advantageous side of the visitor, considering efficiency in reception and deposition. This precision is also expressed by a tendency to deposit the pollen as one mass, the pollinarium. This is in reality "a dangerous gambling-mechanism of a long-term strategist." In this "precision-gambling" there is at the same time ultimate efficiency. If the pollinium is actually delivered only one visit is required to fertilize thousands of ovules. The pollen is no longer deposited loosely with a chance of wastage or of its being consumed.

Efficiency in pollen reception also increased. In ordinary flowers the stigma remains separate in space from the stamens. In orchids there is centralization. The single anther and stigma (and thus their function) were centralized with the deposition of pollinaria by an over-hanging anther on top and reception occurring underneath. Stamen and style are fused into one organ, the column or gynostemium. Thus both functions are accomplished during one visit. This situation can be seen in a primordial phase in the Apostasioideae (see Fig. 6), where the fusion is not complete. The two side stamens are fertile and the pollen still free and granular in *Apostasia*.

Anther and stigma remain separated by the sterile top of the style or the sterile portion of the stigma, which usually changes into an important organ, the rostellum. This sometimes extends over the stigma, preventing self-pollination. In some lower forms such as *Neottia, Cephalanthera, Caladenia,* and *Listera,* the stigma forms a special viscid disc or viscidium which may be single or in pairs and is sometimes covered by a fold of the column before the visit. The fold has been

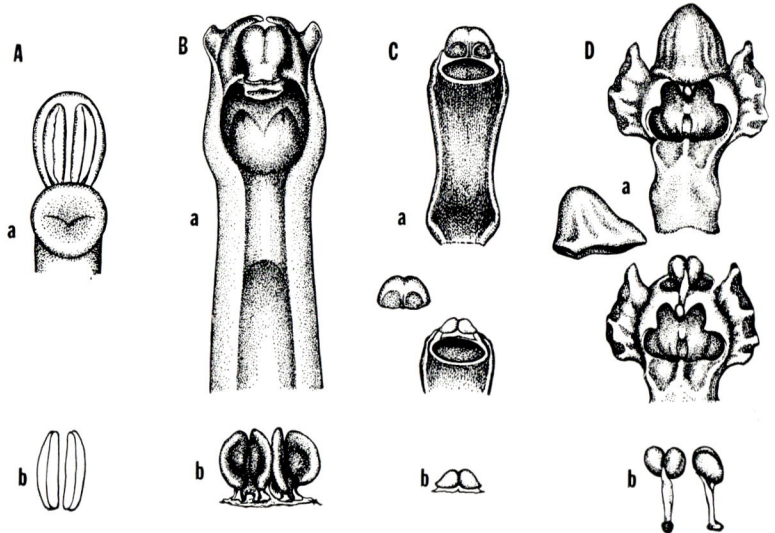

FIG. 7. Column arrangement and pollinarium organization in four groups of orchids. A. Neottieae. a. Column. b. Pollinia. B. *Cattleya*. a. Column. b. Pollinia with caudicles at base. C. *Cymbidium*. a. Two views of column, one with the anther cap removed. b. Pollinia attached to viscidium. D. *Oncidium*. a. Two views of column, one with anther cap removed. b. Two views of pollinarium showing pollinia attached to sterile stipe, which is attached to the viscidium. (Drawing by P. Fawcett.)

called "the bursicle" by some authors. For higher groups of orchids the sticky mass helps in the transport of the pollinarium as a refinement in coadaptive integration. The viscidium (or unset cement) is sometimes freely exposed, sometimes more or less explosively freed by a touch of the visitor (e.g., *Neottia, Listera, Spiranthes* spp. and the Catasetinae).

In some orchids the pollen is still granular. It is powdery in *Cephalanthera* and other primitive Neottioideae such as *Thelymitra*, also more or less so in the Vanillinae and others, where the mass can be divided for subsequent visits. The powderyness is very clear in the Cypripedioideae, an ancient sideline. Loose pollen also occurs in *Pterostylis* (the Greenhood of Australia), where mealy pollen may be a regression for dispersal by very small midges weighing only 1 mg.

In higher forms the pollen grains are not just united by viscin—elastic threads of tapetal origin—but they form a hard, waxy mass, divided into a number of pollinia. Pollinia may, in the first phase, be devoid of further apparatus for transport (Neottieae, Fig. 7A). The first evidence of better adaptation for transport is the development of a caudicle—a specialized part of the pollinium with concentrated threads (*Cattleya*, Fig. 7B). Some authors distinguished an appendicle (from sporogenous tissues) and a frenicle (from the tapetum).

Often the pollinia are directly connected to the viscidium (*Cymbidium*, Fig. 7C). This may occur at the base or the apex. Acrotony and basitony are unreliable criteria used in some classification systems. In *Thelymitra*, for example, both modes occur. Sometimes there is a special connection between pollinium and viscidium, the strap-like stipe (the "pedicel" of Darwin), composed of sterile tissue. The entire complex—pollinia, stipe, and viscidium—is called the pollinarium and is transported as such in derived forms in the Vandeae (e.g., *Oncidium*, Fig. 7D).

We remarked above that pre-orchid flowers had already reached centralization of female organs, with one stigma. We do not know whether in the Lilliflorae the three stigma lobes serve as one unit for all ovules or remain functionally apart, each serving its own locule. In the Apostasioideae there are no distinct stigma lobes and the stigma serves all three carpels equally well. When some of the stigma lobes become reduced such integration is necessary anyhow. Perhaps the disappearance of septa in orchids must be considered—as a new phenomenon in monocotyledons—to be regulated in this respect.

There has been much discussion on the morphological nature of the column, its anther and other organs. The rostellum may have developed independently in separate groups of orchids. Doubts as to its nature make taxonomy based on the rostellum difficult. In the structure of pollinaria—the basis of Schlechter's classification system—much convergence also may be hidden, as we shall demonstrate by showing many parallelisms within the family. But as our book is not meant solely for professional botanists, we shall preferably keep to functions.

The numbers of pollen grains must be correlated with the number of ovules (or the reverse). In *Orchis mascula*, Darwin counted 120,000 pollen grains in one pollinarium and 6,200 ovules in the ovary. The packing in one unit thus has two aspects: a) on the receptive side the fertilization of very numerous ovules in one visit, b) the deposition of the unit as an "all-or-none" precision effort in transport by the right pollinator at the right place. As pointed out in the general summary of differentiation (Chapter 12), the functions of seed dispersal and pollen dispersal are not always coupled. Amidst all this luxury there is economy in pollinia.

In the lower orchids pollinaria do not adhere (or do not adhere firmly) to the visitor at entrance but are firmly attached when it leaves. In some higher orchids the pollinarium is attached upon entrance and during transport the stipe can bend, directing the pollinia straight into the stigma on the following visit. The lapse of time in transport varies, as does the time needed for hardening of the glue. For a discussion of the pollinaria-ejecting Catasetinae see p. 57. We will not discuss in detail the various changes which occur in the pollinaria between reception by the pollinator and their deposition*. Darwin discussed this phase extensively and we have little to add other than to point out that the changes have two different and important functions. First, in many species of the Orchideae and the Vandinae, the stipe must depress in order for the pollinia to line up with the stigma. This occurs at varying rates of speed from almost instantly to several hours duration. Second, in a number of species, rapid torsion of the stipe tends to prevent the pollination of another flower from the same inflorescence. After a period of time, with the pollinator presumably flying on to another plant, the stipe straightens and deposition can occur (*Mormodes* and *Cycnoches*, Fig. 41).

---

*The terms pollen-deposition and pollen-presentation seem ambiguous. The two oppositie terms, deposition and reception may indeed be used for both flower and animal, an analogy that is of bookkeeping by business firms. The incomings and outgoings of firm A may refer in a reverse sequence to firm B. The context seems to make things so clear that bookkeeping has not been handicapped by just two terms. In the same way, pollen-deposition by the flower is pollen-reception for the insect and vice-versa.

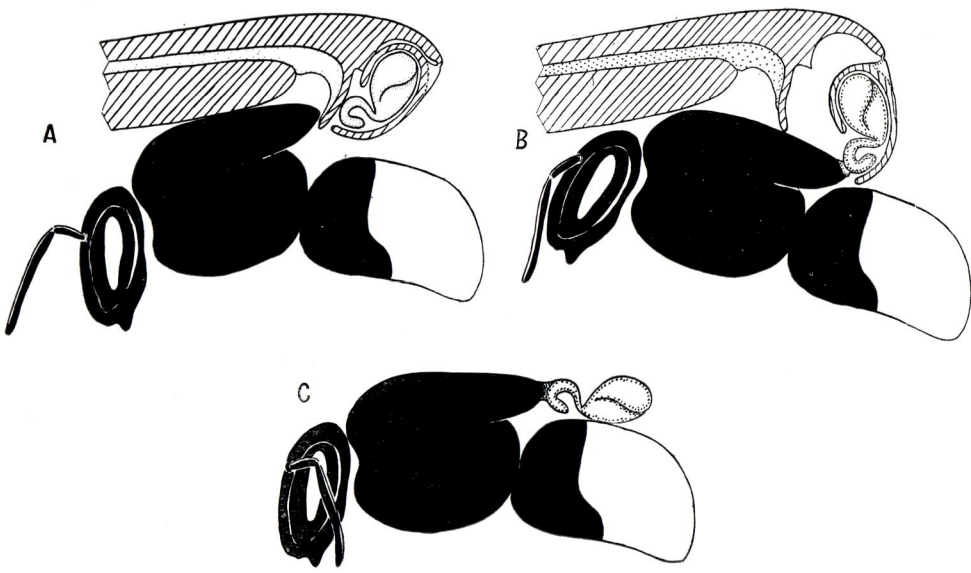

FIG. 8. Mechanism for attachment of pollinarium in a simple bee-pollinated orchid flower. A. Position of bee in relation to the column after the bee has completely entered the flower. B. As the bee backs out, the dorsal thorax pushes against the rostellar flap and sticky liquid from the stigma cements the base of the pollinarium to the bee. C. Position of the pollinarium as the bee flies to another flower. (Drawing by G. P. Frymire.)

Proceeding to the receptive aspect, the stigma is usually sticky and holds the incoming pollinia. In some cases of plants with pollen not having elaborate transport contrivances (e.g., *Cephalanthera, Sobralia, Cattleya,* and others), first the stigmatic fluid is smeared over the visitor so that the pollen can stick to it (Figs. 8 and 9). The absence of real viscidia and rostellum is considered as primitive in simple Neottioideae. The curious female column in *Cycnoches* (Fig. 10) strips the pollinia from the stipe, attached to the falling bee, by special notches near the stigma, which itself is dry.

In the Catasetinae and Stanhopeinae, the functions of deposition and reception of pollen became separated again, leading to dichogamy (separation in time) and unisexuality (separation in space). We shall explain the reason for this departure from the one-visit method of the family on p. 52.

The stigmatic fluid sometimes contains a mass of loose cells (*Coelogyne, Dendrobium,* Molisch, 1930). We do not know if this also may be used as food but it seems highly unlikely and all current observations would indicate that it is not. The same holds true for the callus and hair tufts on the column of some orchids (*Thelymitra*). Such appendages (auricles) are usually considered as rudimentary stamens in the Orchidinae. In *Thelymitra* they are known as "stelidia" (plumed structures which may play a role in pollination). The "glands" near its base in *Calochilus* (as in *Ophrys*) are not glands but "eyes." The function of the glistening "tabula infrastigmatica" in *Oncidium* is apparently associated with pollination by bees which grasp it with their mandibles. Also, the imperfect flowers in the group *Heterantha* of this genus may serve as food but this seems doubtful from what is known of the pollination of similar members of the genus. The presence of raphids (bundles of sharp needles) in the column may have the function of protecting this precious organ against being eaten by gnawing visitors. However, in the Andes, Scarabid beetles (*Macrodactylus* sp.) eat pollen, column, lip and other tepals of many orchids indiscriminately and without hesitation.

The column may have other secondary, more physiological functions. It regulates the provision with, and the transport of, ergastic substances for the belated growth of ovules, which occurs only after pollination. The column also transports substances that are toxic to the petals, that stop the production of fragrances and that close the stigma. This group of phenomena, to be discussed more fully on p. 159, have been called "a dangerous gambling on one card." We mention them here because they not only delay growth of ovules until pollination is insured, but because they also affect pollination ecology. They restrict the visits of scarce pollinators by causing rapid cessation of attraction and prevent unnecessarily prolonged florescence.

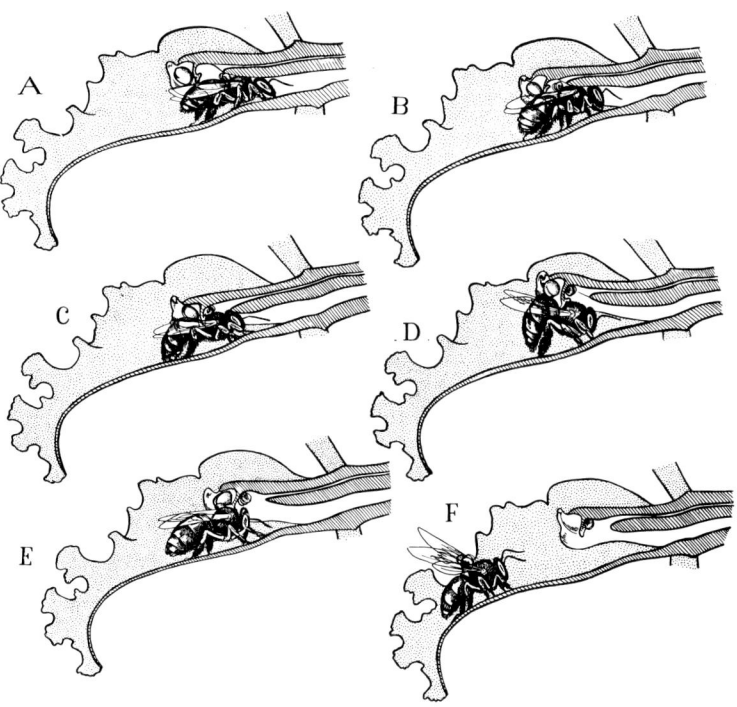

FIG. 9. Pollination mechanism for a simple bee-pollinated orchid flower such as a *Cattleya*. A. The bee, carrying pollinia from another flower, entering the flower. B. Bee starts to back out; pollinia move into the stigmatic cavity. C. Pollinia on the back of the bee come in contact with the stigmatic fluid as the thorax of the bee contacts the flap of the rostellum. D. Bee forces backward to pass the flap of the rostellum, leaving the pollinia on the stigma and rocking back the anther cap of the flower. E. The flap of the rostellum wipes sticky liquid on the thorax of the bee and the caudicles of the pollinia of the flower become attached as the bee backs farther from the flower. F. The bee begins to fly, carrying a new set of pollinia after pollinating the flower with the set of pollinia brought from a previous flower. (Drawing by P. Fawcett.)

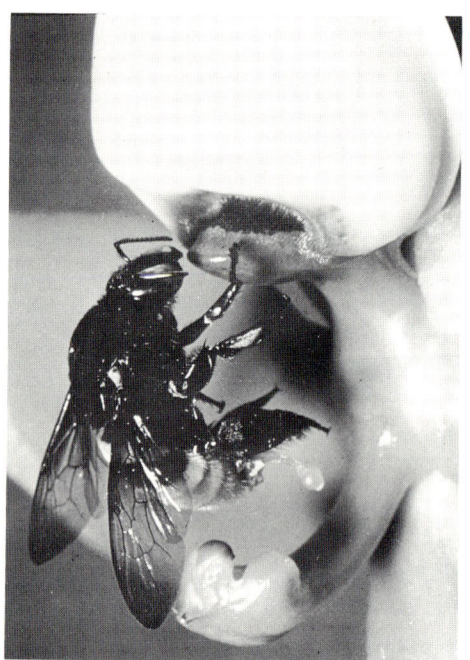

FIG. 10. Female flower of *Cycnoches warszewiczii* showing the thick column with grooves into which the round pollinia slide.

CHAPTER 4

Attraction in the Flower

We shall use the term "attraction" somewhat loosely. Zoologists might distinguish signals that advertize from food substances associated with them which offer the real recompense. The one, however, is primary in time, the other in importance. Consequently we shall not consider one more important than the other. Often, moreover, in the orchids, there is no final food, only the signal itself acting on instincts—which condition we call "deceit."

NECTAR

Orchids as a group have nectar as the major attractant, whereas pollen, the protein-rich food in lower families, has been withdrawn. This was, as we saw, tied to the exactness of pollination, but it means at the same time that orchids can no longer provide sole sustenance for the pollinator and must rely indirectly on other flowers in the biotope to maintain visitors. For butterflies, moths and birds, this is no particular problem, nor to some flies, but it is to most syrphid flies. For lower Hymenoptera with a mixed diet the inability to obtain pollen from orchids is not of much consequence. Also, for social, polytropic Hymenoptera it is not so important as long as other pollen sources are present. Nevertheless it is not surprising that orchids tend to provide other, stronger enticements for Hymenoptera with narrower, oligotropic tastes. Nectar then remains a sweet delicacy and the switch to other luxuries for the satisfaction of special instincts could follow.

Nectar is not produced from septal glands in the orchids and it appears that this condition was either left in the basal stock of the Liliiflorae from which the orchids arose or disappeared with the septa. Reminiscent of them (implying no relationship) are the tubular nectar tubes of *Cattleya*, *Brassavola*, and others, which are embedded in the ovary (Fig. 11A). Study of *Apostasia* should be most interesting on this point. As in many of the Liliiflorae, nectaries have arisen on tepals, mostly on the labellum. In unspecialized orchids (*Listera, Epipactis*) and in some fly-pollinated forms (e.g., *Bulbophyllum* and *Cirrhopetalum*) they are superficial grooves. In more specialized forms a spur is formed on the labellum. This is usually fitted to higher pollinators and sometimes occurs in duplicate and on other tepals (Disinae). The mentum (chin)—a hook formed between the lateral outgrowth of the column and the parallel labellum-base implanted on it—may also act as a nectar-spur (*Scaphyglottis* and *Dendrobium*, see Fig. 11C). Butterfly and moth-pollinated orchids develop long spurs or tubes (see p. 84). Quite rarely the column secretes nectar. Porsch (1906b) described this for *Stelis*.

The nectar in the spur is not always free; sometimes it must be obtained from the tissues by piercing the wall with the mouthparts (e.g., some species of *Cattleya, Epidendrum* and *Sobralia*). This does not (contrary to Darwin's opinion) include some *Orchis* species, such as *O.* "latifolia," where the spur is in fact empty and the visits accordingly scarce—limited to newcomers in the first days of blooming. In *Diuris* (Coleman, 1932) the bees must pierce tissues to obtain nectar from a glandular ring on top of the receptacle—a seemingly primitive condition.

The ecological function of nectaries on the outer surface of the tepals, as in *Spathoglottis plicata, Notylia barkeri* and species of *Phajus*, remains uncertain and it seems that the "glands" at the tip of the tepals of *Pleurothallis redmondii* are merely odorous. For false nectaries in pseudocopulation see p. 132. Some species of *Vanda, Cymbidium* and *Grammatophyllum* produce nectar at the base of the outer surface of tepals. This may result in the ant-guard discussed under *Xylocopa*-flowers on p. 42. The purely extrafloral nectaries on the bracts below the flowers of *Spathoglottis plicata* and some *Cymbidium* and *Oncidium* species must—as in other flowers—remain in the domain of plant physiology.

POLLEN, POLLEN-IMITATION AND FOOD-HAIRS

In flowers in general, pollen was an earlier attractant than nectar and it usually remained as a partial attraction. For oligolectic bees (Linsley, 1958) pollen is the main object of their visits to flowers. The circumstance that in orchids pollen is placed apart, made uncollectable, and occasionally, perhaps, inedible, prevented the development of bonds with obligate pollen-eaters. In the extensive lists of Linsley, not a single orchid is mentioned.

Porsch (1908) estimated that 1,000 species of orchids have little or no nectar. We would extend that estimate to at least one-third of the known orchids, perhaps as many as 8,000 species. These nectarless orchids have developed other means of attracting pollinators, largely by deceptive attractants in one form or another. Deception is by no means a new phenomenon and may be considered as a return to the archaic systems of beetle-flowers.

Many orchids produce pseudo-pollen for the attraction of pollinators. A powdery mass resembling pollen occurs on the labellum of a number of species of *Maxillaria*, e.g., *M. lehmannii, M. venusta, M. grandiflora, M. sanderiana*, and others, on *Eria monostachya, E. paniculata* (Beck, 1914) and on most species of *Polystachya*. Sometimes the grains are detached papillae, sometimes disintegrated multicellular hairs filled with starch. It was assumed that this pseudo-pollen was collected by bees. Only recently we have been able to prove this for *Maxillaria grandiflora* and *M. Sanderiana* (Dodson and Frymire, 1961b and Dodson, 1962). In Ecuador, at least 50 species of *Maxillaria* have been encountered which produce this pseudo-pollen. In all of these species no nectar is produced.

When the hairs remain intact in moniliform strings, as in *Polystachya luteola* (Beck, 1914) and *P. lineata* (Porsch, 1906) we see a transition to food-hairs. *Maxillaria rufescens* and other species (Porsch, 1905) have unicellular hairs, filled with aleurone grains and oil drops and have delicate walls. In other species they are multicellular. *Oncidium pulvinatum* also has unicellular hairs on the pad-like callus.

It has been assumed (Beck, 1912) that the labellum hairs and scales of *Vanilla*, *Coelogyne* and *Cymbidium* species are also "grazed" on by bees. Beck found them thin-walled and filled with plasma, oil and sugar.

The hairs and "glands" attracting bees to the vertical lip of species of *Calopogon* are perhaps edible but appear to deceive the pollinator by their similarity to massed stamens. Robertson (1887) considered this condition as pollen imitation. The hairs on sapromyophilous orchids serve other functions (see p. 104). Those inside the labellum of the Cypripedioideae help form a one-way passage out of the sac for trapped flies, but in the European *Cypripedium calceolus* they are eaten or licked by the captured *Andrena* bee (Porsch, 1906). Ziegenspeck (1928) denies the presence of food here.

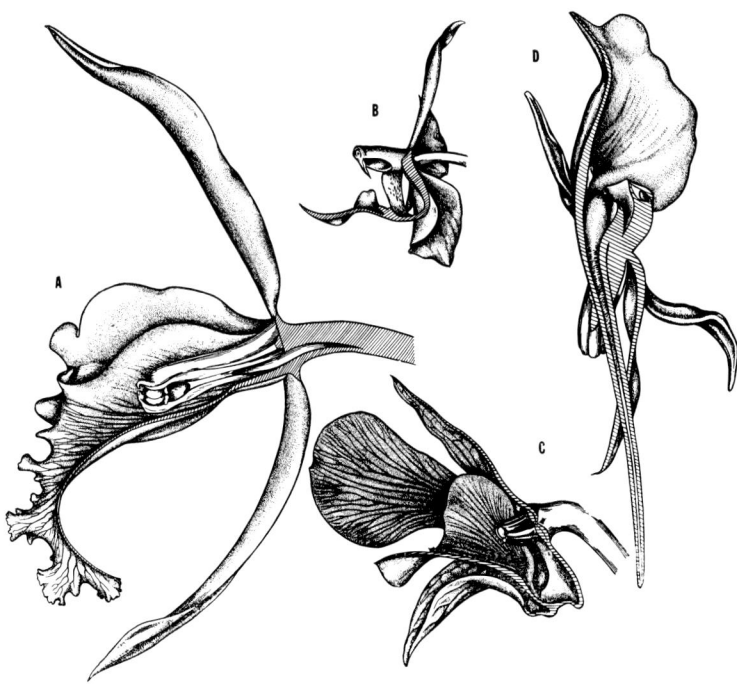

FIG. 11. Longitudinal sections of various types of orchid flowers showing the development of nectaries. A. *Cattleya maxima* with the nectar tube inside the ovary. B. *Phalaenopsis* with nectar on the column foot, which is developed from the column base. C. *Dendrobium* with nectar in a cavity composed of both column foot and the base of the lip. D. *Angraecum* with a nectar tube. (Drawing by P. Fawcett.)

CALLUS

The demarcation of a true callus—a coherent, locally changed swelling of the general tissue—is often vague. In many genera hairs and calli vicariate. Though Kirchner (1925) demonstrated oil in the callus of *Oncidium longicorne*, and Gellert (1923) in those of *Cymbidium, Gongora, Vandopsis,* and *Zygopetalum*, and Porsch (1908) found protein in the callus of *Maxillaria nana*, we have found no evidence that the actual pollinator feeds on the calli of any of these or similar plants. The oil and protein may be metabolic material for the production of odorous substances. Our extensive evidence indicates that the pollinators, at least in Central and South America, are not interested in the callus as food. Numerous reports of bees such as *Euglossa* gnawing on the callus of orchids appear to be erroneous. We have carefully observed the visits of these bees to *Catasetum, Mormodes, Cycnoches, Gongora, Pescatorea* and numerous other orchids and have never noted the bees biting the callus in any of them. The bees scratch the surface of the callus but do not ingest callus material (corroborated by Vogel, 1963). In other orchids such as *Oncidium macranthum. O. hyphaematicum, O. planilabre, Odontoglossum grande, O. kegeljani*, all of which have prominent calli, the pollinators apparently came for other reasons than to eat the callus for it was left undisturbed. We did note considerable damage to the calli of *Oncidium macranthum* and *Odontoglossum kegeljani* which was done by a scarabid beetle, *Macrodactylus* sp. This beetle caused severe damage to the flowers in general and to the callus in particular. An incautious observer might attribute such damage to the pollinator. The beetles did not accomplish pollination.

We do not mean to infer that callus material cannot be considered as an attractant to a pollinator; however, in our experience it has apparently served other purposes such as guidance. Kullenberg (1961) reports xylocopas tearing at the base of the lip of *Eulophia horsfallii* and then licking the exposed areas. In some instances bees may actually gnaw at callus tissue when natural food is scarce, as observed by *Cymbidium* growers in Holland.

SPECIAL SECRETIONS

In Brazil insects were observed collecting the large masses of white wax secreted on the labellum of *Maxillaria divaricata* (nectarless). Porsch (1905) also studied *M. veriferum* and *M. flavo-viride* and found that the wax is formed in the epidermal cells and secreted through the intact cuticula. Many species of bees have been found to collect wax and resins for nest-building. Kirchner (1925) found that the callus of *Eria vulpina* secretes a viscid, oily substance and the flower is nectarless.

The shiny, slippery layer of oil on the surface of some petals has a different function and shall be discussed later.

VISUAL ATTRACTION (COLOR AND SHAPE)

Sensitivity of pollinators to certain colors is important in attraction and should be classified. In some pollinators there is a measurable difference in sensitivity to color. In others an individual constancy for certain colors exists and in some groups a general, unanalyzed fidelity occurs—as is immediately obvious in the behavior of certain butterflies.

The distribution of coloring among orchids shows but few remarkable points. The rarity of pure red seems connected with the primary bond with bees (often red-blind). Some butterfly-pollinated orchids, e.g., species of *Disa* and *Epidendrum*, have shades of red. The bird-pollinated species (see p. 93) are also red. For a discussion of the dull-purple colors of fly-pollinated species, their return to a radial shape, their hairiness and fluttering motions, see p. 102 and p. 103. For consideration of light colors, flags and frayed petals in moth-flowers see p. 84.

In the Stanhopeinae and Catasetinae many kinds of colors and designs, lurid and vivid, without apparent functions, occur in narrowly related taxa. We have observed vivid colors to vary there to such an extent that color seemed of no importance for visits and speciation (Dodson and Frymire, 1961a).

ODOR

Insects are differentially attracted by odors as well as colors, and attraction by this means appears to be the oldest. It works at a distance and often at night. In beetle-flowers, in many fly-flowers, and in some bee-flowers the sense of smell of the visitors is practically the only one involved.

The scale of odors in orchid flowers is enormous, an inexhaustible basis for specificity of visitors. Odors mostly affect innate instincts. Flowers often deceive visitors by producing putrid aminoid substances occurring in decaying organisms. In some instances odors are produced which insects perceive and distinguish but which are not perceived by the human nose. Sometimes forms of orchid species from different regions produce different odors. Of the famous moon-orchid, *Phalaenopsis amabilis*, only a form from New Guinea has a strong sweetish odor.

Sometimes special odor-glands produce different odors in a single flower. In *Arachnis flos-aeris* only the tip of the median sepal, far from the column, produces the musk-odor. The rhythm of odor production determines the time of visitation and thereby helps in speciation. Sometimes the odor is limited to—or of a special nature in—the labellum or parts thereof as an odor guide. The vanillin of *Maxillaria rufescens* is limited to the labellum parts around the food hairs. In *Disa lugens* and *Ceratandra atrata* only the petals are odorous. In *Habenaria polyphylla* only the paired petals, and in the Antelope-orchids, *Dendrobium* spp., only the spirally wound "horns" produce odor. Some of the tail-like appendages (see p. 102) may be considered as special glands (osmophores) with strong metabolism for odor production.

Even social bees have traces of some innate preferences left, though they rely mostly on constancy by association with neutral signals (v. Frisch, 1947).

In the *Diuris* mentioned above (*D. pedunculata*, see p. 138) the odor or the nectar has a curious influence on the pollinators (*Halictus languinosis* and *Paracolletes* sp.), of which only males are attracted. They remain stupefied in the flower and females do not visit the species.

The strong, aromatic odors of the Catasetinae and Stanhopeinae (see the analysis by Porsch, 1955) have a striking effect, but only on male *Euglossa*,

Euplusia and *Eulaema*. The nervousness and ardor of the males, even during rain, and their fighting for a place on the flower suggest that here too the odor touches the sexual sphere. The odor production is clearly of an ecological nature and in many species of *Stanhopea, Gongora, Coryanthes, Cycnoches, Mormodes* and *Catasetum* specific species of bees are attracted. The odor may cease after one visit in some orchids when the pollen is removed (see *Catasetum*, p. 63). Studies using gas-chromatography have shown that different chemical compounds are present in the fragrances produced by the flowers when distinct species of pollinators are attracted (Dodson and Hills, 1966).

The optimal effect in this direction is reached in the cases of pseudocopulation (see p. 131). Kullenberg (1956) could identify the odor of the substances involved in this process and compared their effect successfully, first with the pure chemicals and later with the substances produced by bees in connection with mating. A chemical of the farnesol type plays an important role, but shape, hairiness and colors contribute to the deceptive syndrome.

CHAPTER 5
The Pollinators

Although bees appear to be the most frequent pollinators of the orchids a number of other insects and a few specialized birds also function as pollinators. Some large genera of orchids are entirely dependent on bees, flies or moths for the pollination of their flowers. In other genera there may be species adapted to each of these agents. Sometimes the adaptation within a genus of a few species to a different type of pollinator results in morphological changes that lead taxonomists to separate them as distinct genera. A prime example is that of *Brassavola*, which has been separated from *Laelia*. Brassavolas (Fig. 12) are moth-pollinated while *Laelia* (Fig. 13) is probably pollinated by bees. The bright yellow or orange species from Brazil (Fig. 14) which are bird-pollinated are an exception. The change to moth-pollination resulted in characteristic morphological reorganizations which make many *Brassavola* clearly distinct from *Laelia*. Some, like *Brassavola digbyana*, however, are less distinct (Fig. 15), and as a result cause difficulties in taxonomic placement. Another example of difficulty in taxonomic treatment resulting from failure of taxonomists to recognize function is that of *Encyclia* and *Epidendrum*. Some taxonomists place *Encyclia* as a section of *Epidendrum*, others as a distinct genus. Ecologically the two groups differ in their adaptation to different pollinators, *Encyclia* being adapted to bee-pollination and *Epidendrum* to moth-, butterfly- or bird-pollination. The morphological characteristics resulting from adaption to the different characteristics of the pollinators (placement of the pollinaria on the body in the case of the bee-pollinated *Encyclia* and on the proboscis or beak of the pollinators of *Epidendrum*) are clearly distinct but have not been the characters taken into consideration by taxonomists working with the group. Dressler (1960) was the first to fully understand why the two groups are distinct. Such problems have made it difficult to classify easily the orchid flowers. We also face a paucity of information in these critical groups.

FIG. 12. *Brassavola nodosa*, a moth-pollinated orchid.

FIG. 13. Flower of *Laelia anceps*, a bee-pollinated orchid.

FIG. 14. *Laelia harpophylla*, a hummingbird-pollinated orchid.

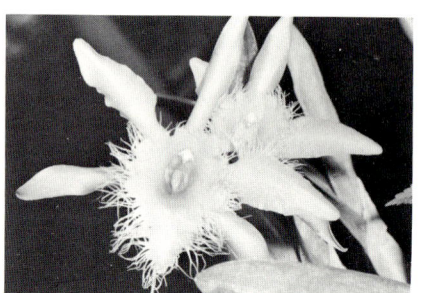

FIG. 15. *Brassavola digbyana*, a moth-pollinated orchid.

POLLINATION CLASSES AND SYNDROMES

In the following chapters we will discuss the pollinators and their relationships with the orchids. This we will do according to the pollination class to which the flowers belong (keeping in mind that we will encounter difficulties in demarcations as indicated below). Each flower class (originally described by Delpino about 1870) tends to exhibit a complex of characteristics which are a direct result of being adapted to the behavior and characteristics of the pollinator. The characteristics of the flowers usually are easily recognizable and when listed, describe what is called a syndrome. The syndromes are partly positive, clearly showing the adaptations between the flowers and the animals which pollinate them. They may also be negative, showing how illegitimate visitors are excluded, as in the curving away of petals, thereby removing the landing platform and restricting visitors to those which can hover. Not all of the characteristics of the syndrome may be present in each flower. There are initial stages in development toward a given syndrome and one stimulus for the visitors may lower the threshold for others. These may suffice to a rudimentary degree and further development may be arrested. In cases where we do not know the pollinator of an orchid which we wish to discuss, we are able to compare the organization of the flower with that of other flowering plants in which the pollinators are known and hopefully place them in their proper flower class. In many cases this has led to confirmation in the field.

Our aim is not primarily demarcation—as we have said the borders often are not clear and in other instances there are neutral forms which attract diverse visitors—but to indicate centers of directed evolution, leading to a certain style. As a secondary result we hope that this light on evolutionary backgrounds may inform us somewhat as to the dynamics of the process and the nature of differences and similarities.

1. *Hymenopterous Flowers*

Flowers which are adapted for pollination by bees, in the broad sense, are called melittophilous (*melitto*=bee, *philous*=loving). The term also covers flowers which are adapted to wasps. These insects belong to the large and advanced order Hymenoptera but the whole group of flowers which they visit are referred to as "bee-flowers."

The syndrome of bee-flowers is listed in the following chapter but it might be wise to point out some of the primary characteristics of this flower class. The vast majority of bees fly during the day and flowers which they visit are open at that time. Bees have highly developed senses of smell and taste. Flowers adapted to them tend to produce odors agreeable to the human nose. The flowers also have bright colors in order to attract the pollinator. The light that bees perceive is in the direction of the ultraviolet end of the spectrum. Von Frisch and his associates have demonstrated that the bees react to four primary colors: violet, blue, green and yellow. They do not differentiate the red end of the spectrum as we do but they react to ultraviolet. Bee-flowers tend to be zygomorphic with the development of a prominent landing platform. Nectar-guides in the form of colored lines running into the depths of the flower toward the nectaries are common; occasionally they are raised as nerves or keels. Some white flowers have nectar guides in the ultraviolet range which we are unable to see. There are other characteristics or tendencies of bee-flowers but we will take them up in the chapter on bees.

2. *Moth- and Butterfly-Flowers*

Moths and butterflies belong to the order Lepidoptera. Adults of this order are primarily adapted to flowers which produce nectar for their food. Their mouthparts are developed into a tube—called a proboscis—for the uptake of nectar. Flowers which are adapted to moths in general are called phalenophilous (*phaleno*=moth, *philous*=loving) while those adapted to butterflies are called psychopilous (*phsycho*=butterfly, *philous*=loving). The separation into two parts is attributable to the basic differences in behavior of moths and butterflies. Most moths fly at night and flowers which are adapted to them have a different syndrome from those which are adapted to day-flying butterflies.

Moth-flowers are divided into two groups: those adapted to such families as the Noctuidae, which tend to land on the flower, and those adapted to the Sphingidae (commonly called hawk-moths), which are stronger fliers and hover in front of the flower. There is consequently a difference in the morphology of the flowers visited by the two groups. Flowers adapted to hawk-moths often are called sphingophilous. The noctuid-type flower permits landing, tends toward deposition of pollinia on the feet of the pollinator and usually has shorter nectar tubes. The sphingophilous type leads toward avoidance of alighting, deposition of pollen on the proboscis and longer nectar-tubes.

Moth-flowers tend to open at night and some even close during the day. They produce strong odors at night which are musky-sweet or vegetable-like (some epidendrums produce an odor at night reminiscent of rotting vegetables on the refuse-heap of a market). Landing platforms tend to be either turned back out of the way or turned upwards. Colors are commonly white, creamy, or may be green when they lack a particular function. Abundant nectar is produced but is hidden in deep cavities or tubes (the distance between nectar and the sexual organs is great).

In contrast to moths, butterflies fly in the daytime and in a sense are not strong fliers. They rarely hover. Therefore they need ample landing space. Butterfly-flowers are commonly highly colored and have fresh, agreeable fragrances. They have abundant nectar usually in deep nectar containers. As in the moths which land on flowers, the pollen is often deposited on the feet rather than on the proboscis.

3. Bird-Flowers

Bird-flowers are called ornithophilous (*ornitho* = bird, *philous* = loving). In the New World, hummingbirds and the small family of sugar-birds, the Coerebidae, are adapted to flowers for a major portion of their food, while the Old World several groups of birds visit flowers. The Old World flower-birds are rarely as highly adapted as the hummingbirds and in transitional cases fruit and insects form the main diet with nectar as a supplement. Some insects (rarely pollen) provide protein for even the highly adapted hummingbirds, honey-eaters and sun-birds (or nectar-birds).

Flowers adapted to bird pollination tend to be highly colored with red predominating. They usually have little fragrance since the birds have almost no sense of smell. The flowers are often pendant, for the birds do not normally land on the flower itself. Abundant nectar in deep, reinforced nectar-containers is common.

4. Fly-Flowers

Flowers adapted to fly-pollination are called myophilous (*myo* = fly, *philous* = loving). Flies belong to the very large order of insects called Diptera. Some groups are adapted to securing their food from flowers but others are attracted to flowers by deception. That is, the flower imitates the natural food or substrate of the fly. These flies visit decaying substances, dung or carrion either for food or to deposit their eggs and are attracted by the odors and colors of those substances. Flowers which imitate these substances in order to attract the flies for their pollination are called sapromyophilous (*sapro* = rotten). The syndromes of myophilous and sapromyophilous flowers are somewhat different. The flies which seek food in the form of nectar go to flowers with shallow nectaries, sweet odors and open flowers. The sapromyophilous flowers produce putrescent odors and often do not produce nectar. These flowers commonly form traps which hold the pollinator, have various complex attracting devices, and are colored as rotting meat or other foul substances.

5. Beetle-Flowers

Beetle-flowers are called cantharophilous (*cantharo* = beetle, *philous* = loving). This class is archaic but is still present in primitive flower families. Very few reports are available of beetles pollinating orchid flowers and it does not seem likely that they will prove important as pollinators of these advanced and specialized plants. In most cases where they have been reported as pollinators of orchids they act as co-pollinators with other insects. They are often found eating the flower parts indiscriminately. This is called dystropic (destructive) behavior. Several other insects, such as small bees, wasps and thrips, eat the flowers, but sometimes act as pollinators as well.

6. Bat-, Wind- and Water-Flowers

To date there are no reports of any orchids pollinated by these agents and it seems highly dubious that there will be. For that reason we will not discuss the syndromes of these types of flowers.

7. Autogamous Flowers

There are a number of strictly autogamous species in the orchids as well as a number of species which are facultatively autogamous. They will be discussed at length in Chapter 10.

POLLINATOR-FLOWER BONDS

It is well known that a given honeybee tends to travel to similar flowers during its visits. They rarely mix species of plants on a trip to and from the hive. However, honeybees from other groups may be working other plants in the same garden. This phenomenon is called constancy and should not be confused with the phenomena discussed in the next paragraph. Constancy is a learned reaction and may change from day to day or even within an hour or so. If the food supply presented by a certain species of plant is depleted, or no longer profitable to work, the bees will shift to another species. This phenomenon has been well studied for the honeybee but very little is known about constancy in other social bees and in solitary bees. It has become apparent in our observations that solitary bees must be included when constancy is discussed, but they provide a much more difficult subject for study than social bees.

A very different group of phenomena are involved in instances which superficially may appear similar. These have to do with the flowers which bees visit "instinctively." Animals which visit many different kinds of flowering plants for nectar are called polytropic (poly = many, tropic = tending toward). Those which visit related groups of flowering plants are called oligotropic. Monotropic animals only visit single or closely related plant species.

The progression from polytropy to oligotropy to monotropy is not based on phylogeny. When deceit by odor occurs we find monotropy in such insects as flies which are not adapted to flowers. Further, it is often the more primitive Hymenoptera which most clearly demonstrate monotropy. In their short life span they may be associated with but one or a few plant species. The association rests, just as in cases of deceit or of intoxication, on innate instinctive behavior in the animal.

In the social bees polytropy may be present as a secondary character. As a result of the formation of long-lived colonies with division of labor, it is necessary for them to spread their activities over many flower species since they have to collect both nectar and pollen in large quantities in order to maintain their extensive hive systems. Thus polytropy led to difficulties in pollination of flowers, such as the wastage of pollen on foreign flowers. It also resulted in inefficiency for bees, since it required frequent changes of technique in working the flowers. Therefore the social bees apparently perfected constancy, which had developed in the solitary and semisocial bees. Thus constancy may be defined as a temporal bond of an individual bee or colony to certain flowers; an association with certain colors and odors, which do not act directly through instinct but rather become fixed as signals for recognition by the insect. The association with such neutral stimuli arises by experience and learning, and can be changed when the source of food loses its attraction.

The advantages to bee and flower are obvious. Constancy also helps in speciation. We would like to point out that the term has been misused by some authors, causing confusion with oligotropy.

The terms "polylectic" and "oligolectic" are used by entomologists for insects that collect pollen only from many or just a few related species of flowers. This relationship is irrelevant for flowers and especially so for orchids. The terms are useful from the zoological point of view concerning nutritive bonds of insects to flowers, but the zoological lists may refer to visits only. Botanists have been misled by them.* An oligolectic bee is not necessarily the pollinator of the flower, and from the botanical point of view, may be just a thief.

For the delineation of pollinators of flowers (an entirely different aspect) the terms "poly-, oligo-, and monophily" should be used.

---

*An example is that of *Onagrandrena* spp. which, as Percival (1965, p. 128) failed to understand, are not the pollinators of the onagraceous flowers they visited as listed by Linsley (1958).

# CHAPTER 6
Orchids and Bees

The form of the *Cattleya*, with its large lip, is typical of the bee-flower in the orchids. The color of the three sepals and two petals aid in attraction of the bee and the large platform-like lip serves for landing and attraction. The flower is ideally suited for the characteristics and behavior of large bees, and the majority of the bee-flowers in the Orchidaceae follow this basic form (Fig. 16). In accordance with this type of flower the syndrome (adapted in part from Vogel 1954) is as follows:

1. Anthesis diurnal.
2. Flowers zygomorphic with a prominent landing platform.
3. Colors blue, violet, purple, yellow or white.
4. Nectar guides often present and complex.
5. Odors fresh and sweet.
6. Nectar more or less hidden, in shallow or rather deep containers.
7. Flower horizontal.

Certain bees (Euglossini and Xylocopini) seem to exhibit a kind of fidelity in the flower-insect relationship in that they have some specific preference for certain kinds of flowers without clear constancy. Euglossine bees were found with mixed loads of pollinia and were observed bringing foreign pollinia to flowers. Neither group is simply constant or oligotropic, but may visit many flowers on their rounds. This is a characteristic which could be dangerous to orchids but which is often overcome in one of two ways. First, the preference given to some flowers narrowly adapted to the bees is clear when they grow together with differently adapted flowers. The latter are visited elsewhere, where there is no competition with favorites. Second, floral mechanisms developed by genetically compatible, sympatric species may act as physical barriers to pollination. For instance, the

FIG. 16. A typical bee-pollinated orchid. (Drawing by G. P. Frymire.)

pollinarium may be deposited upon the insect by one species at a specific position so that pollination is not possible when the pollinator visits a flower of another species. An example would be *Catasetum bicolor, Cycnoches* cf. *egertonianum* and *Mormodes powellii* which are all pollinated by one species of *Euglossa* and grow sympatrically in Panama (Dressler, personal communication). Another example is that of *Gongora grossa* and *Coryanthes elegantium* which grow together and are pollinated by the same bee, *Euglossa hemichlora*, in western Ecuador. These genera of orchids are genetically compatible but due to extremely different pollination mechanisms and placement of the pollinia do not produce hybrids in nature.

The Euglossini and Xylocopini (as well as some species of *Bombus* and *Centris*) developed a new system to foster the efficiency of their visits. They avoid emptied flowers better than do species of *Apis*. In visited flowers they leave an odor behind (probably from their integumentary scent glands) which repels further visitors for some time (van der Pijl, 1954 on *Xylocopa* and unpublished observations by Dodson on Euglossini, *Bombus* and *Centris* in Ecuador). In this manner a few bees can visit many flowers effectively. It may be that the Euglossini are simply more sensitive to the odors left by other bees for they tended to avoid flowers recently visited by any other bee, whereas the *Bombus* and *Centris* only avoided flowers visited by other members of their respective genera and species.

As mentioned in the previous chapter, an interesting point in the physiology of bumblebees, honeybees and some lower bees and wasps is their "blindness" for red, in reality, a shift of spectral sensitivity toward the ultraviolet end of the spectrum. This explains the rarity of red in bee-flowers. Those flowers in which red does occur often reflect ultraviolet rays so that the bees can perceive them.

What we know of "language" and psychological tendencies of social bees, such as a preference for deeper flowers, finer contours, special shapes, etc., should not be applied automatically to more primitive bees and their influence on flowers in history.

THE GROUPS OF HYMENOPTERA

The insect order Hymenoptera is a very large and diverse group including the wasps, ants and bees. Several members of the Hymenoptera are involved, to a greater or lesser degree, in the pollination of orchids. Other members of this order are known to pollinate other flowering plants and there is the possibility that some of them may be encountered as effective orchid pollinators. Therefore, we feel that it may be useful to give a general review of the groups of Hymenoptera having relations with flowering plants.

The oldest group in the Hymenoptera, in terms of evolutionary advancement, are the Tenthredinidae or sawflies (not true flies). The larvae of these insects are herbivorous. Their activities are not connected with nectar consumption. Adults, however, do take nectar from flowers. The sawflies may have developed in the Jurassic period.

Out of the sawflies arose the ichneumon flies (once again the reference to flies is a misnomer). Families of these insects are the Braconidae, Ichneumonidae and the Chalididae. These Hymenoptera may be considered as primitive wasps and are solitary in behavior. They rarely use nectar as an important source of food and if so, often collect for themselves the small drops of nectar in extrafloral nectaries of leaves and on the outside of sepals and petals as do many of the higher wasps. These "parasitic wasps" lay their eggs in the bodies of other organisms and the larvae feed on the host. In this manner the provision of nests is not involved in the life cycle of these wasps. Consequently there is no need for the collection and storage of nectar or pollen. Certain orchids have developed pollination mechanisms (pseudocopulation in certain species of *Cryptostylis* and perhaps pseudoparasitism in *Calochilus*) as adaptions to reproductive behavior of these insects.

In the course of time, the ovipositor changed—in some early terebranthes—into a stinging mechanism which, by injecting venom, serves to paralyze the prey while the parasitic larvae consume its body tissues. From this stage a number of diverse lines were evolved, all commonly called aculeate or "stinging" Hymenoptera. The most primitive of these lines are known as the stinging digger wasps, composed of the Scoliidae, Pompilidae (often placed in the Vespoidea) and the Sphecidae. They still are solitary and attack other insects as food for the larvae. Adults take some open nectar as food (mainly extrafloral) but collect no pollen.

From this point several separate lines arose with different methods of food collection. Among these are two groups which are important as pollinators. These are often considered as superfamilies: the "true" or folding wasps (Vespoidea) and the bees (Apoidea). The true wasps comprise the solitary wasps (Eumenidae) and the social wasps (Vespidae). The latter collect nectar as part of their diet and therefore act as effective pollinators of many flowering plants which have open nectaries. They still retain the chewing mouthparts typical of the lower Hymenoptera and take the nectar from plant tissues and extrafloral or open floral nectaries. The mouthparts of the bees, on the other hand, are specialized in varying degrees for the consumption of nectar. They also have other devices for collecting pollen and nectar from flowers.

The oldest group of Apoidea—which still retains short mouthparts—is the Colletidae (which includes *Prosopis*, the stomach-collecting mask-bee and *Ptiloglossa*, the night-flying pollinator of *Miltonia endresii*). These bees are mainly found in southern regions and have probably existed since the Cretaceous period, synchronous with flowers. The Halictidae are also old, as is the slightly more advanced group, the Andrenidae. The next step is the Megachilidae (including *Heriades*, *Osmia* and *Anthidium*) with the further specialization of tending to deposit and carry pollen on their ventral side (sternotriby).

The highest bees (family Apidae) developed later, probably after the middle of the Tertiary period, and achieved other devices for pollen transport. They tend to nototriby (primary deposition of pollen on the back). The Apidae developed into specialists for higher flower families, but as we shall see, not all of their subfamilies accompanied the further development of orchids.

Of the subfamilies of the Apidae three have proven especially important in orchid pollination, i.e., the solitary Anthophorinae (including the Centridini), the Xylocopinae (carpenter bees) and the Apinae. The latter are social bees and form a parallel to the social wasps. One isolated group of Apinae, the Euglossini (occurring only in tropical America), have remained more or less gregarious rather than social. Three genera act as important pollinators of orchids and will be discussed at length below. Social genera of the Apinae are *Bombus* (the bumblebees), *Trigona*, *Melipona* and *Apis* (the honeybees). *Apis* is originally non-American. *Bombus* is primarily found in temperate zones but is common in the higher mountains of tropical America and Asia (a few species occur even in tropical rainforests).

VISITS OF DIFFERENT HYMENOPTERA AND THEIR INFLUENCES

1. Wasps

Wasps, except in certain unique situations, are not particularly efficient pollinators. Their behavior, resulting from their life-cycle pattern, tends to be erratic. Ichneumonid wasps (and occasionally sphecids) are visitors of open extra-floral nectaries. Uniquely, they are the regular pollinators of *Listera ovata* (the European twayblade orchid, Fig. 17). This orchid has small, apparently odorless, greenish flowers and offers nectar in an open groove on the labellum. The insects automatically take the right position in the flower. Schremmer (1961) published fine photographs of the visits and Sprengel placed a picture of *Listera* with an ichneumon-fly on the title page of his famous book on pollination in 1793. Some beetles also visit this orchid but are rarely effective as pollinators. Porsch mentioned a primitive stone-fly (Plecopterid) as a pollinator. Darwin reported the ichneumonids *Hemiteles* and *Cryptus* as pollinators of *Listera ovata*. Godfery (1931) added the primitive bee *Eucera longicornis*. Since the stigma does not become accessible until the pollinia have been removed, some protandry exists, making successive visits necessary. Others saw icheumonids together with *Andrena* and *Collyria* spp. acting as pollinators.

In the morphologically more primitive genus *Cephalanthera* some species in

Europe belong to the same ecological class. Godfery (1931, 1933) even caught a saw-fly (*Dolerus*) on *C. ensifolia*, other wasps and also *Halictus* spp.

On *Coeloglossum viride* he also saw a saw-fly (*Tenthredopsis*) take away the pollinia. Evidently this small, greenish flower may also be a wasp-flower, but occasional hybrids with *Gymnadenia* point to (incidental?) common pollinators. There is a short spur but its nectar flows over the lip. In the Netherlands van der Pijl observed visits of many solitary wasps but they did not function as pollinators. A large ichneumon wasp carried away pollinia. Wasps (*Cryptus* and *Ichneumon*) and beetles (*Cantharis*) carrying pollinia were found on *Coeloglossum viride* in Finland (Silen, 1906 a and b).

Chamaeorchis alpina also fits in here, according to Müller (Mueller) (1881). On the small-flowered *Herminium monorchis* (also European) Darwin reported minute hymenopterous insects with pollinia, mainly *Tetrastichus diaphantus* (Ichneumonidae), also dipterans and beetles. Müller (1881) saw minute ichneumonids as visitors with pollinia on the legs in the Alps. A number of small tropical orchids are probably of this nature, e.g., *Scaphyglottis* and *Liparis*, but have not been investigated.

Pollinia of *Orchis maculata* have been found on a *Cryptus* wasp in Europe.

In the genus *Epipactis* the labellum also offers superficial nectar, which attracts—in *E. palustris*—diverse visitors including flies, honeybees and diggerwasps (*Crabro*). *Epipactis latifolia* is well known as a wasp-orchid, attracting mainly species of *Vespa*, perhaps helped by a typical reddish-brown tinge. *Bombus* and *Apis* are not attracted as a rule, but Martens (1928) saw *Apis* visiting (not pollinating) at a place where they were frequent. Godfery (1933) found *Bombus* and *Vespa saxonica* on *E. rubiginosa* in Switzerland. Porter (1896) saw the American *E. viridiflora* pollinated by *Vespa diabolica*.

FIG. 17. An ichneumonid wasp visiting the flower of *Listera ovata*. (Photo by F. Schremmer.)

FIG. 18. The wasp *Campsomeris columba* visiting and pollinating the flowers of *Brassia* aff. *antherotes* in Colombia.

FIG. 19. *Encyclia* (Epidendrum) *pentotis* being pollinated by the tarantula-hawk wasp *Campsomeris columba* in Colombia. The pollinia are deposited under the mandibles of the insect.

Though many of the members of the genus *Ophrys* are pollinated by bees some species are known to be pollinated by wasps (see p. 133).

In Australia four species of the genus *Cryptostylis*, *C. subulata*, *C. ovata*, *C. erecta* and *C. lepitochila* are pollinated by an ichneumonid wasp, *Lissopimpla semipunctata*. Another Australian orchid, *Calochilus campestris*, is pollinated by the scoliid wasp *Campsomeris tasmaniensis*. These appear to be special cases involving mimicry and will be discussed under pseudocopulation (Chapter 11).

Sargent (1907 and 1918) described the pollination of *Caladenia barbarossae* by a large black wasp. It seizes the central labellar appendage, a gland with crystallized sugar, with its mandibles (food or something more intricate?). Coleman (1930a) also saw visits by *Halictus* sp. (see p. 138).

For wasps on *Dendrobium linguiforme* see p. 122.

Dodson (unpublished) found *Brassia antherotes* (Fig. 18) and *Encyclia pentotis* (Fig. 19) to be regularly and efficiently pollinated by *Campsomeris columba* of the Scoliidae in Colombia in 1965. Dressler (personal communication) found *Pachdynerus massidens* to be the pollinator of *Leochilus* sp. in Panama.

The occurrence of wasp-flowers in generally primitive orchids gives the impression of a fundamentally primitive relationship, but this is not necessarily true. Higher dicotyledonous plants also have wasp-flowers. The case of *Pentstemon spectabilis* may be an example. It is (according to Straw, 1955, 1956) possibly a cross between a *Xylocopa*-pollinated species and an ornithophilous parent. The hybrid was at once fitted to a pseudomasarid wasp.

2. Solitary Bees

Many of the terrestrial European orchids are pollinated by solitary bees. *Himantoglossum hircinum* (Schmid, 1912) emits a strong hircine odor from the long lip. *Apis* and *Bombus* avoid it. Some beetles are attracted, though they are ineffective. Even an *Anopheles* mosquito was found with pollinia of this species on its proboscis (Ziegenspeck, 1928). The legitimate pollinator is a primitive bee, *Andrena carbonaria*, and has been reported as such from diverse regions. We shall discuss other bees of this genus later. All are apparently guided by odor and are rather specialized in their activities. *Himantoglossum longibracteatum* has superficial nectar taken by many different Hymenoptera and Diptera (Moggridge, 1865). In southern France, Evans (in letters to Poulton who read them at the Entomological Society of London) found higher pollinators such as *Bombus* and *Apis* on this species. Even a *Xylocopa* was carrying its pollinia.

Evans (1c.) observed solitary bees, from the genera *Heriades* and *Eucera* on *Cephalanthera rubra*. Godfery (1933) observed *Heriades* spp. on this orchid and found species of *Andrena* and *Halictus* as pollinators of *Cephalanthera grandiflora* in southern France. Some autogamy occurs in *C. grandiflora* (see p. 124), especially in northern regions. Godfery (1928) found bees of *Osmia* and *Anthidium* sleeping at night inside the flowers of *Serapias*. *Serapias* (Fig. 20) is closely allied to *Orchis* and has pollinators in common as testified by hybrids. As some of these sleeping bees carried many pollinia they must be regular visitors in the daytime too. An old observation by Darwin of a *Ceratina* in *Serapias* sp. was reported. This bee probably causes the formation of hybrids between species of *Serapias*. *Serapias cordigera*, which also occurs in southern Europe, is pollinated by such solitary bees as *Ceratina albilabris*, *Osmia* sp., and species of *Anthidium*. Godfery (1922) found diverse bees, mostly *Anthidium septemdentatum*, and rarely a *Bombus*, on *Limodorum abortivum* in southern France. Evans (see Godfery, 1933) found

FIG. 20. *Serapias*. (Drawing by P. Fawcett.)

FIG. 21. *Cypripedium arietinum* with bee crawling from under the anther. (Photo by F. G. Irwin, M.D.)

FIG. 22. *Phragmopedium longifolium* with a bee of the genus *Chlerogella* crawling from under the column.

Andrena spp. on *Orchis militaris* and *O. purpurea*. In Britain, flies (*Odyneros parietum*) seem to take over on the latter species.

In the Cypripedioideae, the genus *Cypripedium* (Fig 21) appears to be pollinated by several species of *Andrena* or *Megachile* (*M. melanophora* was observed by Robertson [1887] on *Cypripedium spectabile*). The bees are apparently attracted by deceit and after falling in the pouch, are forced to crawl out under the stigma and anthers. There is some indication that the tropical genera *Paphiopedilum*, *Selenipedium* and *Phragmopedium* may be pollinated by both bees and flies (see p. 104). *Phragmopedium longifolium* var. *hartwegii* was observed to be pollinated by Halictine bees of the genera *Chlerogella* and *Caenohalictus* (Dodson, 1965a) (Fig. 22). Flies of the genus *Syrphus* were also observed as pollinators. Both bees and flies approached the flowers and landed on the lip. They walked to the broad slide formed by the infolded sides of the lip. They then worked their way down the slide to the green spots (imitating food?). The area around these spots is slick and the insect falls on into the pouch. It is not possible for them to fly out of the pouch and the only means of exit is by crawling up the backside of the pouch, under the stigma and out through an orifice on either side of the column just under the petals. The orifice is small and partially blocked by both the petal and an anther. In squeezing past the petal the insect pushes against the anther and a pollen mass is attached to its back. As the same insect passes under the stigma of a succeeding flower the pollen mass is brushed off.

Remarkably little is known about *Calopogon*, the "grass-pink" of the eastern United States (Fig. 23). Robertson (1887) found two species of an andrenid bee, *Augochlora festiva* and *A.* sp., on *C. barbatus* (*parviflorus*) as the effective pollinators. Dodson (unpublished) found *Xylocopa micans* to be the pollinator of *C. pulchellus* in Florida (p. 43).

Halictus languinosus and *Paracolletes* sp. pollinate *Diuris pedunculata* in Australia. According to Coleman (1932), the attractant—acting directly on instincts —has a stupefying and sexually directed effect, as only the males of the *Halictus* were attracted. They remain immobilized for hours, but become active again after removal. The females caught on flowers of other plants carried no pollinia.

Ornithocephalus avicula (Pl. Ia) and *O.* cf. *patentilobus* are pollinated by *Paratetrapedia testacea* (Dodson, 1965a) while Dressler (personal communication) reports *Paratetrapedia calcarata* as the pollinator of *O. bicornis* and *O. powellii* in Panama.

The pollination of *Oncidium hyphaematicum* and *O. planilabre* by species of *Centris* (Dodson and Frymire, 1961b) is based upon the simulation by the flowers of an enemy insect to be driven away by male bees which establish and defend a territory (see p. 141). Female bees of the same genus, however, have been observed pollinating other species of *Oncidium*, e.g., *O. ochmatochilum* by *Centris* sp., and the same species of bee was captured pollinating *Odontoglossum grande* (Dodson, 1965a) (Pl.Ib).

Bletia purpurea is pollinated by mixed groups of bees (Dodson and Frymire, 1961b). These included *Euglossa*, *Thygater* and possibly *Melipona*.

Wasps and lower bees may be said to have "stood at the cradle of the orchid flower." Such primitive Hymenoptera as the digger wasps possessed the necessary instincts for choosing the precise position in pollinating orchids as well as specificity for odor and prey.

3. *Xylocopa* and Orchids

The carpenter bees (Xylocopini) have been said to be backward and of little interest in pollination of modern flowers (Popov, 1956 as cited by Linsley, 1958). In our experience (van der Pijl, 1954 and Dodson, 1962a and 1965a) the reverse is true in southern Asia and in the tropical zones of America. Vogel does not mention *Xylocopa* at all for South African orchids. There are occasional reports,

FIG. 23. *Calopogon pulchellus*, commonly known as the "grass-pink" of the eastern United States. Note the imitation stamens projecting from the lip.

e.g., Kullenberg (1961, p. 281) observed the powerfully built flower of *Eulophia* (*Lissochilus*) *horsfallii* being visited in Africa by a species which tore holes in the labellum base with the mandibles and licked the surface. Some species live in the Mediterranean region and Darwin reported pollinia of *Himantoglossum longibracteatum* on one of them. In the latter case it was acting as a co-visitor.

The carpenter bees tend to visit flowers with sweet, but fresh odors, unsaturated soft colors, rather deep but broad shape and thick walls, with a fair quantity of nectar to be reached by effort only. They, however, are not loath to visit small open flowers in some regions when there is a paucity of larger types. These bees have tremendous mandibles enabling them to bore their tunnels in wood. They are therefore quite capable of penetrating and robbing a flower which cannot be entered in a normal manner. This creates a danger for some flowers, as the bees take the nectar without pollinating. For the most part, this is not important in the orchids since the majority of large-flowered, nectar producing types are pollinated by several kinds of bees, at least one of which is an efficient pollinator.

The flowers especially adapted to *Xylocopa* have developed special provisions against this danger, i.e., extra bracts, very hard bases, or an ant-guard, attracted by extra-floral nectaries at the outside of the flower-base. The significance of such ant-guards at the bases of *Xylocopa*-adapted flowers in Asia was proved experimentally by van der Pijl (1954). The bees tried to puncture flowers at the base instead of using force to open the way to the nectar but were prevented from doing so by the ants at the base of the flowers. In some orchids such ant attracting nectaries are present at the base or top of the ovary and are often beset with ants, especially in species of *Vanda*, which are very popular with the bees when grown in gardens. The odors of these (*V. teres, V. hookeriana* and their hybrids) agree with those of specialized *Xylocopa*-flowers (large *Centrosema, Cavanallia, Bauhinia* and *Thunbergia* flowers). In *Vanda teres* dead specimens of the large *Xylocopa latipes* have been found in the flowers and *Vanda* pollinia are frequent on captured bees. Orchid growers in Java fear these bees inside greenhouses where they can pollinate and destroy the whole stock. Growers there protect the flowers with cotton plugs. Carpenter bees have a preference for flowers with a secluded ante-room and this is provided by the upturned side lobes of the labellum of species of *Vanda*.

Phajus tankervilliae and *Arundina speciosa* have the same character and are visited by species of Xylocopa. The *Phajus*, at least, has external perianth nectaries and some cymbidiums have them also on the small bract below the ovary. The moon-orchid, *Phalaenopsis amabilis*, does not appear to be adapted to *Xylocopa* but is sometimes pollinated by them in nature. *Grammatophyllum speciosum* is sometimes visited by the large *Xylocopa* types, but the bees are apparently too heavy and depress the lip so much that the pollinarium cannot be deposited (Ridley, 1905 and Burkill, 1919). *Bromheadia palustris, B. aporoides* and *B. alticola* were reported by Ridley (1890) as being pollinated by a species of *Xylocopa*. Perhaps the robust flowers of *Vandopsis*, with nectar-secreting bracts, belong to this type. We lack observations in the wild on the many species of *Coelogyne, Cymbidium* and *Pleione* which appear to belong here. However, *Cymbidium aloifolium* was reported to be pollinated by a *Xylocopa* (Ridley, 1905). The sturdy flowers of the cultivated *Cymbidium* hybrids are good examples of the type. *Cymbidium* hybrids in Holland may be pollinated by *Bombus* in the greenhouse.

In tropical America observations indicate that *Xylocopa* may be of major importance in certain groups of especially adapted orchids. Also in many instances they act as co-pollinators in unadapted nectar-producing species such as *Sobralia* and *Cattleya*. *Cattleya warszewiczii* was observed (Dodson, unpublished) being visited by *Xylocopa viridis* in northwestern Colombia. This species is also visited by species of *Eulaema* (see p. 48). *Xylocopa* cf. *transitoria* and *X. frontalis*, males and females, were reported as pollinators of *Sobralia violacea* in western Ecuador (Dodson and Frymire, 1961a and Dodson, 1965a). *Sobralia weberbaueriana* is pollinated in Colombia by species of *Xylocopa* and *Eulaema* (Dodson, unpublished). *Xylocopa frontalis* was observed pollinating *Encyclia crassilabia* (Fig. 24) in the Andes of Ecuador (Dodson, 1962a). Female *Xylocopa* cf. *transitoria* pollinates *Oncidium onustum* in the desert regions of coastal Ecuador where the plants grow on cacti. In the garden, the bees seemed to take some time to learn to visit the fragrant flowers but were very effective pollinators thereafter (Fig. 25). *Apis mellifera* also learned to visit the flowers but was unable to pollinate them.

Bennett (personal communication) reported *Bletia catenulata* to be pollinated by *Xylocopa tricuspidifera* in Peru. In Ecuador a *Xylocopa* was observed visiting *Epidendrum* cf. *acuminatum* (Dodson, 1965a).

Dodson (unpublished) encountered *Xylocopa micans* pollinating *Calopogon pulchellus* in Florida. No other bee was observed visiting the flowers and the difference in dimensions between *C. pulchellus* and *C. barbatus* would indicate that the size of the pollinators acts as an effective barrier to hybridization. Robertson (see p. 40) reported *C. barbatus* to be pollinated by much smaller bees of the genus *Auglochlora*.

Xylocopa tabaniformis was captured while pollinating *Barkeria lindleyana* in Costa Rica (Dodson, 1965a). A single bee pollinated about 150 flowers of an estimated 700 to 800 in two days. After the bee was captured no further pollination occurred. Several smaller bees visited the flowers but were unable to force their

FIG. 24. *Xylocopa frontalis* pollinating *Encyclia* (Epidendrum) *crassilabia*.

FIG. 25. *Xilocopa* cf. *transitoria* pollinating *Oncidium onustum*.

FIG. 26. *Xilocopa tabaniformis* visiting the flowers of *Barkeria lindleyana*. (Posed.)

way between the column and the lip as did the *Xylocopa* (Fig. 26). The pollination mechanism in this species is very similar to that encountered in *Encyclia* and there is indication that species of *Xylocopa* may pollinate many of the species in that genus.

Xylocopa fimbriata were forwarded from the Barbados Islands by F. Bennett with pollinia of *Schomburgkia lyonsii* on their heads. *Schomburgkia splendida* is pollinated by *Xylocopa lachnea* (Dodson, unpublished) in Colombia.

4. *Euglossini and Orchids*

The taxonomy of this group of bees has been confused but the excellent work of Moure (1950, etc.) and Dressler promises clarification in the not too distant future. The group probably consists of nearly 200 species of long-tongued, tropical, gregarious Apidae. Their similarities are many and they are considered to constitute a separate tribe. Unfortunately their similarities are so marked as to cause taxonomic problems on the generic as well as specific level. Early entomologists considered them as constituting a single genus, *Euglossa*. About the middle of the last century they were divided into two genera, *Euglossa* and *Eulaema*.

Unfortunately, confusion existed with the use of the generic name *Centris* in place of *Eulaema*. The later name was conserved. After the turn of the century the whole group was again considered as a single genus, *Euglossa*. Moure (1950) studied the group and divided them into four genera: *Euglossa, Eulaema, Eufriesia* and *Euplusia*, and considered the two parasitic genera *Exaerete* and *Aglae* as belonging to a separate subtribe.

a. *Euglossa*

The species of *Euglossa* are sparsely haired, metallic green, blue or golden, brilliantly colored bees. They are generally rapid fliers.

The subgenus *Euglossa* is taxonomically chaotic. The bees are all approximately the same size but vary in color even when emerging from the same nest. At present there is no taxonomic treatment of this subgenus. There may be from fifty to a hundred species.

The subgenus *Glossura* consists of seven to ten species. These are somewhat larger than members of the subgenus *Euglossa*, being approximately intermediate in size between the latter and *Eulaema*. Reports (Ducke, 1902, Dodson, 1965 and Dressler, unpublished) indicate that they may have a slightly different spectrum of floral fidelity than either the subgenus *Euglossa* or *Eulaema*.

b. *Eulaema*

The species of *Eulaema* are markedly larger than those of *Euglossa* (the smallest about the size of an average bumblebee) and are covered with dense hair. The head and thorax are black in all and covered with black hair. The color of the abdomen varies from species to species, being completely black, orange-yellow or banded with yellow and black and red. There are 17 species in the genus.

c. *Euplusia*

The species of *Euplusia* are generally similar in appearance to those of *Eulaema* except that the head and thorax are brilliantly metallic green or blue.

FIG. 27. The flower of *Sobralia violacea* being pollinated by *Euplusia surinamensis*. Note the pollinia on the thorax of the bee.

FIG. 28. *Maxillaria grandiflora* with a female bee of *Eulaema cingulata* entering. (Posed.)

Moure lists a number of other differences. There are probably more than 40 species in the genus.

Moure (1950) includes another genus in the group, *Eufriesia*, with a single species. This bee has not been observed visiting orchids.

Behavior of Euglossine Bees

The Euglossini do not occur outside the tropical zone of the Western Hemisphere and though they have been captured at elevations of 10,000 feet on warm sunny days, we have not observed them visiting orchids higher than 6,000 feet. The species within each genus are often widely distributed, some occurring from central Mexico to southern Brazil.

In many older botanical publications, including those of Darwin, they have been called—together with *Xylocopa*—"Hummeln," Humblebees, Bumblebees or simply "Abelhas."

The behavior of the members of the tribe is for the most part similar. The female bees forage in the field from dawn to dusk, bringing in construction materials and food for storage in the cells. There appears to be little division of labor, with each female constructing her own cells, storing them with a honey-pollen mixture, and then sealing them over. In *Euglossa* and *Euplusia* this seems to be strictly true; however, in a large nest of *Eulaema cingulata* some 25 female bees were found working the nest but only five partially constructed cells were in evidence (Dodson and Frymire, 1961b). Surely there was a cooperative effort in this case. The female bees are to be seen at all hours of the day visiting the local plants, but we have never observed a female bee visiting an orchid which did not provide food of some sort.

The male bees apparently leave the nest immediately upon emerging and do not return. They seem to lead a vagabond life, feeding on various flowers which provide nectar.

They are relatively long-lived bees for males—living to at least six months of age (Dodson, 1962a). It is their between-feeding activities which are of interest to us. They visit and pollinate a large number of orchids which do not provide food.

Aside from the different nest building habits of each genus, and their consequent differences in habits concerning the collection of nest building materials, there are marked differences in their overall fidelity in regard to the visits to orchid flowers by male bees. *Euglossa*, partially due to their size, have orchid flowers adapted to them which are usually somewhat distinct from those adapted to species of *Eulaema* and *Euplusia*. The latter two genera, however, are essentially of the same size and both sexes do act as co-pollinators of many orchids such as *Sobralia* (Fig. 27 and Pl. Ic). On the other hand, male bees are rarely encountered visiting the same higher orchids which use deception as a basis for attraction. Male and female *Eulaema* visit a number of larger-flowered species of orchids from tropical zones, such as *Maxillaria grandiflora* (Fig. 28), *M. sanderiana* (Pl. Id), and *Cattleya maxima* (Pl. IIa). Male *Eulaema* visit *Huntleya meleagris* (Fig. 29), *Cochleanthes aromatica* (Pl. IIb), and *Trichocentrum tigrinum* (Fig. 30), etc. (see Appendix). Male *Euplusia* visit higher orchids including species of *Stanhopea*, *Kegeliella*, *Cycnoches*, *Coryanthes*, some of the tiny-flowered *Notylia* (Fig. 31 and Pl. IIc), and *Pterostemma*, which has very small flowers with the tiny, long-stiped pollinia being found on the femurs of *Euplusia surinamensis* in coastal Ecuador.

FIG. 29. *Huntleya meleagris*.

FIG. 30. *Trichocentrum tigrinum* being pollinated by a male *Eulaema cingulata*.

FIG. 31. Male *Euplusia surinamensis* pollinating the flowers of *Notylia xyphorius*.

Euplusia were also observed visiting flowers of such cultivated plants as hibiscus, roses, ginger and poinciana which were not seen being visited by species of *Eulaema*. All three genera, on the other hand, visit *Maranta, Calathea, Costus, Solanum* and *Thevetia*. *Eulaema* visit, in addition, *Casia, Prestonia, Canna*, large-flowered tecomas, snapdragons and anthuriums. *Euglossa* visit *Impatiens*, species of *Anthurium*, and small-flowered Bignoniaceae.

Bees of this group have been encountered pollinating three species of the horticulturally popular genus *Cattleya*. *Cattleya maxima* was observed being visited by *Eulaema polychroma* in Ecuador (Dodson and Frymire, 1961b). The same bee pollinates *Cattleya warszewiczii* (Pl. IId) in Colombia (Dodson, unpublished). *Cattleya mendelii* was visited by *Eulaema cingulata* in a garden in Medellín, Colombia (Dodson, unpublished). The bees enter the flowers by landing on the lip and forcing their way between the column and lip. On backing out of the flower first the tip of the dorsum comes in contact with the sticky material (from the stigma) on the underside of the rostellum, which adheres to the bee (Fig. 9a-d). The bee backs farther out and comes in contact with the caudicles of the pollinia which become cemented to the dorsum of the bee (Fig. 9e). The bee in leaving the flower withdraws the pollinia from the anther cap (Fig. 9f). On visiting another flower the pollinia are left on the large, sticky stigma. Though species of *Eulaema* commonly visit the large-flowered species of *Cattleya* there is an indication that species of *Xylocopa* are better adapted to these flowers and tend to be more constant in their visits. In the garden of Mariano Ospina in Medellín, where hundreds of plants of *Cattleya* species are cultivated, species of *Eulaema* only rarely visited the many available flowers. However, flowering plants of *Cattleya warszewiczii* were observed in their natural habitat in tall trees near Amalfi north of Medellín, being regularly visited by species of *Xylocopa* which went from flower to flower. Several instances of hybrid cattleyas under cultivation in the American tropics being visited by *Euglossa* (which were trapped in the stigma and died there) are known. The hybrid nature of the flowers apparently disturbs the balance between size relations and proper odor so that bees which are of incorrect size to manipulate the flower are fatally attracted. In temperate regions bumblebees and honeybees often pollinate hybrid cattleyas in the greenhouse.

The fidelity of a given species in the Euglossini seems to be largely determined by the odors produced by the flowers which attract them. Each species of bee apparently responds to a spectrum of odors. In many cases these odor spectra overlap for species of bees with the result, for example, that four species of *Eulaema* were encountered visiting *Catasetum macroglossum* (Dodson and Frymire, 1961b). Only one of those species was interested in flowers of *Cycnoches lehmanii* which were placed alongside. One species of *Eulaema*, one of *Euplusia* and four of *Euglossa* visited *Sievekingia fimbriata* in Panama but only 2 of the *Euglossa* were effective pollinators (Dressler, personal communication). The *Eulaema*, *Euplusia* and two of the species of *Euglossa* were attracted to the flowers by the odor but did not enter them correctly or were too large to enter. The odor appears to act on instinct and leads the proper pollinator to behave in such a manner that pollination can occur. Dodson observed numerous instances of male euglossine bees being attracted to orchids and scratching on the sepals for long periods of time. However, the proper species of bee would immediately enter the flower correctly and effect pollination. In other cases the odor spectrum of one species may come very near to that of another and elicit a hovering in front of the flower, while testing the odor, but the bee will not continue the sequence by landing. The odor-attraction spectrum may well vary within a particular species of bee in various portions of its geographical range, as indicated by reports of certain species of bee visiting orchid species in Brazil or Venezuela which they do not visit in Costa Rica and Panama (misdetermination of the bees or orchids in the early reports may contribute to this variance).

The male bees in all of the genera tend to be attracted by the strong fragrances of a number of orchids which provide no food but do exude intoxicating liquids when scratched, e.g., *Catasetum*, *Cycnoches*, *Stanhopea* and *Gongora*. The bees apparently absorb these liquids through pads located on the tarsi of the front pair of legs (Fig. 32). Only male bees of these genera have such pads. Experiments conducted by Dodson (unpublished) in Ecuador, in which the inside of the lip of *Catasetum* flowers was scratched and the exuding liquid sopped up with filter paper and which when saturated was applied to freshly captured male bees by

FIG. 32. Legs from a male and female bee of *Eulaema*. Note the brushes on the front feet of the male bee (top right).

FIG. 33. Male bees of *Euplusia purpurata* scratching on the surface of a board that had been sprayed with aldrin several months previously.

FIG. 34. Male *Eulaema cingulata* scratching at the spadix of a flower of *Spathiphyllum cannaefolium*.

FIG. 35. Male *Euplusia surinamensis* at the petals of *Sobralia violacea*.

holding the paper against the pads on the tarsi, resulted in extreme grogginess on the part of the treated bees. The same process using distilled water in place of the liquid from the flowers left the bees unaffected. Vogel (1963) found no sense cells in the pads on the tarsi of the bees and suggested that they only absorb the fluids to transport them to organs located in the swollen tibia of the hind legs. The male bees also scratch on wood (Fig. 33) and certain other flowers such as *Anthurium* spp. and *Spathiphyllum* spp. (Fig. 34).

The immediate reaction of the male bees to the liquid can only be called intoxication. They lose motor control to a considerable degree and become clumsy and sluggish and are no longer wary. They apparently "enjoy" the sensation for they return continually over long periods of time before tiring and flying away, only to return to other similar flowers which may or may not be of the same genus or species. Most of the orchids which produce these effects appear to be rather advanced but there may be some special stimulant or depressant in the nectar of the "simple" genera. Darwin reported that a British bumblebee was seen stupified after drinking from *Sobralia macrantha* in a hothouse. We have observed similar reactions from *Sobralia violacea* and *S. rosea* in *Euplusia*, *Eulaema* and *Xylocopa* in Ecuador. In one instance a male *Euplusia surinamensis* scratched on the inside of the petals of *Sobralia violacea* (Fig. 35). Often euglossine bees are observed scratching on the sepals or petal of orchids that they do not pollinate (Fig. 36). As no details were given on a reported case of bees drugged by *Cymbidium devonianum* in northern India, we simply mention it (Ghose, 1955). The excessively long visit of *Halictus subinclinans*, the pollinator of the Australian *Caladenia deformis*, is also unexplained (Rogers, 1931). Pollination of *Diuris* is mentioned on p. 138.

The habits of these bees have made it possible for the orchids to develop surprisingly intricate pollination mechanisms which by shape or placement of pollinaria on the bee preclude pollination of other flowers of compatible genera or species. The groggy, intoxicated bees can be manipulated by the flowers in a manner which would scare away a "sober" bee, or in other cases, the "sober" bee would be too nimble to effect pollination.

Relations Between Male Euglossine Bees and Orchids

The advanced orchids which produce intoxicating substances appear to attract the male bees by means of strong odors alone. No apparent food is produced. On the contrary, not even rudimentary nectaries are present. Some of the species possess extremely variable colors which obviously have little significance in attraction. Though this ecological group of orchids contains several unrelated genera, e.g., *Pescatorea* (Pl. IIIa), *Cyrtopodium*, *Lycaste* and *Trichopilia*, two subtribes are strongly specialized in this direction: the Stanhopeinae and Catasetinae.

Crüger (1865) in a short paper published the basic observations (from Trinidad) on this most curious group of orchids, and Darwin devoted considerable space in the second edition of his book to Crüger's remarks. Unfortunately, Crüger did not observe carefully for his paper contains several errors.

The queer morphological forms of the flowers are connected with ultimate precision, forcing the male bee to follow more or less involuntarily a prescribed path of reaction after being drugged. In the Catasetinae the pollinarium is ejected onto the visitor when he comes in contact with special organs (the antennae of *Catasetum*, structures developed from the sides of the column near the rostellum, called horns by Darwin; see Pl. IIIb-d). This reaction has long been the subject of controversy as to whether it is sensitivity with conduction or just mechanical triggering of a leverage-tension system. Knoll (1958) presented good arguments for considering it as a mechanism working with release of tension. Dodson (1962b) demonstrated conclusively that the expulsion of the pollinaria in all of the genera is based on the leverage-tension system.

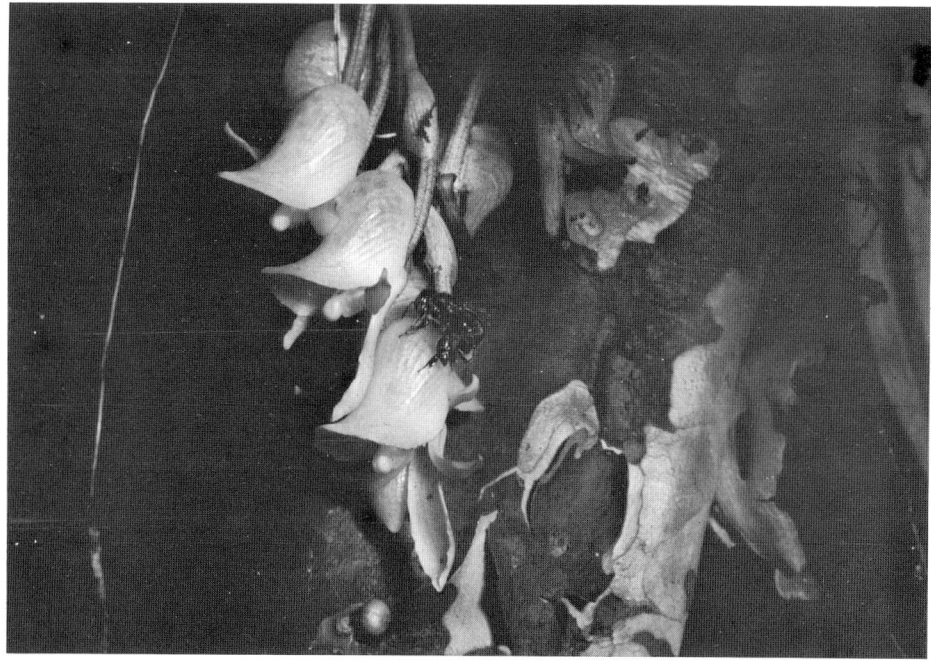

FIG. 36. Male *Euglossa townsendii*, an associate visitor but not a pollinator, scratching at the exterior of the sepals of *Schlimia trifida*.

FIG. 37. Male *Eulaema cingulata* scratching inside the lip of *Catasetum eburneum*. (Posed.)

The two subtribes, endlines of evolution, followed special paths deviating from the general trend of orchid evolution. They abandoned, as we have previously pointed out, the one-visit method. The Stanhopeinae do this by dichogamy, making two visits necessary. The flowers first have a male phase, with the stigma aperture too narrow for reception, and a later female phase in which the stigma aperture opens sufficiently for deposition of pollinia (the pollinia dry and become thinner with exposure as well), often separated by hours. This dichogamy explains the difficulties Crüger and Darwin experienced when trying to fit the pollinia into the narrow stigma aperture.

Catasetinae

In the Catasetinae the flowers have "taken a further step" in this direction largely becoming "unisexual," which we considered previously (p. 17) as simply separation of the receptive and deposition functions (dicliny). The difference in function of the two "sexes" is expressed in differences in shape and position. In *Catasetum*, the female flowers have the column underneath and in most species the male flowers have the column above. In *Cycnoches egertonianum* the female flowers sometimes are twenty times as heavy as the male flowers. The usual preponderance in number of male flowers (here about 25:1) is reached in a curious manner. Only plants which receive an optimum amount of sunlight produce female flowers. In other species of both *Catasetum* and *Cycnoches* the ratio of male flowers to female is maintained by natural conditions in the habitat which produce sufficient shade to keep the plants from producing female flowers in excess of those ratios (for a longer discussion of these phenomena and their importance in evolution in the group see Dodson, 1962b).

Pollination is effected in *Catasetum eburneum*, which has both male and female elements in the same flower, by males of *Eulaema cingulata* (Dodson and Frymire, 1961b). The bees approach the flowers, which are carried on spikes of 10-20 flowers each, land upon the open surface of a flower and attempt to reach the source of the strong, clove oil-like fragrance which emanates from the cavity of the lip (Fig. 37) In attempting to thrust its head into the cavity of the non-resupinate lip, the bee moves a small hump on the anther cap and the stipe is released, flinging the sticky viscidium upwards where it strikes the bee either on the trochanters of his legs or in front of the first pair of legs. The stipe of the pollinarium, immediately after attachment to the bee, is curled and does not dry and straighten out for several minutes. This tends to insure that the bee will have flown on to another plant and will effect cross-fertilization. The viscidium covers the stigmatic surface of the flower and requires that the pollinarium be removed before pollination can occur. When a bee with pollinarium attached comes to a flower and repeats the attempt to enter, the pollinia are forced into the stigmatic cavity and are trapped by the narrow extremities of the cavity and pulled from the bee upon his exit from the flower.

Lankester (1960) reported the pollination of *Catasetum dilectum*, a very similar but smaller-flowered species from Costa Rica, by male bees of the genus *Euglossa*.

The pollination of *Catasetum russellianum*, also a species with perfect flowers, by *Eulaema cingulata* was observed by Dodson (1965a) in Nicaragua (Fig. 38). The anther of this species is only slightly motile and therefore a different

FIG. 38. Male *Eulaema cingulata* visiting *Catasetum russellianum*. (Drawing by P. Fawcett.)

FIG. 39. Male bees of *Eulaema polychroma*, *E. cingulata* and *E. bomboides* visiting and scratching at the inside of the lip of *Catasetum macroglossum*. (Posed.)

All of the color illustrations were taken by C. H. Dodson

PLATE I a (upper left): *Ornithocephalus avicula* being visited and pollinated by the bee *Paratetrapedia testacea*. IQUITOS, PERU.

PLATE I b (upper right): *Centris sp.*, a female bee, pollinating *Odontoglossum grande*. CARTAGO, COSTA RICA.

PLATE I c (lower left): *Eulaema polychroma* entering the flower of *Sobralia* aff. *weberbaueriana*. MEDELLIN, COLOMBIA.

PLATE I d (lower right): Female *Eulaema cingulata* entering the flower of *Maxillaria sanderiana*. BAÑOS, ECUADOR.

PLATE II a (above left): Male *Eulaema polychroma* entering the flower of *Cattleya maxima*. Note the pollinia on the thorax of the bee. (Posed.) GUAYAQUIL, ECUADOR.

PLATE II c (middle left): Male *Euglossa augaspis* (mss. Moure) hovering in front of the flowers of *Notylia buchtenii*. IQUITOS, PERU.

PLATE III a (lower left): Male *Eulaema polychroma* pollinating the flowers of *Pescatorea vallisii*. GUAYAQUIL, ECUADOR.

PLATE II b (above right): Male *Eulaema seabrae* visiting and pollinating the flower of *Cochleanthes aromatica*. Note the pollinarium on the head of the bee. CARTAGO, COSTA RICA.

PLATE II d (middle right): Male *Eulaema polychroma* entering the flower of *Cattleya warszewiczii*. Note the pollinarium on the thorax of the bee. MEDELLIN, COLOMBIA.

PLATES III b-c-d: Pollination of *Catasetum platyglossum* by a male bee of *Eulaema cingulata*. GUAYAQUIL, ECUADOR.

PLATE IIIb (lower right): The bee scratching in the cavity of the lip of the male flower.

PLATE III b-c-d: Pollination of *Catasetum platyglossum* by a male bee of *Eulaena cingulata*. GUAYAQUIL, ECUADOR.

PLATE III c (above left): The bee touching the antennae and releasing the pollinarium, which is thrown downward by leverage tension and becomes cemented to the thorax of the bee by the sticky viscidium.

PLATE III d (above right): The bee crawls inside the hood-shaped lip of the female flower to scratch. (Posed.) Note the pollinarium hanging over the flower.

PLATE IV a (middle left): Male bee of *Eulaena cingulata* visiting the male flower of *Cycnoches lehmanii*. GUAYAQUIL, ECUADOR.

PLATE IV b (middle right): Male bee of *Eulaena cingulata* falling from the lip of *Cycnoches lehmanii*, where it had been scratching. Note the pollinarium from a male flower extending from the abdomen of the bee. GUAYAQUIL, ECUADOR.

PLATE IV c-d: Male bee of Euglossa pollinating a form of *Cycnoches egertonianum*.

PLATE IV c (lower left): Male bee hanging from the flexible lip of the male flower. Note the pollinarium extending from the abdomen of the bee. TURRIALBA, COSTA RICA.

PLATE IV d (lower right): Bee visiting and scratching on the lip of the female flower. TURRIALBA, COSTA RICA.

PLATES V a-b: Male bee of *Eulaema nigrita* pollinating *Cycnoches aureum*. EL VALLE, PANAMA.

PLATE V a (above left): Bee on male flower.

PLATES V c-d: Male bee of *Euglossa ignita* pollinating *Cycnoches egertonianum*. COSTA RICA.

PLATE V c (middle left): Bee on male flower.

PLATE VI a (lower left): Male *Euglossa hemichlora* scratching at the lip of *Mormodes* cf. *buccinator*. Note the freshly deposited pollinarium on the thorax of the bee with the stipe still tightly curled. GUAYAQUIL, ECUADOR.

PLATE V b (above right): Bee on female flower.

PLATE V d (middle right): Bee on female flower.

PLATE VI b (lower right): Male *Eulaema meriana*, one of four species of bee which visit and pollinate the flowers of *Coeliopsis hyacinthosma*. EL VALLE, PANAMA.

PLATE VIc (above left): Male *Euglossa ignita* crawling on the balanced lip of *Peristeria pendula*. Note the pollinarium on the thorax of the bee. IQUITOS, PERU.

PLATE VId (above right): Male *Euglossa purpurea* scratching at the lip of *Polycycnis gratiosa*. Note that the weight of the bee has depressed the flower so that contact with the column of the flower is assured when the bee exits. EL VALLE, PANAMA.

system for attaching the pollinarium is presented. The bee, in attempting to enter the orifice of the saccate lip near the base of the column, touches the stipe of the pollinarium. The viscidium is released and swings down into such a position that in withdrawing from the flower the bee must push against it with its thorax. The sticky pad of the viscidium becomes fixed to the top of his thorax and upon entrance to, and exit from, another flower—allowing time for the anther cap to dry and fall off—the pollinia are left behind in the narrow stigmatic cavity. This is one of the more primitive species in the subtribe.

In the more advanced species of *Catasetum* a different system of pollination exists because the sexes are in separate flowers. Pollination of several species in this group has been reported. Crüger (1865) described the pollination of *C. macrocarpum*; Allen (1952) and Dodson (1965a) observed the pollination of *C. maculatum* (*C. oerstedii*) by *Eulaema cingulata* and *E. polychroma*; Hoehne (1933) reported pollination of *C. cernuum* by *Euplusia violacea*; Ostlund (in notes) mentioned *C. integerrimum* as pollinated by *Eulaema* and *C. costatum* by *Euglossa* while Pollard (personal communication) photographed *Eulaema cingulata* and *E. polychroma* working *C. integerrimum* species. Dodson and Frymire (1961b) described the pollination of *C. macroglossum* (Fig. 39) and *C. platyglossum* (Pl. IIIb-d). *Catasetum fimbriatum* was observed being visited by *Euplusia auriceps*, *Catasetum bicolor* by *Euglossa cordata*, and *C. viridiflavum* by *Eulaema cingulata* by Dressler (personal communication). *Catasetum saccatum* is visited by *Eulaema cingulata* in Peru (Dodson, 1965a) and *C. hookeri* and *C. barbatum* by *Euglossa cordata* in Brazil (Dodson and Dressler, unpublished). *Catasetum tabulare* is pollinated by *Eulaema cingulata* in northwestern Colombia (Dodson, unpublished).

In all of these species, two or three days after opening the male flowers begin emitting a strong musky-sweet odor. Male bees land upon, and enter the flower, and proceed to scratch at the source of the odor. This is normally located just under the antennae which, when contacted by the bee, move the rostellum which holds the viscidium in place. The viscidium is released and is flung by the tension-bound stipe onto the back of the bee. The adhesive substance on the viscidium sets rapidly and the stipe hangs back along the dorsal midline of the abdomen of the bee. The anther cap does not fall from the pollinia for at least 20 minutes. The bee may then proceed in its wandering to a mature, aromatic, female flower (Pl. IIIc). The odor production in the male flowers has been found to change in its major components as early as 15 minutes after the anther has been discharged. Within 25 minutes the odor production had decreased more than 50%, as shown with a gas-chromatograph (Dodson, unpublished).

The female flower takes somewhat longer to mature than does the male and begins to give off a strong odor on the third or fourth day after opening. The non-resupinate female flowers last up to a month if not pollinated and continue to emit their strong fragrance during the day. The fragrance, however, disappears within hours after pollination and the stigma swells shut. Bees enter the female flowers much as they do the hooded male flowers of some species. All of the female flowers are hood-shaped and in most cases it is not possible to separate species on the basis of the female flowers alone. When a bee with a pollinarium attached to the dorsum of its thorax enters a flower, the stipe, hinged at the viscidium, swings down in line with the stigmatic cleft. As the bee backs out to leave the flower, one or both of the pollen masses are guided down on the backside of the lip and are caught in the stigmatic cleft. They are then wrenched free—due to leverage—from the weak bonds with the stipe and are left to fertilize the flower.

Porsch (1955) observed the nervous conduct of male bees on a *Catasetum*, and made the same mistake as earlier observers in believing that they gnawed the callus inside the galeate, upright labellum. He pointed out, however, that the quantity of tissue consumed seemed so small that it could not act as food. He also compiled data on intoxicating odors in the genus.

Cycnoches is called the swan-orchid because of its white lip and slender, arched column, down-turned in both sexes. The pollination process in *Cycnoches lehmannii*, a member of the group in which the male and female flowers are similar, appears very complex but in reality is quite simple. The system depends on perfect placement of the bee in relation to the lip and column of the flower. In order for the bee to be properly placed the flower has developed a non-resupinate lip, forcing the bee to land in an inverted position. The female flower appears to have an odor that is a little stronger and more penetrating than the male flower. Male bees of *Eulaema cingulata* approach the male flower and land on the inverted lip, gradually swinging around into an inverted position with the 2nd and 3rd pair of legs grasping the edges of the lip (Pl. IVa). The tarsi of the first pair of legs are brushed back and forth on the apex of the callus. The odor appears to emanate from between the apex of the callus and the lip. The extended callus of the male flower forces the bee, in attempting to get closer to the source of the odor, to swing his abdomen down and release his lower pair of legs. This is an awkward position and the lower portion of the abdomen of the bee brushes the trigger mechanism of the column. The brushing of the tip of the anther cap releases the viscidium, which is held under tension in what would normally be the stigmatic region in a bisexual flower. The stipe whips the viscidium around, striking the bee on the apex of the abdomen where it sticks by means of its rapidly drying cement. The anther cap remains over the pollinia and the stipe is curled around the end of the bee's abdomen. The stipe of the pollinarium, through differential drying of the two sides, gradually straightens and after about 40 minutes reaches a stiff, pendant position. The anther cap remains in place, covering the pollinia for about two to three hours before drying sufficiently to fall. The pollinarium is now ready for the bee to pollinate the female flower.

The female flower is constructed similarly to that of the male but the position of the column and stigma is different in relation to the callus of the lip, the column being much shorter and thicker. The callus is not as extended as in the male flower and the bee has little difficulty in hanging and scratching on the callus tip. When the bee is ready to fly he must fall for a short distance to be able to revert to a flying position. In falling, the bee, through his position on the callus, is oriented in such a manner that in passing the column the pollinia are caught by the finger-like processes of that structure (Pl. IVb). One of the pollinia is caught between the processes and is stripped from the stipe. Within a few hours the stigma swells, closing around the pollinium and the odor ceases. The sepals and petals wither and the pod ripens about a year after pollination. Pollination of this species was reported in Dodson and Frymire (1961b). Allen (1952) reported similar phenomena in the pollination of *Cycnoches warscewiczii* by *Eulaema cingulata* in Central America. *Cycnoches ventricosum* was observed being worked by *Eulaema cingulata* in Nicaragua by Dodson (1965a). Pollinia of *Cycnoches pentadactylon* were found on *Euplusia superba* in Peru by Dodson (1965a).

Pollination of *Cycnoches egertonianum* is similar in most respects except that special adaptions for the much smaller *Euglossa* have resulted in different male flowers. *Cycnoches egertonianum* is a member of the heteromorphic group of *Cycnoches* in which the male flowers—unlike the subgenus *Cycnoches* to which C. *lehmannii* and C. *ventricosum* belong—are strikingly different from the female flowers. The male flowers of this species and its close allies are small and are carried on long pendant spikes. The lip is somewhat different from that of *C. lehmannii* in that the claw is thin and flexible and the blade is divided into numerous fleshy terete divisions. Male bees of *Euglossa hemichlora* were observed pollinating a form of this species (described as *C. peruviana*) in eastern Ecuador (Dodson and Frymire, 1961b). The bees land on the blade of the lip, which then swings down with the weight of the bee (Pl. IVc). This action causes the tip of the bee's abdomen to touch and lift the anther cap on the apex of the column, discharging the pollinarium, which becomes affixed to the bee much as in *Cycnoches lehmannii*. The female flowers are nearly identical to those of *C. lehmannii* except that they are smaller and are darker green in color. The pollination of the female flower is essentially the same as discussed above for *C. lehmannii*. Allen (1952) placed the numerous described species in the heteromorphic section as synonymous with *C. egertonianum*. This treatment now appears to be in error. One of the species, which Allen considered as a sub-species of *C. egertonianum*, is *C. aureum* and was found to be exclusively pollinated by *Eulaema nigrita* (Pl. Va and b) in Panama (Dressler and Dodson, unpublished). Four forms of *C. egertonianum* from Panama and Costa Rica were found to be exclusively pollinated by specific species of *Euglossa* (Pl. V) which do not visit other forms even if placed together in the same area (Dressler, personal communication and Dressler

FIG. 40. Male *Euglossa viridissima* visiting the female flowers of *Mormodes lineatum*. (Photo by G. Pollard.)

FIG. 41. Male *Euglossa hemichlora* on the lip of *Mormodes* cf. *buccinator*. Note the dried pollinarium on the thorax of the bee. The stipe uncurled as the drying process took place and the pollinia are now held erect where they can be caught in the broad stigma of the flower.

and Dodson, unpublished). These allies of *C. egertonianum* are unquestionably distinct species and are maintained as such by the exclusiveness of their pollinators. When carefully examined distinguishing morphological characters between the kinds can be found in the male flowers.

Pollination of *Mormodes* has been reported for twelve species. Darwin (1872) extensively and accurately described the mechanism of the flower of *M. ignea* and we recommend his discussion for further details. He, unfortunately, had no information as to the actual pollinators and we therefore include supplemental information from observations of their pollination. Allen (1954) reported *M. ignea* as pollinated by *Euglossa cordata*; Oestlund (in notes) recorded *Euglossa* pollinating *M. buccinator*, *M. lineatum* and *M. uncia*; Pollard photographed *Euglossa viridissima* visiting *M. lineatum* (Fig. 40); Dressler (personal communication) observed pollination of *M. atropurpurea* by *Euglossa championi*, *M. colossus* by *Euglossa* spp., *M. cartonii* by *Euglossa cordata*, *M. powellii* by *Euglossa* sp., and *M. flavidum* by *Euglossa viridissima* in Panama and Costa Rica, and Dodson (1962a) observed the pollination of *M.* aff. *buccinator* in Ecuador. In the latter observation, male *Euglossa hemichlora* with pollinia attached to their thorax were seen visiting female flowers of *M.* aff. *buccinator*. The bees land on the outstretched lip and proceed to scratch the surface of the lip with their front pair of legs. While moving around on the flat lip, the pollinia, standing erect from the stipe of the pollinarium, on the backs of the bees, come in contact with the very broad stigmatic surface and the pollinia become detached. Though the anther of the pistillate flower in *Mormodes* is capable of discharging the pollinarium, it is held up and far away from the lip of the flower in a position which would be very difficult for a bee to encounter and discharge. In many species the flowers are first male until the anther has been discharged and then become female by unwinding and raising the column (Dodson, 1962b). In purely male flowers the column is twisted in such a manner that the apex of the column lies in contact with the lip (Fig. 41). Usually the twisting places the back of the column in contact with the lip. The anther thus faces outward. A small terete finger or tubercle formed from the tip of the column is in contact with the anther cap (the filament and hinge of Darwin). This tubercle lies on the surface of the lip and the slightest movement moves the anther cap off of the small pedicel around which it is clasped and allows the viscidium to be released. The viscidium, carried by the stipe, springs around and strikes any object which has moved the tubercle. The cement on the viscidium quickly dries, leaving the pollinarium attached to the insect but tightly curled (Pl. VIa). After about 30 minutes the stipe straightens and the pollinia are held erect from the thorax of the bee (Fig. 41). When the bee walks under the stigma of the flower contact is made.

Stanhopeinae

The pollination phenomena of the *Stanhopea* alliance is based on the same principles as in the Catasetinae but with the separation in sexes being in time rather than in space. Self-pollination is averted by dichogamy. The stigma is narrow when the bee first visits and the pollinia are thick before drying and therefore cannot be inserted (Dodson and Frymire, 1961a and b). The intoxicating liquids and powerful fragrances for attraction are present. In the Catasetinae, male flowers are organized to position the bee perfectly so that when the pollinarium is discharged the viscidium becomes attached at a specific location. In this manner it will fit properly in the stigmatic cleft when the bee visits a female flower. In most species of the Stanhopeinae the flowers are organized so as to take advantage of the erratic flight habits and slowed reflexes of drugged male bees. Their pollination mechanisms, in the more spectacular forms, manipulate the bees so as to make them fall either through a chute, down a slide, or into a "bucket" of water.

Relatively simple mechanisms are found in the flowers of some genera in the *Stanhopea* alliance. Probably the simplest system—and apparently the most effective in terms of successful pollination—is that of *Coeliopsis hyacinthosma*. The long lasting, highly fragrant, white flowers of the single species are typical of the bee-pollinated orchid model and are produced in head-like clusters. Male bees of *Eulaema cingulata*, *E. meriana*, *Euplusia schmidtiana* and *E.* cf. *surinamensis* were observed pollinating this species in Panama (Dodson and Dressler, unpublished). The bees land on the inflorescence and reach into the bell-shaped flowers to scratch at the base of the simple 3-lobed lip (Pl. VIb). The bees force their way in as far as possible and contact the sticky viscidium with the tip of the frons of the head. The viscidium becomes attached and the two tiny flattened pollinia are held erect on the stipe. On visiting another flower the pollinia slide into the stigmatic pocket as the bee backs from the flower. Numerous seed pods are produced from each inflorescence and an abundance of seed is released. The species is often quite common but has a very restricted local distribution in Panama and Costa Rica. The populations are only found in the dampest of cloud forest

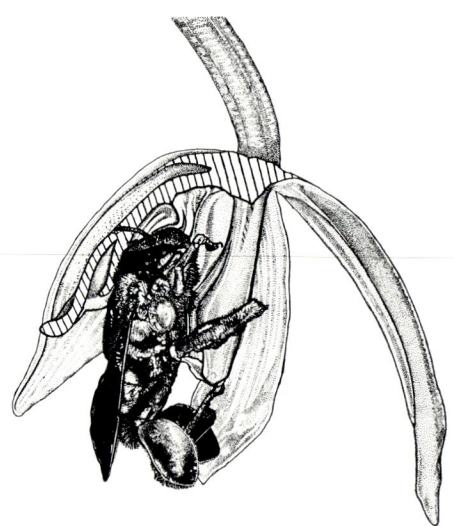

FIG. 42. Male *Euglossa nigropilosa* entering the flower of *Sievekingia jenmannii*. The bee lands on the petals of the flower rather than on the lip, and the pollinaria are attached to the bases of the middle pair of legs. (Drawing by L. Mourré.)

associations at intermediate elevations. Perhaps the success of the pollination system equalizes the relative lack of success in terms of adaption to varied habitats.

In *Acineta* the flowers are each pointed downward on a pendant raceme. The sepals and petals hood the lip and column, leaving a tunnel for the bee to enter. The bee crawls upward into the flower, scratches at the inside of the saccate base of the lip and on the way out picks up the viscidium of the pollinarium on its scutellum. *Acineta chrysantha, A. barkeri* and *A. superba* are all pollinated by *Euplusia concava* (Dodson, 1965a, Grant, personal communication, and Dressler, personal communication) but are geographically isolated.

The genus *Peristeria* is allied to *Acineta* but the flowers have a distinct pollination system. The sepals and petals form a cup but the lip is articulated with the column and overbalances with the added weight of the pollinator, throwing the bee against the column and trapping it between the lip and the column. The pollinarium is attached to the thorax of the bee as it struggles to get out of the flower. *Peristeria pendula* was observed to be pollinated by *Euglossa ignita* (Pl. VIc) in Peru (Dodson, 1965a) while *P. elata* is pollinated by *Euplusia concava* in Panama (Dressler, personal communication).

The pollination mechanism of *Sievekingia jenmannii* is quite unique. In all the species of *Sievekingia* the flowers are pointed downward on a pendant spike as in *Acineta* but are densely clustered in a head-like inflorescence. Male bees of *Euglossa nigropilosa* hover under the inflorescence of *S. jenmannii* and crawl upward into the flowers but use the petals as a landing platform rather than the lip. Spine-like processes from the callus inhibit their entrance and guide the bees into position over the column where the cupped viscidium is attached to one end of the tibia of the second pair of legs (Fig. 42). Entry into a subsequent flower results in placement of the pollinia in the stigmatic pocket (Dodson, 1965a). The same mechanism is reported for *S. suavis* which is pollinated by

Euglossa dodsoni and for *S. fimbriata* which is pollinated by two unnamed species of *Euglossa* (Dressler #117 and 120). Both species of *Sievekingia* are visited by other species of *Euglossa*, *Eulaema* and *Euplusia* but they are either of improper size or do not seem oriented properly to enter the flowers facing the column and therefore are not effective pollinators (Dressler, personal communication). In *Paphinia clausula* the white flowers are pendant and the papillate lip is uppermost in the semi-closed flowers. Bees of *Euglossa gorgonensis* swarm around the flowers. While entering and leaving the flowers the pollinaria are attached to the legs of the bees (Fig. 43) (Dodson and Dressler, unpublished).

The flowers of *Schlimia trifida* are unusual in that the sepals are united to form a hood and the lip is greatly reduced. Bees of *Euplusia* cf. *purpurata* were observed entering and scratching at the lip in Colombia (Dodson, unpublished). The pollinarium is apparently deposited under the projection at the back of the dorsal thorax of the bee.

Dressler (personal communication) reported the pollination of *Kegeliella atropilosa* by *Euplusia concava*. Details of the pollination mechanism was not given but apparently it is not particularly complex. The complexities of the lip must function in positioning the bees while the pollinarium is deposited on the back of the head.

Polycycnis depends upon the weight of the bee to depress the entire flower sufficiently so that the viscidium which projects from the long slender column will slide under the dorsal thorax of the bee (Pl. VId). Bees of *Euglossa* sp. (RLD 77) were observed pollinating *Polycycnis gratiosa* in Panama (Dodson and Dressler, unpublished).

In *Stanhopea* two systems occur but some species show intergradation. In the more primitive species such as *S. pulla*, *S. ecornuta* and *S. annulata* pollination is similar to that of *Acineta* with the pollinarium being deposited on the bee as it leaves the flower. *Stanhopea ecornuta* has been reported to be pollinated by *Euplusia schmidtiana* (Dressler, personal communication). *Stanhopea cirrhata*

FIG. 43. The pollination of *Paphinia clausula* by *Euglossa gorgonensis*. (Left) Bee entering the pendant inverted flower. Note pollinarium attached to the middle leg of the bee and hanging below the abdomen. (Right) Bee inside the flower in the position for pollination.

FIG. 44. Male *Eulaema seabrae* scratching at the basal concavity of the lip of *Stanhopea costaricensis*.

has the flowers pointed downward and the bees fall a bit as they leave. *S. cirrhata* is pollinated by an *Euglossa* (Wilson, personal communication). *Stanhopea tricornis* (Pl. VIIa) is pollinated by *Eulaema meriana* (Dodson and Frymire, 1961a). In the advanced species, e.g., *S. costaricensis* (Fig. 44), the flowers are turned so as to face downward with the lip and column pendant while the sepals and petals are reflexed. The base of the lip is saccate and separated from the arched column. The bee enters here rather than at the apex of the lip and column, which are close together and developed so as to form a chute. The rostellum with the viscidium attached projects into the chute. After becoming intoxicated the bee attempts to fly out. The column interferes with his hampered flying equilibrium and he falls, abdomen first, down through the chute, picking up the viscidium under his metathorax as he passes (Fig. 45). Species of *Stanhopea* which employ this advanced system are listed below with their pollinators:

Species	Pollinator	Reported by
S. candida	*Euglossa ignita* (Pl. VIIb)	Dodson (1965a)
S. connata	*Eulaema speciosa* (Pl. VIIc)	Dodson (1965a)
S. costaricensis	*Eulaema seabrae* (Fig. 44)	Dodson (1965a)
S. florida	*Euglossa nigropilosa* (Fig. 46)	Dodson (1965a)
S. gibbosa	*Eulaema meriana* (Fig. 45)	Dodson (1965a)
S. grandiflora	*Eulaema meriana*	Ducke (1902) and Dressler (pers. comm.)
S. aff. *jenishiana*	*Eulaema bomboides*	Dodson and Frymire (1961a)

S. oculata	*Eulaema cingulata*	Heller (in Litt.)
S. reichenbachiana	*Eulaema leucopyga*	Dodson (unpublished)
S. saccata	*Euglossa viridissima* (Fig. 47)	Dressler, Swartz, Pollard (in Litt.)
S. tigrina	*Euglossa viridissima* (Pl. VIId)	Friese (1899)
S. wardii	*Eulaema polychroma*	Dodson (1965a)
S. warszewicziana	*Euplusia macroglossa* (Fig. 48)	Dodson (1965a)

The genus *Gongora* has developed rather unique pollination mechanisms based on inverted bees. Bees of *Euglossa viridissima* were observed to land on the flower of *Gongora armeniaca* and enter between the lip and the column after turning upsidedown (Pl. VIIIa). After scratching at the opening at the base of the lip the bee backs slightly, held in position by the petals at each side, and picks up the viscidium of the pollinarium on its scutellum. The pollinia are left in the stigma on a succeeding visit (Dodson, 1965a). The sympatric and similar G. *horichiana* (previously known as G. *armeniaca* var. *bicornuta*) is pollinated in the same manner but by a different species of bee, *Euglossa dodsoni* (Pl. VIIIb). The two forms produce distinct odors and apparently attract different species of pollinators on that basis.

Gongora quinquenervis and G. *grossa* have a similar system (Allen, 1954 and Dodson and Frymire, 1961b and Dressler, personal communication) with the exception that the column is longer and arched downward under the lip, leaving

FIG. 45. Male bee of *Eulaema meriana* falling through the flower of *Stanhopea gibbosa* after having become intoxicated by scratching at the base of the lip of the flower. The pollinarium is attached to the thorax of the bee as it falls through the flower.

FIG. 46. Male bee of *Euglossa nigropilosa* landing in the basal part of the lip of *Stanhopea florida*.

considerable space between the two. The *Euglossa* which pollinate these species land and crawl around to the underside of the lip and are positioned by projecting spines on each side of the lip (Fig. 49). The bees scratch at the cavity of the hypochile and drop loose occasionally. When they drop they must fall for a short distance to regain their balance and turn over. While falling they slide down the inside surface of the column, back first (Fig. 50). The rostellum projects from the line of the slide and the passing bees pick up the pollinarium under their dorsal abdomen. Later a bee with pollinarium attached can pollinate the flower.

More complex is the pollination of members of the genus *Cirrhaea*. Here the inflorescence is pendant but the flowers are turned so as to stand erect. Bees of the genus *Euglossa* or *Euplusia* land on the erect lip. They touch the extended rostellum, where the sticky viscidium is attached to the legs. Hoehne (1933) reported a species of this genus to be pollinated by an *Euplusia violacea* and six bees of *Euglossa mandibularis* were found in the Museum of the University of Kansas with a total of seventeen pollinaria attached to their legs.

The pollination of *Coryanthes* is an old story first reported by Crüger (1865) for *C. macrantha* and amplified by Allen (1951) for *C. speciosa* (Fig. 51) and Dodson (1965b) for the genus. The flowers are very large and might be considered to be grotesque. The sepals and petals fold back out of the way when the flowers open—like sails on a boat—revealing the strangely formed lip. The lip is divided into three parts: a globular or hood-shaped hypochile above, an elongate, sometimes fluted, mesochile and a bucket-shaped epichile. The epichile is partially filled with water during the last few hours before the flower opens and for a short time after anthesis by two faucet-like organs at the base of the column which drip water. *Euglossa, Euplusia* or *Eulaema* are attracted by the strong odor produced by the hypochile where they scratch (Pl. VIIIc). They then fall or are knocked into the water-filled bucket of the epichile. In order to escape they must leave by way of a tunnel formed by the apex of the column and the epichile of the lip and the pollinarium is deposited upon their abdomen as they crawl out (Pl. VIIId). The pollinia are deposited in the stigma of the succeeding flower visited.

In Iquitos, Peru, Dodson (1965b) observed pollination of three of the five species of *Coryanthes* which occur sympatrically there. *Coryanthes macrantha* is pollinated there by *Eulaema cingulata* (F. Bennett forwarded 32 bees of *Eulaema basalis* and one of *E. cingulata* carrying pollinia of *C. macrantha* from Trinidad). *Coryanthes trifoliata* is pollinated by *Euglossa ignita* (Pl. IXa-b) and *C. rodriguezii* by *Euplusia superba* (Pl. IXc-d). *Coryanthes albo-rosea* did not attract pollinators during the single period of observation. *C. maculata* was not encountered in flower during the period but has been reported by Dressler (personal communication) to be pollinated by *Euglossa azureoviridis* and is probably pollinated by the same bee in Iquitos. Flowering plants of *Coryanthes leucocorys* in the garden of Lee Moore near Iquitos attracted many bees of *Euglossa ignita* (Pl. IXc) and one *Eulaema meriana*. The latter bee could have been an effective pollinator but *Euglossa ignita* is too small and passed under the anther without dislodging it. *Coryanthes bicalcarata* (Pl. IXd) also was pollinated by *Euglossa cordata* in the same garden. These species occur sympatrically near Moyobamba in Peru, about 400 miles from Iquitos, where they may be pollinated by other bees. From their dimensions, however, it can be deduced that *C. leucocorys* must be pollinated by a large bee and *C. bicalcarata* by an *Euglossa* similar to *E. cordata* if not that species.

FIG. 47. Male bee of *Euglossa viridissima* hovering in front of the flower of *Stanhopea saccata*. (Photo by G. Pollard.)

FIG. 48. Male bee of *Euplusia macroglossa* entering the base of the lip of *Stanhopea warscewicziana*.

FIG. 49. Male bee of *Euglossa hemichlora* scratching at the lip of *Gongora grossa*.

FIG. 50. Male bee of *Euglossa hemichlora* falling and sliding through the flower of *Gongora grossa*. (Posed.) The pollinaria are attached to the bee as it slides past the apex of the column.

Coryanthes wolfii was reported by Jativa (personal communication) to be pollinated by *Euglossa hemichlora* in western Ecuador.

No natural hybrids between the five sympatric species of *Coryanthes* at Iquitos were encountered. The species would appear to be effectively isolated by attraction of specific pollinators. The attraction would appear to be strictly based on production of different odors by each species of *Coryanthes*.

Pohl (1927) studied the anatomical aspects of the slide-flower as found in *Stanhopea* and found that the odor is almost exclusively produced by the callus tissue of the hypochile. Analyses of the odors produced by several species of *Stanhopea* made with a gas-chromatograph indicate that each species produces a distinctive odor (Dodson and Hills, 1966). This is probably fundamental to the maintenance of species differences in the more advanced members in the genus, particularly where they occur sympatrically. Each distinct odor seems to attract different species of bees of the Euglossini.

Crüger described the pollination of *Gongora maculata* on Trinidad as being accomplished by "the tip of the extremely long pendant tongues of *Euglossa* which hung down and touched the rostellum while the bee gnawed the callus tissue of the lip." This report has been discredited by both Allen (1954) and Dodson and Frymire (1961b).

Three important phenomena which are uncommon in other orchids have been brought out in the above discussion: dichogamy, dicliny and the passing of a long period of time before the pollinia are ready for deposition. These phenomena have been considered as mysterious expressions of orthogenic, exaggerated sexuality, or refinement. If taken from a functional approach, however, they are completely logical and occur in a rational sequence. In regular flowers a bee leaves an emptied flower for others. In these orchids, drugged male bees try immediately to re-enter the same flower which has kept its charm intact. This upsets the basic principle of avoidance of self-pollination and the three devices mentioned above provide a detour.

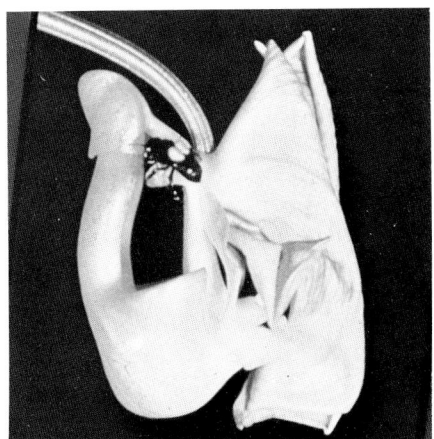 

FIG. 51. (Left) *Euglossa cordata* crawling on the flower of *Coryanthes speciosa* after exiting from the bucket of the lip, right. (Right) Bee emerging from flower. Note the pollinarium on the abdomen of the bee. (Photos by Paul Allen.)

The pollination of *Anguloa*, a relative of *Lycaste*, has long been a matter of conjecture. The sepals and petals form a large cup rather like a tulip. The lip stands erect and is articulated to the base of the column by a thin strap which allows the lip flexibility so that it easily moves back to the lateral sepals or forward to be appressed against the column. Male bees of *Eulaema boliviensis* were observed pollinating *Anguloa clowesii* in eastern Colombia by Dodson, (1966c). The bees at first attempt to enter the flower head first (Pl. Xa) but find the small shelf near the apex of the lip, which is the source of the odor, inaccessible from that position. They then turn and back into the flower, where they retain their position while scratching on the shelf by holding the edges of the petals with the second pair of legs (Pl. Xb). However, on exiting from the flower the bee releases its hold on the petals and grasps the lip with all six legs. The lip falls toward the column with the additional weight of the bee and the bee falls against the column. The long slender rostellum slips between the thorax and abdomen of the bee and as the bee struggles to escape the viscidium becomes attached to the abdomen. The pollinia are then withdrawn and carried away by the bee.

Male bees of *Eulaema cingulata* were captured pollinating flowers of *Anguloa ruckeri* in the garden by Mr. Robert Wilson of San Vito, Costa Rica. *Eulaema cingulata* may therefore be the pollinator of this species in its natural habitat in Venezuela and Colombia.

5. Social Bees and Orchids

As an anticlimax we now proceed to the social bees, which became large-scale, modern flower visitors on a different basis. The individual and instinctively determined behavior of the solitary ancestors of the social bees was sufficient for securing specific pollination during the short lives of bee and flower. This was replaced by the plastic, collectivistic and more socially oriented life of colonies. The colonies had to work during a long season and on a large number of flower species, shifting from one to another and away to different species for nectar or pollen for larval food. Perhaps orchids as a group could not follow this modern pollination trend. In addition, they could not obtain specificity from bonds with such widely polytropic pollinators.

The introduction of the superior honey bee in America is said to have had deleterious effects on the old populations of solitary bees with serious consequences for plants dependent on them as pollinators (Pearson, 1933). This may be a repetition of what happened in historical times in Europe where *Apis* is not native, certainly not in northern regions. In southern Asia the four species of *Apis* have had an ancient role in the pollination of orchids.

The genus *Melipona* was considered by Ducke as seen on diverse nectar-secreting orchids in South America. One common species, *M. beechii*, has been supposed to be the natural pollinator of *Vanilla* in Mexico. There is reason for doubt, however, as the pollinator of this flower must apparently comply with special requirements, for no other bee could take over in plantations elsewhere. The pollinating bee is either so local in Mexico or so inefficient that even there pollination is effected primarily by hand for commerce.

Several bees of *Melipona eburnea* were observed pollinating *Maxillaria furstenbergae* in Ecuador (Dodson, 1962a). The pollination mechanism is quite simple, with the bee simply landing on the lip, entering the flower between the column and lip and upon withdrawing having the yoke-shaped viscidium stuck to the apex of the metathorax (Pl. Xc). The pollinia are then withdrawn from the anther cap. The bees were apparently collecting the starch cells on the inside of the lip. *Melipona flavipennis* was encountered on numerous occasions by Dodson (1965a) pollinating *Cattleya luteola* before dawn in Amazonian Peru (see p. 81).

Bees of the genus *Trigona* tend to be erratic fliers and dystrophic feeders on all kinds of flowers. Therefore, they would not be expected to be efficient orchid pollinators. However, two species, *T. testacea* and *T. amalthea*, were encountered as pollinators of *Maxillaria reichenheimiana*. Several bees were involved and appeared to be acting in an efficient manner. An unusual observation of a bee of *T. amalthea* visiting flowers of *Coelogyne lawrenciana* (native of Asia), under cultivation in Costa Rica, was made recently (Dodson, unpublished). The bee in a state of excitation entered flower after flower, pollinating each with pollinia from a previous flower. No food was available and the bee entered and left each flower very quickly.

Trigona amalthea visit and pollinate the nectarless flowers of *Xylobium latilabium* (Pl. Xd) in Peru (Dodson, 1965a). Smaller *Trigona* (determined as *T. amalthea* also) pollinates *Xylobium variegatum* in Peru and Costa Rica but never visited *X. latilabium* even though they flew past that species in order to visit the flowers of *X. variegatum*.

Trigona (Partamona) nigrior was observed to effectively pollinate *Schomburgkia crispa* (*S. moyobambae*) by Dodson (1965a) in Amazonian Peru. Kerr

FIG. 52. The flower of *Trigonidium obtusum*.

and Lopez (1963) observed pollination of an orchid closely allied to *Maxillaria*, *Trigonidium obtusum* (Fig. 52) which was visited by *Trigona doryana* (males only). The bees attempted to copulate with both paired petals, which are glandular and produce odors (see p. 137 for further discussion). In Africa Kullenberg (1956) found worker-bees of *Trigona nebulata* very busy on *Eulophia* (*Lissochilus*) *horsfallii*. He saw them carrying pollinia, but was not certain of ensuing pollination.

Pollinia have been found on the hive-bee, *Apis mellifera*, in Europe from *Orchis morio*, *O. maculata*, *Epipactis palustris* and others, which they sometimes visit (the horn-disease of apiculture). A prominent bee-keeper there doubts that the bees are hindered severely and does not think that the pollinaria are used as food-pollen. The absence of easily collectable and serviceable pollen and the nuisance of the pollinia may help in explaining the unsatisfactory relationship. In addition the worker-bees are neuter and do not react to imitative sex scents. Many dicotyledonous families (Labiatae, Papilionaceae) went much further in the "quaternary," "democratic" direction toward pollination by collectivistic bees as outlined above.

Honeybees were observed visiting the flowers of the sweet-scented *Oncidium onustum* in the garden in Guayaquil but they were ineffective as pollinators. They also visit and pollinate orchids in greenhouses in temperate zones where they can become a pest to the commercial orchid grower.

Of the four natural species of *Apis*, the giant Indian honeybee, *A. dorsata*, has been reported most often as a pollinator of Malaysian orchids. *Apis dorsata* was mentioned as a rare, but efficient visitor on *Dendrobium crumenatum* and *Cymbidium finlaysonianum*, by Burkill (1919). Burkill also observed *Dendrobium superbum* being visited by *A. dorsata* and *A. indica*. Ridley (1905) reported *A. dorsata* as the effective pollinator of *Grammatophyllum speciosum*. That orchid is also visited by *Xylocopa* but they do not act as pollinators. Cultivated plants of *Grammatophyllum speciosum* are pollinated by *Augochlora pura* in Florida (L. C. Vaughn, personal communication).

In temperate zones *Bombus* has some importance in a few cases, according to the old literature. One instance is hyacinth-scented *Spiranthes autumnalis* in Europe, on which Darwin saw bumblebees, beginning their visits from the base of the spike. Another is *S. gracilis* of North America, on which Robertson (1893) saw *Bombus americanorum* and some solitary bees (*Calliopsis andreniformis* and *Megachile brevis*). The latter bore pollinia on the mandibles.

It seems dangerous to consider both small-flowered species as *Bombus*-flowers, the more so as *S. romanzoffiana* (also mentioned as such by Godfery, 1931, 1933) represents clearly an incidental case and since Godfrey never reported *Bombus* on *S. autumnalis*.

Saprophytic *Epipogium* (*Epipogon*) *aphyllum* (in dark forests) is usually placed in this class on the basis of one observation of two specimens of *Bombus lucorum* visiting it (Rohrbach, 1866). This observation is ever again cited—extensively in Knuth-Loew II/2—though the vanilla-scented flower with a non-resupinate lip and rather superficial nectar secretion, does not seem to fit *Bombus*. The old report mentions, moreover, the difficulties the bees encountered, leaving actual pollination uncertain. The construction of the flower reminds one of *Stanhopea*. Werth (1956) confirmed the visits in Germany, but Ziegenspeck (1928) reported that fruits are never produced there. The south Asian mountain species *E. Roseum* is autogamous (D. van Leeuwen, 1937). It fruits three to four days abundantly after anthesis.

Müller (1873) saw *Bombus* on *Goodyera*, but he expressed doubt as to whether it was a legitimate pollinator.

Like those to be discussed next, all cases require further investigation. Exploratory, ineffective visits of *Bombus* occur everywhere, even in *Gymnadenia*.

Let us consider the case of *Orchis* (*Dactylorchis*), of which large-flowered Asiatic and American species may help to indicate the original use and users of the spur. Robertson (1928) found on *O. spectabilis* in Illinois *Bombus separatus* and *B. americanorum* as pollinators—especially the females. The flower has a broad spur, 12-15 mm. long, with free nectar.

In most west European species the spur is empty and apparently functionless. It is absent in the closely related European species of *Serapias*, for which the source of attraction should be ascertained.

In Europe bumblebees have also been described as pollinators of *O. mascula* (H. Müller, 1873), *O. latifolia*, *O. maculata* and, at least as co-visitor with solitary bees, for *O. morio* (Darwin). Even *Apis* is mentioned as such in the literature. Keller (1930) mentions seeing *Bombus hortensis* on *O. tridentatus* and *Apis* on *O. lactea*, without giving exact data on his observations.

There are many objections to considering these observations as indicating a legitimate or regular bond. *Orchis morio* was never seen visited by *Bombus* by Godfery (1933), a good field-observer. In Jersey, Evans (1934) over the years found only solitary *Anthophora acervorum* as the pollinator of *O. morio*. Entomologists have reported that for many years they have found no pollinia of *Orchis* on specimens of *Bombus*. Godfery (1918) observed very few visits of *Bombus* to *O. mascula* in a field, with an abundance of *O. mascula* and *O. morio* and no hybrids between the species. *Orchis morio* was sometimes visited there by *Apathus* (*Psithyrus*) *rupestris* (cuckoo bumblebee).

Social bees must rapidly discover that there is no food in the lumen or wall of the spur of the marsh-orchids. This fact was unknown to Darwin and H. Müller, who thought that the lining of the empty spur was pierced by the tongue. Daumann (1941) proved the contrary and emphasized the rareness of *Bombus* visits (also butterflies). The few visits are just exploration ending in deception. Delpino, after observations in 1870, commented that only newcomers were deceived. Observations in Holland by van der Pijl (unpublished) in a field where different species of *Orchis* are cultivated (including *O. praetermissa*) confirmed that bumblebees throughout the season visited only other flowering plants.

After scrutinizing the often-cited report of H. Müller (1873) mentioned above, it becomes clear that for long periods he observed no *Bombus* on *Orchis mascula*. He only did so on one day, the first favorable day early in the flowering season after a long cold spell.

FIG. 53. *Odontoglossum kegeljani* being pollinated by male *Bombus robustus* var. *hortulans*.

The rather unbalanced and unsatisfactory pollination system of these *Orchis* spp. is more or less unspecialized, though solitary bees still assist as do beetles, butterflies, moths and flies (for observations concerning *Eristalis* and *Empis* see p. 122). Illustrative is the enumeration by Richards (1931) and Silen (1906) of visitors to *O. maculata* in Europe (no *Plusia*). The Dutch orchidologist, Dr. Vermeulen, thought (personal communication) that the occasional visits of *Plusia* moths to species of the subgenus *Dactylorchis* and never to *Orchis s. str.* might form an ecological barrier between the two (see p. 170). This supposition might also serve to explain the hybrids of *Orchis* (*Dactylorchis*) (*O. maculata* and *O. latifolia*) with *Gymnadenia*.

According to Martens (1926, 1928), if *O. morio*, *O. maculata* and *O. latifolia* are not pollinated, autogamy may occur at the end of anthesis. Self-incompatibility is absent in this group.

Bombus is a very widely distributed genus of social bees occurring throughout the temperate zones of the world in considerable quantities. They are also abundant at higher elevations in the mountains of tropical America. From 1500 to 3500 meters elevation they are perhaps the commonest bees in the Andes; however, they are not uncommon in the tropical zone even though the number is reduced. The male bees loaf around the nest or set up territories and defend them diligently (Dodson, 1962a). Meanwhile, they have time available for visiting flowers from which they do not receive food.

In the case of *Odontoglossum kegeljani* in Ecuador, male bees of *Bombus robustus* var. *hortulans* come to the flowers and attempt to reach nectar in the false nectaries (Fig. 53). The teeth of the callus act to impede the advance into the flower and in their struggles they detach the viscidium of the pollinarium with their heads. The stipe curves downward, carrying the pollinia to a position in front of the head and in visiting a subsequent flower they leave the pollinia on the sticky surface of the stigma. Other smaller bees were observed attempting to reach the false nectaries, forcing the lip back from the column and struggling with the flower, but these bees were too small to contact the sticky viscidium.

The same species of bumblebee works *Oncidium macranthum* (Pl. XIa) in Ecuador looking for nectar, which does not exist (Dodson, 1962a). Later observations indicate that a species of *Centris* may be the principal pollinator of this orchid. The flowers produce a sweet fragrance for a short period (one or two days) during the natural long life of the flower. There is no false nectary in the flower but a large yellow spot at the base of the column (tabula infrastigmatica) may act to attract the bee to that locality.

Bombus morio has been encountered in Ecuador pollinating both *Sobralia violacea* and *S. rosea* and *Bombus volucellioides* was captured with pollinaria of *Maxillaria fletcheriana* on its thorax (Dodson, 1965a).

It seems probable that the importance in the pollination of orchids of both *Bombus* and the tropical Asian species of *Apis* will be found to be greater.

6. *Nocturnal Bees*

Not a great amount of information is available on nocturnal bees and only two have been reported as pollinators of orchids adapted to their behavior. However, several orchids appear to have a syndrome which might indicate such a possibility.

Linsley (1958) discussed several kinds of bees which are known to be nocturnal or crepuscular (flying at dawn or dusk). Bees of the Anthophorinae, Halictidae, Andrenidae and Colletidae are known to fly at night and occur in tropical or sub-tropical regions of the Western Hemisphere.

Ptiloglossa ducalis of the Colletidae was captured while pollinating the flowers of *Miltonia endresii* (Pl. XIb) (Dodson, 1965a). The flowers were visited at about 4:30 a.m. in complete darkness and the pollinator was very efficient. A population of *M. vexillaria* was observed in Ecuador for three days from dawn to dusk and no pollinator visited. Each flower, however, was pollinated apparently before dawn. There was no opportunity to observe the population at night, however. The other two species in this section of the genus, *M. phalaenopsis* and *M. roezlii* are very likely pollinated in the same manner. All species in this section tend to be white or glowing pink and are easily observable in the dimmest of light. The true species of *Miltonia* of Brazil are probably not pollinated at night since they do not exhibit similar colors and are constructed differently.

In Iquitos, Peru, Dodson (1965a) observed many inflorescences of *Cattleya luteola* which were pollinated and produced seed pods though no pollinators were observed visiting them during the day. By selectively leaving plants outdoors during certain hours it was determined that the flowers were pollinated at hours just before dawn. At approximately 5:30 a.m., in the predawn darkness, large numbers of *Melipona flavipennis* (Pl. XIc) swarmed to the flowers, which were

FIG. 54. *Lycaste denningiana*.

fragrant at that time. Pollination was very effective. The visits only lasted until 5:45 a.m. when daybreak began. After first light no visits occurred.

Dodson (unpublished) spent considerable time observing *Lycaste gigantea*, *L. ciliata* (*L. costata*) and *L. denningiana* (Fig. 54) in Ecuador. The plants were particularly abundant and thousands of flowers were at hand. Though they were observed from early in the morning until late afternoon, no animal which could have acted as an effective pollinator visited the flowers. However, pollination was occurring regularly as evidenced by the production of seed pods and by flowers with the column swelling around freshly deposited pollinia. Their odor was noted to increase markedly just after sundown and by 7:30 p.m. was actually oppressive in the natural areas. Autogamy apparently is not involved. Though no nocturnal bees were observed visiting these flowers there seems little question that they will be found to be the pollinators. The flowers are constructed like typical orchid bee-flowers.

CHAPTER 7
Orchids and Lepidoptera

Flowers which are adapted to moths or to butterflies tend to be somewhat distinct from each other. This is based primarily on one of the basic differences between the two kinds of insects, i.e., moth-flowers are designed for attraction of the night-flying moths whereas butterfly-flowers are adapted to day-flying butterflies and skippers. Most floral ecologists separate them into two classes and we will follow that practice.

MOTHS AND ORCHIDS

This class concerns the ordinary moth (i.e., Noctuidae and related families) —the flowers adapted to them are called phalenophilous—and hawk-moths (Sphingidae)—the flowers they pollinate being called sphingophilous. The former usually land on the flower whereas the latter are better fliers and hover before the flower.

Among the sphingids there is one group, *Macroglossa*, which makes the transition between the two gradual (and vaguely toward the butterfly syndrome) as it leads a diurnal life and shows clear sensitivity for colors. Other moths, however, may also be able to distinguish colors, though these may have less effect at night. For a comparative table of all moth- and butterfly-flowers see Faegri and van der Pijl, 1966.

The syndrome of moth-flowers, in accordance with the ethology of moths, is the following:

1. Anthesis (opening, receptivity, pollen and odor production) at night; closing during day-time frequent as a negative character.
2. Weakly zygomorphic (in orchids nevertheless present as organizational).

3. Landing place curved backwards or turned upwards, deeply dissected when functioning as a showplace only.
4. Color white, cream or often greenish (then lacking a function).
5. Odor heavy-sweet or vegetable-like, very strong, not fruity as in beetle-flowers.
6. Nectar abundant, deeply hidden in narrow tubes for long tongues.
7. Colored nectar guides absent, replaced by guidance through the form of the flower, with a star shape or fringe points indicating the center (sometimes with grooves as mechanical tongue-guides).
8. Position of the flower rarely erect, mostly horizontal or hanging.
9. Sexual organs protruding, anthers versatile.

The last character, common in other night-flowers, cannot be realized in orchids; however, elongation and sideward shift of the rostellum and stigma can be indications in this direction. Some authors consider linear viscidia as specially fit to curl around a thin proboscis. A perianth tube is also difficult to realize and is usually improvised by spurs. Pollinia are normally deposited on the proboscis or head. Therefore sternotriby and nototriby are without significance in this class of flower.

The vagueness of the boundaries between this class of flowers and others is demonstrated by the case of *Gymnadenia conopsea*, which is worked by butterflies (most frequently *Zygaena filipendulae*) and several different moths including *Macroglossa*. A consequence is the frequent production of hybrids (see Fig. 114).

The genera *Angraecum*, *Platanthera*, *Brassavola* and some species of *Habenaria* agree with the the syndrome. In the best studied species of *Angraecum*, *A. eburneum*, the labellum is upturned, making landing impossible. The genus includes the acme of sphingophilous adaption, the classical *A. sesquipedale* (Fig. 55), described by Darwin (1862) as having an exaggerated spur-length (21-35 cm.). It would therefore require a moth with at least a 25 cm. tongue length to effect pollination in the home country of Madagascar. Forty years later this moth, *Xanthopan* (Macrosila) *morgani* f. *praedicta*, was found. Its visits have not yet been observed (see p. 165 for a discussion of Darwin's statement in regard to the concurrent evolution of the orchid and the pollinator).

The literature on *Habenaria* and *Platanthera* (cf. Darwin) mentions many moths for each species, but specificity exists nevertheless. The graded difference of attractivity by odor is reinforced by the specific length of the spur, according to tongue lengths, and by specific deposition of pollinaria on head, body, feet or proboscis as an isolating barrier.

Fragrant, nocturnal *Platanthera* has either a narrow and linear labellum (excluding many visitors) or a fringed one, as expressed by the names *P. fimbriata* and *P. ciliaris*. Darwin and H. Müller described the isolating barriers between *P. chlorantha* and *P.* (Habenaria) *bifolia*. They result (see Percival, 1965) in pollination in Britain for the former by *Plusia* spp. plus *Hadenia dentina* and for the latter by *Anaites plagiata* plus *Agrotis segetum*. On the European continent *P. bifolia* (see Knuth-Loew II/2) was observed to have the same visitors, but longer spurred forms there tend to be pollinated by hawk-moths, such as *Macroglossa* and *Deilephila*. Asa Gray (1862, 1863) was cited by Darwin as describing the differentiating structures of American species of *Habenaria* and some of their visitors. The North American species *H. psycodes* var. *grandiflora* and *H. dialata* var. *leucostachys* are considered as sphingophilous. The far-northern *H. hyperborea* has a tendency toward autogamy.

In Java Docters van Leeuwen (1933) found *P. blumei* on the summit of Mt. Gedeh to be pollinated by the noctuid *Agrotis nigrum*. Robertson (1893) saw *Sphinx* spp. on *H. leucophaea* in Illinois.

The elongated stigmatic projections of *Habenaria* seem typical for specialized moth-flowers (in *H. roeperocharis* these are even branched). Vogel (1954) studied many South-African species, e.g., *H. polyphylla*, pollinated by the sphingid *Hippotion celerio*. This pollinator curiously, when hovering before the flower, supports itself with the front legs, which extract the pollinia. *Habenaria tetrapetala* has sternotribic pollen deposition on its sphingid visitors; other species such as *H. drageana*, *H. galpini* and *H. polyphyodontha* (all greenish-white) have various methods of deposition on various noctuids and sphingids.

For a discussion of mosquities on *Habenaria* see p. 122.

FIG. 55. *Angraecum sesquipedale*, the Christmas-star orchid.

FIG. 56. *Epidendrum difforme* being visited by the moth *Amastas acona*. (Drawing by G. P. Frymire.)

The African "spider-orchids" *Bonatea*, *Holothrix* and *Bartholina*, close relatives of *Habenaria*, comply ecologically as was clear to Darwin when he discussed *Bonatea*. Vogel (1954) confirmed this for *Bartholina* and *Holothrix* without finding pollinators.

In the multi-class African genus *Disa* the moth-pollinated type is rare, perhaps occurring in *D. fragrans* and *D. macrantha*. In the related genus *Satyrium*, reorganized on a two-spur basis, more species have developed in this direction, e.g., *S. odorum* and others. In the American genus *Epidendrum* perhaps a major portion of the species belong to this type, for example, *E. nocturnum*, *E. arachnoglossum*, *E. ciliare*, *E. purpurescens*, and others. Dodson and Frymire

(1961b) found pollinia of *E. difforme* (Fig. 56) on the moth *Amastus acona* and the same species of moth was found to pollinate *E. latilabre*, a species very closely related to *E. difforme*, in Costa Rica (Dodson, 1965a). Epidendrums have a deep tube inside the ovary—which in some species lacks free nectar but does have thin-walled cells lining the tube—augmented by coalescence of the sides of the labellum-claw and the column. This flower is un-orchid-like, forming a simple horizontal tube, with the free part of the labellum used as an appendage for attraction. The other tepals tend to form a less conspicuous, commonly greenish, narrow-lobed, five-pointed star on the spatial and ecological background, as in non-orchid night-flowers.

Nephelaphyllum, totally unrelated, shows an erect (non-resupinate) white lip, whereas the other tepals are curved back and greenish as described above.

The small *Orchis* (Leucorchis) *albida* has been observed being visited in Europe by a small moth, a Tineid (K. Fritsch, 1933). It is sweet-scented and has free nectar in the spur. Godfery (1933) observed solitary bees as visitors to this orchid but they did not remove the pollinia. Rare hybrids occur between *O. albida* and *Gymnadenia conopsea*.

In the genus *Spiranthes*, which is pollinated by many agents, the species *S. aestivalis* in Europe seems dependent on moths (Godfery, 1933). The flowers are slightly fragrant in the evening and have linear viscidia.

Brassavola digbyana was observed being visited by sphingid moths in Honduras by F. Fuchs (personal communication).

BUTTERFLIES AND ORCHIDS

Butterfly-flowers are called psychophilous. In contrast to moths, butterflies fly in the daytime and are, in a sense, inferior fliers which rarely hover. They therefore need ample landing space. Some have fidelity to colors and can discern them well, including red. An inborn preference for certain colors by some butterflies has been demonstrated (Ilse, 1928). The trumpet-shape with tube and flat rim seems ideal for them. Since orchids have primarily a gullet-type flower it is interesting to contemplate how the change has been achieved.

A closely allied group, the skippers (Hesperiidae), is separated by entomologists. It has some characters intermediate between moths and butterflies but flies during the day and has other habits which make it ecologically more closely related to the butterflies.

The general syndrome is:

1. Anthesis diurnal.
2. No zygomorphy necessary.
3. Horizontal landing place, lobes weakly dissected.
4. Colors vivid, including red.
5. Odor agreeable, fresh.
6. Nectar less than in sphingid-flowers, more than in bee-flowers, contained in rather long, narrow tubes.

FIG. 57. *Disa uniflora*. (Drawing by P. Fawcett.)

7. Nectar guides present, simple.
8. Sexual organs usually enclosed, not protruding.
9. Position of flower erect.

How did orchids comply with these requirements, partly strange to their organizational type? The South African *Disa* (Vogel, 1954) contains melittophilous forms such as *D. racemosa*, but these already have a reduced lip and a short spur on the dorsal sepal. The dorsal sepal together with the two lateral petals form an "upper lip" whereas the "lower lip" is formed by the two lateral sepals. It is questionable if this strange reconstruction is primarily melittophilous or just secondary on the basis of psychophily as described below.

Many species of *Disa*—including the famous *D. uniflora* (Fig. 57), commonly known as "The Pride of Table Mountain"—are psychophilous, for example, *D. crassicornis*, *D. draconis* and *D. polygonoides*. These have a new type of long spur on the dorsal sepal containing copious nectar. Their labellum is reduced and replaced as a landing platform by the enlarged, horizontally projecting, lateral sepals. The column is placed below, thus forsaking nototriby. The colors are often orange or red.

All this indicates fundamental psychophily in the genus. Species of *Meneris* (butterflies) have been found as pollinators of *D. uniflora* and other species (Vogel, 1954). In *D. draconis* one of the curious long-tongued bee-flies of the genus *Pangonia*, with 6 cm. tongue-length, has been caught on the flower with pollinia attached (Vogel, 1959). Such flies (tabanids and nemestrinids) are also presumed as pollinators of *Disperis* and can take the place (niche) of butterflies with ease (Vogel, 1954). Darwin (1872) mentioned such flies as pollinators of *D. polygonoides*.

Ridley (1896) reported the pollination of *Haemaria discolor* (Fig. 58) by *Pleisconeura asmara*. *Haemaria* belongs to the artificial group of largely unrelated orchids which are called "Jewel Orchids" and are grown for their striking foliage. The pollinaria are deposited on the legs of the butterfly. To facilitate the deposition of the pollinarium the column is twisted to one side. The anther and viscidium form a hook at the apex to catch the legs of the visiting butterflies. *Macodes* is a genus of similar orchids; however, the column is even more twisted so that the anther faces the dorsal sepal. Ecologically this would presumably result in the same system of deposition of pollinaria.

In America we find psychophily in some *Epidendrum* species with the improvised erect tube described above. For *E. secundum* Dodson and Frymire (1961b) corroborated the psychophily predicted by Vogel for the comparable hybrid, *E.* X *O'brienianum*. Pollination by a skipper, *Urbanus proteus*, was observed. Dodson (1962a) indicated that the skipper was a co-pollinator and that hummingbirds were also observed as pollinators of this orchid. Later observations at a different site show the same species of orchid to be pollinated by a butterfly, *Papilio polyxemes* v. *americus* (Pl. XId), and an unidentified skipper. *Epidendrum radicans* was found to be pollinated by five kinds of butterflies in Costa Rica by Dodson (unpublished). *Epidendrum paniculatum* is pollinated by *Heliconia* spp. in Costa Rica (Dodson, unpublished) (Pl. XIIa).

Butterflies or skippers were seen from a distance visiting *Cochlioda vulcanica* in Ecuador; however, it was determined from examination of the flowers that the pollinia had not been disturbed. Hummingbirds were also observed, but as effective pollinators.

FIG. 58. Flower of *Haemaria discolor* showing twisted column.

Some temperate orchids with small aggregated reddish flowers—including one or two species of *Orchis*—have adapted exclusively to butterflies. *Orchis ustulata* (Europe) is said to have fragrant day-flowers fitted to butterflies with an entrance too narrow for large bees. Visits have not been observed, but may be presumed from the kind of hybrids in the scheme on p. 169. It seems not to hybridize with other *Orchis* (Dactylorchis) spp. *Orchis* (Traunsteinera) *globosa* has in its dense, globular head a perfect brush-flower for butterflies. Here the position of the labellum is unimportant, as is still more clearly visible in the comparable *Nigritella nigra*, which is non-resupinate. This vanilla-scented orchid, well known from the Alps, is (Knuth II/2, Godfery 1931) visited by butterflies (often *Leucania* and *Zygaena* spp.), though *Apis* and *Bombus* sometimes probe it.

Anacamptis pyramidalis has (as Darwin described) many butterfly—and some moth—visitors which carry the pollinia on the proboscis. The scent is agreeable, the spur long and narrow.

CHAPTER 8
Orchids and Birds

The familiar sight of brilliantly colored hummingbirds visiting various flowers in the garden almost anywhere in America makes it seem incredible that ornithophily as a scientifically recognized phenomenon was not accepted until after the turn of the last century. On all sides we see flowers obviously adapted to birds as pollinators. These flowers are particularly common as horticultural subjects in our gardens, for the very characters which attract the birds as pollinators, such as bright, glowing colors, make the plants esthetically interesting to us. We have introduced them from all parts of the world and particularly from tropical America.

How it is possible that ornithophily was neglected for so long when many observations of birds visiting flowers surely had been reported? Probably this can be attributed to the origins of the study of floral biology having been in Europe where flower-birds do not exist. Only when interest in floral biology in America and tropical Asia and Africa developed did it become obvious that birds were significant pollinating agents.

Several groups of birds independently developed the habit of visiting flowers for their food. Much of the early adaption was probably based on dystrophic behavior where the birds ate parts of the flower and in fact we still encounter less specialized groups of birds which have a mixed diet of flower, fruit and insects. As the birds came to depend more on flower, nectar, and insects associated with flowers, special adaptations arose, probably on a mutual basis, between the birds and the flowers. The apex in adaptation is reached with birds which hover in front of flowers and collect nectar.

The peak of adaptation is found in the hummingbirds (Trochilidae) of the Western Hemisphere. Many hummingbirds still receive much of their protein from insects partly found in the flowers and the young birds are reared primarily on insects. For the most part, however, their basic reason for visiting flowers is to

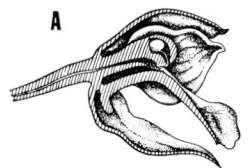
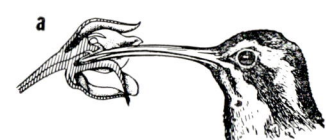
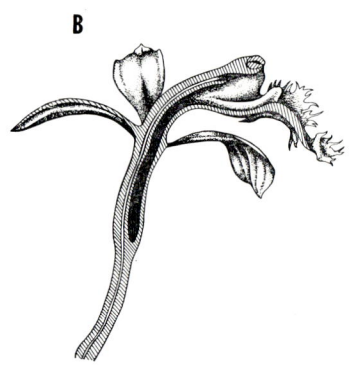

FIG. 59. Bird-pollinated orchids showing guidance of the bill by the form of the lip of the flower. A. *Rodriguezia secunda*. B. *Epidendrum ibaguense*. (Drawing by P. Fawcett.)

collect nectar. Often hummingbirds collect insects much as do fly-catchers, capturing the insects on the wing. Another related family of birds which visit flowers in the tropical regions of the Western Hemisphere are the less-specialized sugar-birds (Coerebidae). These brilliantly-colored birds are perching-birds (related to and often included with the tanagers) with slight beak adaptions for collecting nectar.

In the Old World several families developed characteristics similar to those of the hummingbirds but not as extreme. The most specialized are the sun-birds (Nectariniidae) of Asia and Africa. These spectacular birds can hover in front of flowers to reach nectar but usually land on the inflorescence or nearby perches (as do hummingbirds rather frequently). In Hawaii the honey-creepers (Drepanididae) are intimately associated with *Lobelia*. In the Indo-Australian region the nectar-eaters (Meliphagidae) and the brush-tongued honey-parrots (Trichoglossidae) are less specialized but nevertheless effective as pollinators.

A few members of several other non-flower-adapted families of birds visit flowers and in some instances may demonstrate the first sign of adaptation, such as fringed tongue-tips in tropical woodpeckers (Picidae).

The general syndrome of ornithophilous flowers—in accordance with the peculiarities of flower-birds—mainly consists of the following points (supplemented by an explanation of the descriptive point where required):

1. Diurnal anthesis.
2. Zygomorphy weakly expressed.

3. Lip or margin absent (flower tubular) or lip curved back (birds normally do not land on the flower itself).
4. Vivid colors, often scarlet or with contrasting parrot-like colors (birds depend on strong visual sense).
5. Absence of odor (birds have almost no sense of smell).
6. Nectar very abundant, often in medium-length, rather broad tubes and spurs, with capillary systems in the container.
7. Nectar guide absent (not necessary for birds).
8. Tubular flowers horizontal or hanging freely in space (for hovering birds).
9. Hard flower wall, with protected organs (against the hard beak).

In orchids a further development to increase the efficiency of bird-pollination is that of a barrier to entrance of the beak. The column is usually located at the upper edge of the corolla (or the tube formed by the column and lip) and the simple thrusting of the beak into the tube is not sufficient to ensure the proper placement of the pollinarium. Most bird-pollinated orchids have a strong fold in the lip or a heavy callus which partially closes the floral tube at the level of the anther and stigma. The barrier forces the bird to push its beak against the column to gain entry (Fig. 59). This arrangement has been conspicuous in all of the orchids which have been reported as ornithophilous and seems an important character to be expected in the syndrome of ornithophily in the orchids.

The absence of pollen as food in orchids is no objection in this class. When we consider the points 2, 3, 6, 7 and 8 we see that they are also present to some degree in orchids pollinated by moths and butterflies (which are occasionally co-pollinators with birds [Dodson, 1962]).

FIG. 60. Bird-pollinated *Elleanthus capitatus*.

FIG. 61. Bird-pollinated *Masdevallia rosea*.

Birds appear to be rather late comers in the pollination of orchids and therefore we may expect isolated cases in groups which are basically pollinated by other agents. For the most part, orchids in which bird-pollination has been reported or suspected are from high elevations where flower-visiting insects become rare or are unable to operate effectively due to the cold. This is in line with findings in other plants where the number of ornithophilous species in the flora at high elevations seems overwhelming.

A point which has been generally overlooked in taxonomy in the orchids is that the characters which result from adaptations to bird-pollination are often striking. These characters are commonly employed by taxonomists in separating genera, with the result that closely related species may be placed in distinct genera. Examples are the *Cochlioda-Odontoglossum-Oncidium* and the *Sophronitis- Laelia-Cattleya* complexes where the enormous numbers of artificial hybrids are mute evidence of the failure of taxonomists to understand the ecological background of speciation in these groups.

When we add an environment which is at least subtropical as a requirement for flower-birds it becomes clear why ornithophily arose in South Africa in the genus *Disa*. It was already adapted toward butterflies and therefore had a reduced labellum and possessed other showy parts with red color and a long spur containing much nectar. The species, *D. zeyheri*, *D. ferruginea* and *D. porrecta* are almost sure cases and were suggested as such by Vogel (1954). In *D. ferrugina* a red tube is formed, opening downward. None of the numerous South African sun-birds has been reported yet as its visitor.

Dodson and Frymire (1961b) reported hummingbirds regularly visiting the heads of light purple flowers of *Elleanthus capitatus* (Fig. 60) and the yellow flowers of *E. aureus*. Dodson (1962a) observed pollination by hummingbirds of some sister species with orange or scarlet flowers such as *E. aurantiacus*. In addition, birds were observed visiting *Masdevallia rosea* (Fig. 61), a typical case of the mighty influence of the hummingbird, as the shape, tails, and other characters of the flower are remnants of the original, fly-pollinated condition in the group.

Observations were made (Dodson, 1965a) of hummingbirds visiting several species of *Elleanthus*, e.g., *E. hallii*, *E. rosea* by unidentified birds, *E. arpophyllostachys* by *Ocrateus underwoodii* and *E. hymenophorus* (Fig. 62) by *Amazalia tzacatl*. *Amazalia tzacatl* pollinated *Comparettia falcata* (Fig. 63), *Epidendrum pfavii* and *Isochilus carnosiflorus*. A different bird, *Pantrope insignis*, was observed visiting *Sobralia amabilis* (Fig. 64) and a tubular, pink-flowered species of *Maxillaria*. An unidentified species of hummingbird visited *Cochlioda vulcanica* (Fig. 65) and the flowers were checked and found to be pollinated. *Rodriquezia secunda* is pollinated by hummingbirds at Iquitos, Peru (Dodson, 1965a). *Laelia muelleri* was observed being pollinated by hummingbirds in Brazil (Dodson, unpublished). *Epidendrum pseudepidendrum* is pollinated by hummingbirds in Costa Rica (Dodson, unpublished).

A few observations of sun-birds (also called nectar-birds) pollinating orchids in the Old World have been reported. Burkill (1919) reported *Cyrtostomus pectoralis* pollinating *Dendrobium secundum* in Singapore and Docters van Leeuwen (1933) reported birds visiting *D. hasseltii* on a mountain summit in Java where the birds tried many plants. Slade (1962) reported birds visiting *D. lawesii* (Fig. 66) at elevations above 10,000 feet in New Guinea where many species such as *D. sophronitis*, *D. roscum* and *D. flammula* are similar and brilliantly colored.

FIG. 62. *Elleanthus hymenophorus*.

FIG. 63. *Comparettia falcata*. Note the thickened callus of the lip that guides the beak of the bird against the column.

They too are presumed to be bird-pollinated. All of these species have highly colored flowers with a narrowly-clawed lip which forms a tube with abundant nectar production.

Amongst the bee-flower genus *Cattleya* one species, *C. aurantiaca* (Fig. 67), is a probable case, with its narrow-tubed labellum, though natural hybrids with *C. skinneri* point to some promiscuity. A considerable number of other orchids from the American tropics fit the syndrome, e.g., the species of *Sophronitis, Ada, Meiracyllium, Hartwegia, Hexisia,* and *Symphoglossum* (Fig. 68); and *Stenoptera pilifera, Spiranthes speciosa* (Fig. 69), *S. standleyi, Alemanica punica,* and *Maxillaria fulgens*.

Several orchids from the Old World also fit the syndrome, e.g., *Eria ignea, Cryptochilus sanguinea* and perhaps certain species of *Saccolabium*.

At high elevations in Andean regions, where birds take over from bees in many plant families (including Cactaceae), some interesting situations occur. High in the pass between Loja and Zamora in southern Ecuador a quantity of orchid species occur which appear superficially similar but have origins from diverse sections of the subfamily Epidendroideae (Dodson, 1962a). Strong evidence indicates that all are pollinated by hummingbirds and are so adapted that they resemble the various species of ericaceous shrubs which are constantly in flower in the same area. These shrubs, which include species of *Gaultheria* (Fig. 70C), have been observed on numerous occasions to be pollinated by hummingbirds. The list of orchids would include *Elleanthus aureus* (Fig. 70B), *Odontoglossum*

FIG. 64. The bird-pollinated *Sobralia amabilis*.

FIG. 65. *Cochlioda rosea*, a bird-pollinated species.

FIG. 66. *Dendrobium lawesii*, a bird-pollinated orchid from New Guinea. (Drawn from a photo by H. Slade.)

FIG. 67. *Cattleya aurantiaca*, a small, orange-flowered species probably pollinated by hummingbirds.

FIG. 68. *Symphoglossum sanguineum*, a species that is probably pollinated by hummingbirds.

FIG. 69. *Spiranthes speciosa*, a species with dark red flowers.

FIG. 70. A series of orchid species whose flowers converge in their morphological form and color to mimic those of *Gaultheria* to attract hummingbirds as their pollinators. A. *Epidendrum ardens*. B. *Elleanthus aureus*. C. *Gaultheria* sp. D. *Odontoglossum retusum*. (Drawing by P. Fawcett.)

retusum (Fig. 70D), *O. flavescens*, *O. mystacinum*, *Epidendrum ardens* (Fig. 70A) and *E. scabrum*. The *Elleanthus* was observed being visited by hummingbirds. These plants all have a very similar aspect in regard to the flowers which in most cases is quite atypical of the genera to which they belong. This indicates extreme plasticity on the part of the orchids in adapting to an available pollinator when the normal pollinators for these genera are unable to operate effectively due to the cold.

The instances of possible orithophily in orchids mentioned in the handbook of Knuth-Loew are probably of only incidental character, the plants being adapted otherwise. The liquid of *Coryanthes* mentioned as sucked by a hummingbird is not nectar and the pollinators are bees (see p. 73), the *Angraecum* mentioned is sphingophilous and the sucking described (if true) is just robbery. The *Anguloa* is (with its strong smell, rocking lip and lack of nectar) bee-pollinated (see p. 76). The later study by Porsch (1926) on ornithophily in orchids was hardly more critical, though it came near the truth in *Disa*.

The report of hummingbirds visiting and pollinating *Stanhopea* in Brazil (Ruschi, 1949) is not to be considered as valid. The observations made in the field (reported in the National Geographic Magazine, 1962) seem flights of fancy, particularly when the author describes spiders in unopened flower buds. Caged birds were taught to drink nectar from false flowers and tubes and then many flowers were introduced into the cage to study the reaction of the birds. It only seems reasonable to expect such a conditioned bird to visit a *Stanhopea* flower if only out of curiosity. For the legitimate pollinators of members of this genus see p. 70.

On the other hand, the birds may be encountered examining unfamiliar flowers such as orchids in search of small insects (which may explain Ruschi's observations). This was apparently the case when Dodson (unpublished) observed hummingbirds visiting *Lycaste gigantea* in Ecuador. The birds did not disturb the pollen apparatus, however.

The lack of reports on orchids which seem obviously bird-pollinated can be attributed to no more than simple failure of observers to note birds visiting orchid flowers. Birds as a rule are wary, furtive and illusive in behavior and do not stay long while visiting flowers. The few reports which are available result from sheer coincidence or long tedious hours of observations before results are attained.

CHAPTER 9
Orchids and Flies

Flies belong to the insect order Diptera, which contains numerous families of the most divergent nature. The front pair of wings are usually developed normally while the second pair form balancers. Flowers adapted to flies for their pollination are called myophilous.

MYOPHILY

Most of the families of flies are not primarily adapted as flower visitors; however, a few such as the Syrphidae, Bombylidae and some Tachinidae are restricted to flowers for their food. Many kinds of flies visit unspecialized flowers for part of their food. The flowers which they visit tend to be promiscuous in their pollination relations and attract all manner of pollinators such as beetles, bees and butterflies. They are usually rather shallow, produce abundant nectar on surface nectaries and emit sweet odors. The flies collect the nectar (some syrphids also eat pollen) for their own sustenance and do not store it as do bees.

SAPROMYOPHILY

Some flies become effective pollinators only under special conditions. These flies are usually attracted through deception. Many flies, mosquitos, small midges, gnats, and other Diptera exhibit a predilection for oviposition or food uptake from decaying substances, dung or carrion. Plants have evolved characteristics which emulate these substances and thereby attract the insects to act as agents in their pollination. Flowers which are adapted to this group of insects are called sapromyophilous. The class of sapromyophilous flowers is strongly specialized in the tropics. Oddly enough, though the class is rather frequent in temperate regions, the specialized characters associated with them are seldom strongly expressed, even in stringent climates where flies take over from bees.

Sapromyophilous flowers are most numerous in warm, arid zones, especially in Africa, where flies as regularly present flower visitors are apparently dominant of old. It is curious that this switch to flies is not paralleled in the warm, arid zones of America where sapromyophilous flowers—and orchids—are rare in contrast to the abundance in the American tropics. The switch-over to Diptera in Africa must have some relation to dominance of flies.

Ordinary Diptera (excluding Syrphidae and Bombylidae) are by nature poor orchid pollinators and require special guidance to make them effective. They tend to approach flowers in steps, flying back and forth in the neighborhood, rather than flying directly from flower to flower as do bees. They are not fitted for accurate guidance to a critical spot in the flower and their very presence depends on the incidental occurrence of the real feeding substrate somewhere nearby. The adaptations are entirely on the part of the flower and act on the instincts of the insects, deceiving them by odors that simulate the regular substrate or food. There is rarely a real reward present in the flower such as the offering of a breeding substrate (not yet found in orchids). The sustained guidance system, attracting the insect and carrying through to proper placement for pollen reception and deposition, is all important in this class and is more intricate than for any other system. The odors produced by the flowers may be aminoid, containing true amines, or may remind one of overripe fruits or fermenting juice. They attract beetles in some cases as well. The odors provide strong specificity of pollinator in most cases.

The general syndrome of sapromyophily has been described for flowers, leaf-traps and even for mosses and fungi (Phalloideae) in a general book on pollination ecology (Faegri and van der Pijl, 1966). It is:

1. Anthesis at different times.
2. No zygomorphy; radial-flat or trap-like.
3. Landing by steps possible on a large surface, perhaps helped by long "tails" as guides. The latter often have a glandular surface, and they may act as osmophores (odor-spreaders) like the finer fringes of other flowers (Vogel, 1962).
4. Color often superfluous, dull or greenish, occasionally augmented by a brown-purple color supplemented by checkered or dotted designs.
5. Odor putrescent.
6. Nectar or other food usually absent.
7. No nectar-guides.
8. Often with peculiar slits or holes in the side (corresponding to some instinct of flies) leading to the lantern-type of *Ceropegia* and many others.
9. Transparent windows guide flies to certain places or in and out (consider the behavior of frightened flies against a window).
10. Brown, furry hair-cover, perhaps imitative.
11. Often with motile, club-like hairs vibrating in the wind ("Flimmerkörper" or oscillators) much finer than the fringe in sphingophilous flowers.
12. Trap-devices guiding the unadapted visitors or even catching and holding them with arresting devices.

In orchids it is often difficult to decide where simple myophily ends and sapromyophily begins. Many genera have some species whose pollination is based on simple myophily, attracting various flies on the basis of sweet odors and nectar production, and others which attract specific flies on the basis of rotten odors and provide no food.

It seems hardly plausible that in the orchid flower, the apex of precision, such essential changes could occur that adaptation to insects which are so much lower than bees on a behavioral level, in regard to their relations with flowers, would be possible. However, the switch has occurred in perhaps 3,000 species in the most divergent genera, high and low, in all regions of the world. Unfortunately such forms are seldom represented in our greenhouses with the exception of the tropical members of the Cypripedioideae.

Four large groups of orchids have even become predominantly myophilous, namely, the Pleurothallidinae (in America), the *Bulbophyllum* group (mainly in the Old World), the large genus *Pterostylis* (in Australia) and probably the majority of the tropical Cypripedioideae (cosmopolitan). In many other genera incidental cases occur.

1. *Cypripedioideae* (*slipper-orchids*)

Though the temperate genus *Cypripedium* (Fig. 71) has gaudy, often fragrant flowers which do not trap flies, but rather bees (see p. 40), the tropical genera *Phragmopedium* (Fig. 72) and *Paphiopedilum* (Fig. 73) are fly-pollinated at least partially. The latter genera may represent the original condition of all Cypripedioideae as an old sideline of the first orchids which were already

FIG. 71. *Cypripedium.*

FIG. 72. *Phragmopedium.*   FIG. 73. *Paphiopedilum.*

zygomorphic and labellate in the first bee period. On the other hand, anatomical evidence (Rosso, unpublished) indicates that the genus *Cypripedium* is the more primitive of the genera. Since it is bee-pollinated, fly-pollination may be a later development in the more advanced tropical genera. However, some myophilous traits are found in *Cypripedium*, i.e., brown sepals, hairs, windows and the trapping labellum, which seem out of line for early bee-flowers but may be a transformation of one of the bee line.

The flies slide off the oily, flat, median staminode or other parts and are caught via the large opening of the labellum. They can only escape by climbing along a median, internal ridge armed with stiff, retrorse hairs, and then, after touching the stigma under the staminode, find a way out through one of the side exits, brushing an anther as they pass. Two diaphanous windows on the sides of the labellum, even in *Cypripedium*, seem remnants of the condition when they may have guided flies past the anthers. For food presented see p. 30.

Phragmopedium longifolium var. *hartwegii* was observed to be pollinated by both bees and flies in western Ecuador (Dodson, 1965a and 1966a) (see p. 40). Two species of syrphid flies were effective pollinators and behaved much as the bees, falling into the trap-labellum and working their way out through the exits under the stigma and anthers (Fig. 74). The long tails of *Phragmopedium caudatum* no longer seem "just variety," nor the auxilliary transparent windows in the flag of *Paphiopedilum fairreanum* (serving as a "backboard as in basketball") nor the oily, slippery surface of the parts helping in the slide, nor the purple spots. The significance for attraction of spots for flies (even to their specificity as they must have a relation to the size of the animal) have been proven experimentally (Steiner, 1948 and Vogel, 1958). The curious furry warts on the sepals of some species of *Paphiopedilum* now seem flies attracting other flies (aggregation-instinct).

As to the odor, it is difficult for the human nose to determine that some component of decay is really absent. Also, the odor may occur only at specific periods of the day. In any case, fragrance fails in many tropical forms. A sweet odor has been reported for *Selenipedium palmifolium* but that species may be bee pollinated. Delpino mentioned an "odore spermatico-urinoso" for *Paphiopedilum villosum* and *P. purpuratum* and suggested basic myophily for the group. He also found blue-bottle flies caught in *P. barbatum* in a greenhouse in Italy. Schlechter (1927) also relates such occurrences. Ziegenspeck (1928) indicated the same for *P. insigne*. Vogel (1962) mentions an urinous smell of the tails of *Phragmopedium* X *grande*.

The granular pollen has served to corroborate the primitivity of the group. It also may have been influenced ecologically by myophily. The presence of two anthers is considered as a radical divergence from the main line of orchid evolution but is also ecologically bound to the presence of two exits. Later myophilous orchids managed with one exit after fixation on a single anther.

2. The Bulbophyllum complex

The *Bulbophyllum* complex consists of about 1,000 species and is ecologically characterized by its balanced see-saw labellum which is hinged by a narrow,

FIG. 74. Pollination of *Phragmopedilum longifolium* var. *hartwegii* by a fly, *Syrphus* sp. a. The fly crawling on the lip of the flower just before falling inside the pouch-like trap. b. The fly emerging from the base of the lip under the anther after crawling through the tunnel formed at the back of the lip.

FIG. 75. *Bulbophyllum lobbii*.

springy claw and tips over when its equilibrium is disturbed. Otherwise the flower usually retains the orthodox bee-type characters. The flower has developed the hinged labellum as a means of throwing poorly directed flies against the column so precisely that they function as effective pollinators. Without such a mechanism pollination for these flowers would be well nigh impossible.

In *B. lobbii* (Fig. 75)—the species most commonly cultivated because of its inoffensive, large flowers—the smell of fresh cucumbers is not putrid for man and the color is yellow with purple stripes. Pohl (1935) found oil and sugar on the base of the lip. The flower does catch flies in the tropics. Most other species have either a purple flower or a purplish lip and all the foul smells imaginable, including some new ones. For that reason many species are not considered "safe" for cultivation.

Bulbophyllum macranthum and probably *B. emiliorum* have a non-resupinate flower and are assisted by a sliding trap-device. Flies were observed sliding down the vertical, oily sepals and were then steered onto the column by the lip (Pohl, 1935 and Ridley, 1890b).

Other points of the syndrome appear in more specialized species. Tails occur in the well-known *B. medusae* (Fig. 76) (where they are not osmophores), *B. ornatissimum* (Fig. 77) and *B. arachnites*. Closed flowers with side-slits occur in *B. singaporeanum* and *B. grandiflorum*. Fringe-hairs occur on the lip of *B. barbigerum* (Fig. 78), causing it to flutter in the slightest current of air.

In *Bulbophyllum psittacoides* a minute dipteran settles on the pendant sepals and climbs up them until it reaches the lip upon which it sits. When it has passed beyond the balancing point the fly is pitched onto the column, where it receives the pollinia (Ridley, 1890b).

Figure 77 of *Bulbophyllum ornatissimum* being visited by flies was made in the greenhouse at the Missouri Botanical Garden. The flies were two kinds of ordinary bluebottle flies. They landed on the joined sepals, crawled up to the lip and were flung against the column when the lip became overbalanced. Flies of the proper size for pollination were pinned in the flower for long periods of time by the hooks on each side of the column. These slide over the apex of the inverted thorax of the fly when it is thrown in place. The flies struggled for some time to free themselves but never failed to dislodge the pollinia from the anther cap and firmly cement them on the thorax during their struggles.

Many of the above mentioned species have been separated from *Bulbophyllum* as the genus *Cirrhopetalum* based on their aggregation of flowers in a fan-like whorl, hair-fringe on the tepals and the fused, twisted lateral sepals. In horticulture they are known as the genus *Cirrhopetalum* and will probably continue to be called by that name. It is clear that the points by which they differ from *Bulbophyllum* are simply elaborations within the fly-syndrome and are encountered jointly or separately outside the section *Cirrhopetalum*. The fan-like inflorescence, which is not present in all species of the section *Cirrhopetalum*, indicates a curious return to radiality. The small flexible labellae are more oscillators than traps here. In large, single flowers there is also some return to radiality and to a flat disk when all the tepals become alike (section *Micromonanthe*). Here too, species are known with a lantern-type, i.e., with the large, checkered and spotted sepals fused at the tip (*B. ipanemensis* and *B. fritillariiflorum*). The petals in these

FIG. 76. *Bulbophyllum* (Cirrhopetalum) *medusa*.

FIG. 78. *Bulbophyllum barbigerum*, a species with a lip that moves in the breeze.

FIG. 77. *Bulbophyllum* (Cirrhopetalum) *ornatissimum*, with two flies trapped between the balanced lip and column.

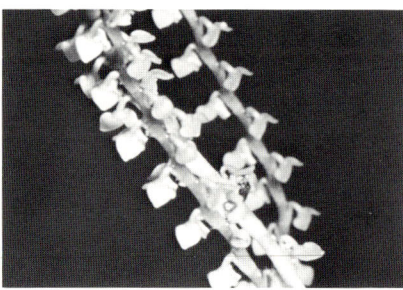

FIG. 79. *Stelis aemula* being pollinated by *Bradysia* sp., a tiny fly which has the pollinia stuck to its legs.

FIG. 80. *Cryptophoranthus* sp., the window-orchid. Note the tiny slits on each side of the joined sepals through which the pollinator must enter.

FIG. 81. *Restrepia xanthopthalma*.

species are extremely small and the sepals long and dominating, a parallel with the sapromyophilous trait predominating in *Masdevallia*.

Some species formerly described as *Megaclinium* have been said—since the days of Lindley and Morren—to possess an autonomous vibrating movement of the lip. This seems incorrect for an air current is necessary. The curious flat rachis, often purplish, may insure the first landing in the gradual approach described for flies. Perhaps the same end is achieved in the tiny-flowered *Oberonia thwaitesii* from Ceylon. It may also be compared to the subtending leaf under the flowers of some species of *Pleurothallis*.

The related genus *Monosepalum* from New Guinea has curious club-like antennae and a motile lip, but fused sepals form a tube.

Occasionally secondary feeding of visitors has arisen. *Bulbophyllum cupreum* has a nectar-groove on the lip, *B. lobbii* has oil and other species have diffuse secretions of sugar and oil on the sepals (*B. macranthum*) or a thick layer of slime on the upturned undersides of the lateral sepals (*B. campanulatum*).

3. Pleurothallidinae

The genera *Scaphosepalum, Stelis, Masdevallia, Restrepia, Lepanthes* and *Pleurothallis*, along with a few small genera, contain another thousand myophiles which are of a different origin and only occur in the American tropics. In *Masdevallia* we recognize myophily in the radial shape, spots, tails, fusion, slits and reduction of the labellum. These characters are well developed in the *M. bella* group. *Masdevallia erythrochaete*, a typical representative, was observed being visited by several drosophila-like flies which wandered around in the cup-like apex of the lip before climbing up onto the pad-like base of the lip under the stigma and anther (Dodson, 1965a). Many species, however, have changed to ornithophily, e.g., *M. rosea* (Dodson, 1962a) and *M. coccinea*. Some species have very offensive odors and are pollinated by flies. Dodson (1962a) reported the pollination of *M. fractiflexa* by flies which were attracted by the foul odor (Pl. XIIb).

Among the many parallels with *Bulbophyllum* we find that at least one species, *M. muscosa*, developed a motile lip for the final guidance. The movement is, however, not passive, but active and the consequence of special sensitivity (cf. *Pterostylis*). The phenomenon was investigated by Oliver (1888), who found the labellar crest to be the sensitive spot and that the reaction followed after two seconds.

Stelis aemula was observed to be visited by several kinds of small flies and mosquitos in Panama (Dodson, unpublished). One type of fly *Bradysia* sp. (*Sciaridae*) was well guided and moved from flower to flower taking nectar from the lip (Fig. 79). The pollinia were attached just under the mouthparts and the anther caps fell from the pollinia after a few moments. They were very effective pollinators. Larger flies and mosquitos took nectar but did not remove pollinia. Smaller flies were found trapped in the flowers apparently unable to free themselves from the sticky apices of the pollinia.

We see another parallelism—a refinement of slits between partially fused

FIG. 83. The flower of *Pleurothallis monocardia* being pollinated by the fly *Lycoria* sp. Note the pollinia hanging from the leg of the fly.

FIG. 82. *Pleurothallis schiedei*. Note the strange dangling bits of wax from each sepal.

FIG. 84. *Pterostylis* sp.

PLATE VII a (upper left): The pollinator of *Stanhopea tricornis*, *Eulaema meriana*, hovering in front of the flower. GUAYAQUIL, ECUADOR.

PLATE VII b (upper right): Male bee of *Euglossa ignita* scratching at the lip of *Stanhopea candida*. IQUITOS, PERU.

PLATE VII c (lower left): Male *Eulaema speciosa* struggling to escape from the flower of *Stanhopea connata*. The pollinarium is attached to the bee as it escapes. BAÑOS, ECUADOR.

PLATE VII d (lower right): Male bee of *Euglossa viridissima* falling through the flower of *Stanhopea tigina*. Note the constriction of the apex of the horns, epichile and column of the flower to fit the small bee. (Posed.)

PLATE VIII a (above left): Male *Euglossa viridissima* pollinating the flowers of *Gongora armeniaca*. CARTAGO, COSTA RICA.

PLATE VIII b (above right): Male *Euglossa dotsoni* pollinating the flowers of *Gongora horichiana* (formerly known as *Gongora armeniaca* var. *bicornuta*). Note the similarity of this species to *G. armeniaca*. TURRIALBA, COSTA RICA.

PLATES VIII c-d: Pollination of *Coryanthes rodriguezii* by male *Euplusia superba*. IQUITOS, PERU.

PLATE VIII c (middle left): Bees approaching and scratching at the lip.

PLATE VIII d (middle right): Bee struggling free from the flower. Note the anther cap which has been forced upward and the pollinarium being attached to the bee's abdomen.

PLATES IX a-b: Pollination of *Coryanthes trifoliata* by male bees of *Euglossa ignita*. IQUITOS, PERU.

PLATE IX a (lower left): Bees hovering in front of a flower.

PLATE IX b (lower right): Bee exiting from the lip of the flower. This species occurs together with *Coryanthes rodriguezii* at IQUITOS, PERU.

PLATE IX d (above right): *Coryanthes bicalcarata* being pollinated by male *Euglossa cordata* at Iquitos, Peru. This plant is from Moyobamba, Peru, and it is not known if the same bee pollinates it in its natural habitat.

PLATE X b (middle right): Bee scratching at the apex of the lip after entering the flower properly. As the bee prepares to exit, the lip falls backward carrying the bee against the column of the flower.

PLATE X d (lower right): *Xylobium latilabium* being pollinated by *Trigona amalthea*. Iquitos, Peru.

PLATE IX c (above left): *Coryanthes leucocorys* being visited by *Euglossa ignita*. This bee is attracted to the flower but does not pollinate it because of its small size. Iquitos, Peru.

PLATES X a-b: Pollination of *Anguloa clowesii* by male *Eulaema boliviensis*. Fusagasuga, Colombia.

PLATE X a (middle left): Bee preliminarily investigating the flower.

PLATE X c (lower left): A female bee of *Melipona eburnea* preparing to enter the flower of *Maxillaria furstenbergae*. Baños, Ecuador.

PLATE XI a (above left): *Oncidium macranthum* being pollinated by male *Bombus robustus* var. *hortulans*. BAÑOS, ECUADOR.

PLATE XI b (above right): *Miltonia endresii* being pollinated by *Ptiloglossa ducalis* in the pre-dawn darkness (4 a.m.) in Costa Rica.

PLATE XI c (middle left): *Cattleya luteola* being pollinated by *Melipona flavipennis* in the pre-dawn darkness at Iquitos, Peru.

PLATE XI d (middle right): *Papilio polyxenes* var. *americus* pollinating the flowers of *Epidendrum secundum*. BAÑOS, ECUADOR.

PLATE XII a (lower left): *Epidendrum paniculatum* being pollinated by a butterfly of the genus *Heliconia*. SAN VITO, COSTA RICA.

PLATE XII b (lower right): A fly visiting the foul-smelling flowers of *Masdevallia fractiflexa*. LOJA, ECUADOR.

PLATES XII c-d: Pollination of *Oncidium planilabre* by male *Centris geminata*. The bee strikes the flower, attempting to drive it away as if it were an enemy insect. GUAYAQUIL, ECUADOR.

PLATE XII c (above left): The bee with a pollinarium from another flower attached to the front of its head. (Posed.)

PLATE XII d (above right): The bee striking the flower and forcing the pollinarium into the stigma of the flower. (Posed.)

sepals—in the species described as window-orchids. These were discussed by Darwin under *Masdevallia* but separated by most authors as the genus *Cryptophoranthus* (Fig. 80). This genus is clearly myophilous but in a more specialized manner than *Masdevallia*, retaining fringes, lurid color and spots. Darwin found insect eggs inside the flowers.

In *Restrepia* the curious, partly glandular and odor-producing tips of some tepals which form the antennae (Fig. 81) are perhaps intermediate between tails and vibrators as in *Bulbophyllum lupeniorum*. The lip is reduced and supplanted by the synsepalum—a pair of fused sepals, which is also parallel with Cypripedioideae. In some species of *Bulbophyllum* and *Monomeria* the fused sepals form a frame around the motile lip.

The large genus *Pleurothallis* is extremely varied ecologically and contains many myophilous forms with features from the syndrome. The long motile hairs of *P. ornata* and the strange dangling white appendages on the edges of the dark colored sepals of *P. schiedei* (Fig. 82) are examples. The *P. cardiothallus* group approaches the genus *Stelis* in its pollination mechanisms. Nectar is secreted around the base of the lip and flies attracted to the flat flowers pick up the pollinia on their legs while drinking the nectar. *Lycoria* sp. (Sciaridae) was observed pollinating *P. monocardia* (Fig. 83), a member of this group, in Ecuador (Dodson, 1962a). The broad stigma which surrounds the anther makes deposition of the pollinia on succeeding flowers an easy matter.

Dodson (l.c.) observed numerous drosophila-like flies visiting the flowers of *P. xanthochlora*, which produce a sweet, fruit-like odor, but did not witness pollination. In Costa Rica numerous similar flies of the genus *Lacodrosophila* were observed visiting the flowers of *P. ruscifolia* and *P. eumecocaulon* (Dodson, 1965a). For a discussion of *Scaphosepalum* and its glands secreting odors see Vogel (1962).

4. Pterostylis

This fairly large genus, known from Australia and New Zealand as the "greenhoods," has a quite different place in taxonomy (Fig. 84). It is placed very low because of its granular pollen, though this may just as well be a derived character in response to the smallness of the visitors. It is almost entirely sapromyophilous and specialized in such minute microdipterans as Psychodidae and Mycetophilidae (Hyett, 1960). In some species such as *P. mutica* the odor is strongly unpleasant for man; in a single species, *P. trullifolia*, the odor is agreeable. The specificity of odors leads to strong specificity of visitors, one dipteran for each species.

The pollination of the flower depends on deceit and they are nectarless. The sepals and petals are connected basally, forming a closed kettle which contains the column and labellum (Fig. 85). The upper part of the sepals and petals opposite the lip is interconnected to form a helmet (galea) covering the kettle like a hood, as in *Arisaema* and other fly-traps such as *Sarracenia* and *Nepenthes*. The tails on the tepal-tips, the translucent windows and the greenish color with purple stripes of the flower are so much like a spathe of *Arisaema* that at first glance the orchid character of the flower is doubtful. The space inside the galea

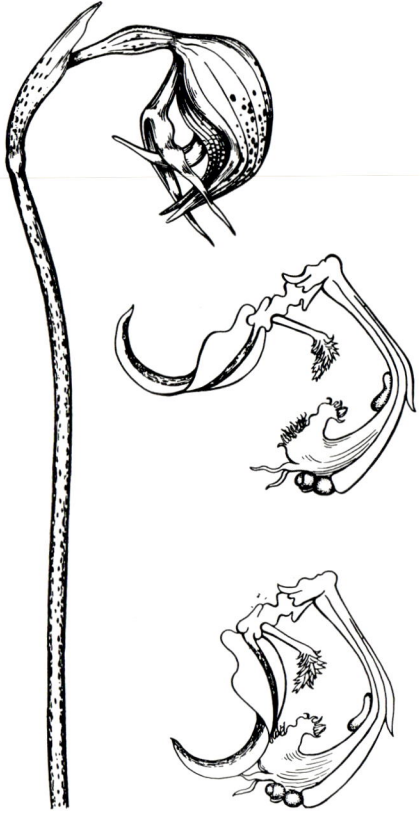

FIG. 85. Drawing of the flower of *Pterostylis* sp. showing the lip open and closed. (Drawing by P. Fawcett.)

is internally divided into an upper and a lower chamber. Small flies landing on the "visor" or stepping on the balanced labellum of most species make it suddenly tip over so that the insect is thrown against the stigma and imprisoned in the lower chamber. Through a tunnel it can escape but touches the anther. The movement of the lip is active, can be repeated, and the stimulation takes place in appendages of the labellum. The sensitivity is great as the insects do not weigh more than 1 mg. The insects appear to become intoxicated. Substances from the flower stupefied even large blow-flies. The mechanism has been described by Sargent (1909), Coleman (1934b), Werth (1911, 1956) and Hyett (1960).

In the related genus *Drakaea* the lip has the same irritability. Two allied genera, *Acianthus* and *Corybas* (Corysanthes)—usually with small flowers—are also myophilous according to observations. Some *Corybas* species from New Zealand are pollinated by gnats (Culicidae) according to Thomson (1927). This country has few bees and flies take their place as pollinators.

The allied genus *Caleana* from Australia has an upward movement of the lip and has a variety of visitors.

The genus *Prasophyllum* is also a member of the subfamily Neottioideae and is a common group of orchids in Australia. The flowers are carried in dense spike-like racemes and are non-resupinate. The labellum is articulated at the base and flexible. When an insect lands upon the lip the added weight causes it to deflex, rapidly lowering the visitor onto the column. The viscidium is attached to the prothorax of the insect and is withdrawn from the anther as the pollinator makes its exit. The stipe depresses and the pollen masses are deposited on the stigma of the succeeding flower. Garnet (1940) reported numerous instances of the pollination of P. morrisii, P. archeri, P. nigricans and P. dispectans by three species of small flies of the family Chloropidae, Claviceps flavipes, Oscinosoma subpilosa and O. sp. Coleman (1933) reported pollination of P. mulleri and P. gracile by the chrysomelid beetles Ametalla spinolae and Trogoderma adelaidae respectively.

Plocoglottis belongs to an entirely different group, the Phajinae in the Malayan region, but the labellum throws the visitors against the column, this time actively by tension released by the visitor, not by sensitivity. Some species are purple-spotted* and foetid. Ridley (1896) mentions P. foetida as fly-pollinated and further describes the pollination mechanism of P. porphyrophylla:

> "In the bud, the lip lies flat against the column, but, as the flower opens, it is drawn down in such a manner as to lie flat at some distance below it. This is affected by the lateral sepals the thickened inner edges of which develop the prolonged angles of the lip, and, as they are deflexed, draw down the lip. When a fly alights on the lip in search of nectar, it sets it free by its weight or by slightly separating the lateral sepals with its feet, and the lip springs up suddenly (its flexible claw acting as a spring) and strikes the face of the column, where it permanently remains, pressing the insect against

---

*As always in syndromes one should not take any one character as decisive. The spots of species of Gongora, Cycnoches, Vandopsis, Grammatophyllum and Arachnis obviously have a different significance, or none.

FIG. 86. *Epidendrum fimbriatum*, a fly-pollinated species.

the pollen masses so that it cannot escape from the trap without withdrawing the pollen."

There are a number of instances of fly-pollinated orchids which belong to essentially non-myophilous genera. In *Epidendrum*, for example, one species, *E. fimbriatum* (Fig. 86) was observed to be visited by flies of the family Tachinidae (Dodson, 1962a). Vogel (1954) mentions flies as the pollinators of African orchids: *Disa lugens* (sometimes with flat umbels and a motile lip as in the *Cirrhopetalum* section of *Bulbophyllum*), *D. cornuta*, *Satyrium pumilum* and *S. saxicolum*. Holttum (1953) observed fly-pollination in *Gastrodia javanica*. Gilbert (1958) reported flies of the family Syrphidae, *Syrphus viridiceps*, and tinnid wasps, as effective co-pollinators of *Dendrobium linguiforme* in Australia.

Some little-adapted flower-visiting flies of the genus *Empis* (dance-fly) have been observed as secondary, but effective visitors on orchids such as *Orchis "latifolia"* and *O. maculata* in Europe. Hagerup (1951) found that in the stringent climate of the Faroes the syrphid fly *Eristalis* is the only pollinator of *Orchis* (Dactylorchis) *maculata*. This form of the orchid has a shorter spur than usual and apparently has some nectar in it.

Dexter (1913) collected several wild mosquitoes with pollinia of *Habenaria obtusata* on their head and eyes in Michigan. He placed several mosquitos in a bottle with inflorescences of the orchid and they worked the flowers. The mosquitos were female. Silen (1906a) found the large *Tipula* mosquitoes sucking on and taking away pollinia from *Coeloglossum viride* and *Listera cordata* as co-visitors with ichneumonids in Finland. He even considers *Corallorhiza invicta* as a special syrphid fly-flower there. *Listera liliifolia* was found by Robertson (1928) to be visited by flies in the southeastern United States.

Flies of the family Tachinidae were observed to pollinate the flowers of *Trichoceros antennifera* in Eucador (Dodson, 1962a). The flies were attracted on a sexual basis and attempted to copulate with the flowers (see p. 136).

CHAPTER 10

Other Pollinators and Autogamy

Few reports of other kinds of orchid pollinators than those discussed in the preceding chapters are available. Of those which do exist certain are probably not valid. For example, reports of orchid pollination by snails and ants seem to have no foundation in fact. Even Knuth-Loew (III/1.) doubted the assumption that ants are pollinators of *Calypso borealis*. A recently published report of frog-pollination of *Lissochilus roseus* (called "batrachophily") seems incredible at best. The instance may well have been a simple misinterpretation of a phenomenon reported by Jones (personal communication) where lizards were observed on numerous occasions on the inflorescences of *Schomburgkia* in the Barbados Islands. The lizards were consuming ants which were attracted to the extrafloral nectaries on the outside of the sepals and bracts. The possibility of such animals acting as pollinators in the normal sense seems remote. Van der Pijl (1933 and 1953) reported lizards and frogs eating insects attracted to *Artocarpus* sp. and *Alocasia* sp.

There have been no reports of pollination by water (hydrophily), wind (anemophily) or bats (chiropterophily). Pollination by these means is not to be expected for orchids are not adapted to them.

ORCHIDS AND BEETLES

Plants adapted to beetles as their pollinators are called cantharophilous. Edith Coleman (1933) reported beetles (species of *Ametalla* and *Trogoderma*) working *Prasophyllum odoratum* in Australia. This orchid has a delightful, fruit-like fragrance and open nectar on the labellum. Other observers reported such beetles as effective pollinators of other species of *Prasophyllum* where the beetles visited for long periods. Darwin (1872) reported a beetle, *Strangalia atrata*, as a co-pollinator of *Orchis maculata*. Ridley (1894) observed beetles (*Rhyncophorus* sp.) creeping about among the nectarless flowers of *Dendrochilum*

(Platyclinus) *longifolia* with pollen masses on their heads. In South Africa Bolus (1893) found a beetle on *Disa bivalvata*, which produces umbels of flowers and appears to be fly-pollinated. Beetles occasionally can be found on some European orchids which have exposed nectar. Sometimes the beetles even extract pollinia and may actually act as pollinators. Species of *Leptura* and *Grammoptera* are regularly encountered on *Herminium monorchis* and *Listera ovata* (Darwin, H. Muller, 1873 and Heimans and Thysse, 1907). These beetles are visitors of specialized flowers and have well oriented flight habits. Beetles regularly visit some species of *Orchis* (see p. 80). Martens (1926, 1928) observed them effecting self-pollination on *Epipactis latifolia*.

These are the only reports of beetle-pollination to date for the orchids. The cases are obviously scattered in the lower orchids and there appears to be no trend toward adaptation to beetles as pollinators. Such a trend would not be expected since it would require too much regression in the orchid. Beetle-pollination as a class is associated with primitive angiosperm flowers for the most part (see p. 146). For this reason it seems hardly necessary to list the points which form the cantharophilous syndrome.

AUTOGAMY

Plants which are self-pollinated successfully are called autogamous. In orchids, seed production after cross-pollination is the general means of reproduction but a certain number deviate from the trend. These cases can often be attributed to special circumstances. Several degrees of this phenomenon may be found in a single genus, from species in which accidental self-pollination results in fertilization to those in which the flowers never open yet fertile seed is produced. In many orchids self-fertilization is not possible due to genetically controlled self-incompatibility. That is, pollen from a plant with a particular combination of genetic factors will not fertilize its own ovules or those of any other plant with the same combination. In several species of *Oncidium* Scott (1864) and Dodson (1957) demonstrated that some clones were self-incompatible and others not. Many species are self-compatible but normally outcross due to their pollination mechanisms (see p. 164).

In most species the pollen is kept separate from the stigma by the rostellar flap (see Chapter 1). This physical barrier is normally quite effective but forms occur in some species in which the rostellum degenerates or becomes stigmatic and self-pollination results. The pollen germinates on contact with the stigmatic fluid and the pollen tubes grow down the column to the ovules. This form of autogamy is clearly derived in normally outcrossing species and is found throughout the orchids. Darwin described the manner by which partial autogamy occurs in *Cephalanthera grandiflora*, a member of the primitive northern genus, where some pollen grains germinate in place due to the absence of a rostellum. After exclusion of visitors this process provides far less fertile seed than open pollination. Some authors (Godfery, 1933) considered this condition as primitive, but we do not necessarily share the view. Sometimes the flowers are pollinated in the bud in this manner and do not expand well (e.g., forms of *Phajus tankervilliae*, *Arundina speciosa* and *Cattleya aurantiaca*); however, normal forms are found either mixed in the population or in separate populations. This form of autogamy approaches cleistogamy where the buds do not open at all (see Knuth-Loew where a number of cases are mentioned and also the paper by Kirchner [1922] on European orchids which are cleistogamous).

In other instances the stigmatic fluid is so abundant that it reaches the pollinia, inducing germination (see Knuth-Loew). This occurs occasionally even in *Vanilla*.

Autogamy may also occur by simple falling of old disintegrated pollinia as a means of averting sterility at the end of a long, normal anthesis without arrival of a pollinator. *Ophrys apifera* in northern Europe demonstrates something similar as an exception in the genus (Fig. 87). The caudicles of the pollinia bend strongly out of the anthers and into the stigma, aided by shaking by the wind or by visitors. In *Herminium*, some species of *Epipactis* and *Orchis* the same happens (Martens, 1926). This phenomenon was studied in autogamous forms of *Oncidium glossomystax* in Ecuador by Dodson (unpublished—see Fig. 88). Recently Dressler and Wirth (personal communication) observed such autogamy in *Oncidium ostlundianum* in western Mexico. For consideration of an autogamous hybrid see p. 165.

In the *Phragmopedium* known as *P. caudatum* var. *lindeni*, an interesting form of autogamy occurs (Dodson, 1966a). A third anther extends from under the column and presses the pollinum directly against the stigma. Self-pollination is therefore automatic. Along with this anomalous morphology the lip is developed into a long narrow petal very similar to the two lateral petals (Fig. 89). Thousands of plants were observed in Ecuador in 1962 and 1963—all of which produced seed without cross-pollination. A single plant was found with "normal" flowers, having the typical slipper-like lip of other species. It demonstrated that this is distinct from *P. caudatum*.

We will not cite all the literature on autogamy in the orchids as it does not throw light on their characteristics. Some of the papers are negativistic in approach, based on an iconoclastic satisfaction of overthrowing Darwinistic views.

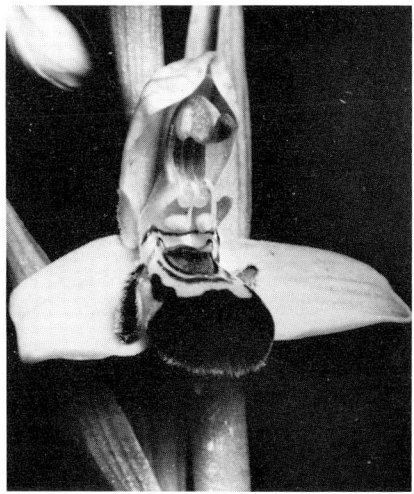 

FIG. 87. The flower of *Ophrys apifera* showing the mechanism whereby the pollinia are twisted on the stipe so that they touch the stigma of the flower and self-pollinate it. (Photos by F. Schremmer.)

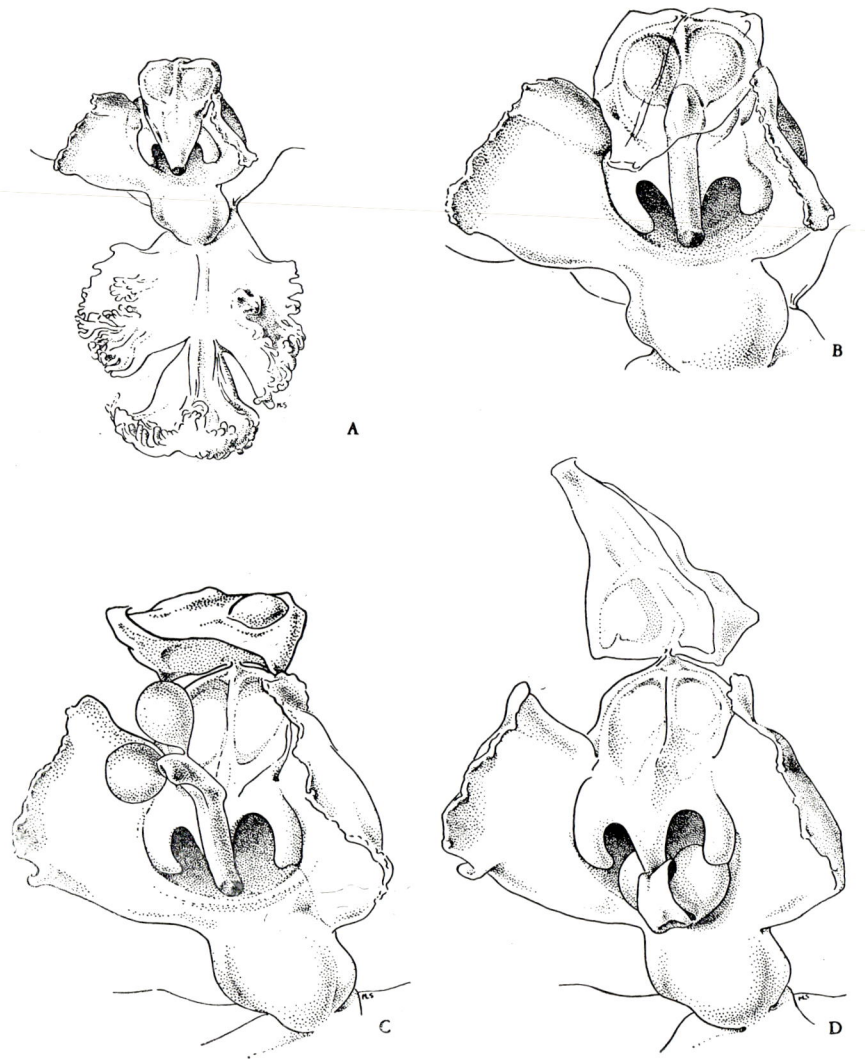

FIG. 88. The mechanism of self-pollination in certain populations of *Oncidium glossomystax* where the stipe curls, forcing the pollinia into the stigma.

The data on the curious Australian subterranean orchids *Rhizanthella* and *Cryptanthemis* are insufficient to indicate whether the minute flowers reach the surface or remain subterraneous with ensuing autogamy. In *Cryptanthemis* they remain underground but do open, and not all flowers form fruit.

In the genera *Thelymitra*, *Prasophyllum* and *Pterostylis* many cases of autogamy are on record. The same is true in certain species of *Cattleya* and *Schomburgkia*. It seems to occur after a long anthesis in all these cases.

Generally speaking, autogamy seems a means of averting extinction in plants growing under conditions adverse for normal pollination relations (Stebbins, 1951 and Grant, 1963). For orchids such a situation may be a cloud forest on a high summit. Schlechter indicated such cases. Species of *Calanthe* in Javanese mountains show a trace of autogamy as do species of *Myrmechis* and *Thelymitra javanica* (Docters van Leeuwen, 1937). Percival (1965) cited *Liparis caespitosa* as cleistogamous in the misty rainforest but chasmogamous (opening) in the drier air outside. Similarly plants growing near the periphery of the range of the species where pollinator frequency is poor or nonexistent may revert to autogamy as a means of survival. Examples are some species of *Orchis* in Europe and several orchids in Florida, such as *Epidendrum nocturnum*, *Encyclia cochleata* and *Bletia purpurea*, all of which have non-autogamous forms in other areas. In Florida seed is blown in from the Caribbean region and normal pollinators do not exist.

Genetically, a certain mixing of autogamy and allogamy (normal outcrossing) can bring equilibrium in population dynamics. For discussion of this point see Stebbins (1950) and Grant (1963).

Cultivation of plants, through unconscious selection, leads to the favoring of autogamous aberrations in the long run when not regulated by genetic countermeasures. A further step away from sexuality is apomixis (the development of unfertilized egg-cells or other cells). Apomixis is against the trend toward out-

FIG. 89. *Phragmopedium lindenii*, a self-pollinating species which has the third petal developed into an elongated structure similar to the other two petals rather than a pouch as in other species which out-cross.

crossing in the family, but occurs in some individuals of temperate orchids (Hagerup, 1947 and Leavitt, 1901). A similar situation has been reported in *Zygopetalum* (Hurst, 1925 and Suessenguth, 1923).

Genetically, autogamy—and more so, apogamy—leads to separation into many varieties and species without gene-flow. Such forms sacrifice the future for maintenance in the present. We estimate that about 200 species of orchids have been reported to be more or less regularly autogamous. Undoubtedly many more exist. We also find that autogamous forms of many species—with their characteristic changes in morphological structure—have been given names and are easily regarded as distinct species. This is particularly true where their real nature is not understood.

GENERAL CONSIDERATIONS ON CLASSES

The published data are insufficient to establish accurately the relative importance of pollinating agents in the family. However, we venture to give a rough estimate in the following chart (see p. 146). This is called the pollinator-spectrum of the family and is expressed in percentages.

HYMENOPTERA		OTHER AGENTS	
Wasps	5%	Moths	8%
Lower bees	16%	Butterflies	3%
Carpenter bees	11%	Birds	3%
Euglossini	10%	Flies	15%
Social bees	8%	Mixed agents	8%
Mixed bees	10%	Autogamous	3%
	60%		40%

Such extreme divergence in pollinators testifies for youth, continuing evolution and adaptive radiation in the family. We have not placed the bee-fly flowers, such as those that occur in *Disa*, in a separate category. With more detailed investigation it should be possible to compare spectra of genera or of particular regions. With the aid of the index and the list on page 181 it is already possible to obtain a review of diversity in pollinators in some genera.

The pollination spectrum of the family Polemoniaceae (Grant, 1961) is based on more thorough and concentrated study in a much smaller and less diverse group.

CHAPTER 11
Mimicry and Deception

The use of the term "mimicry" has been long surrounded with controversy. Mimicry has been used in zoology to signify some adaptation leading to a close external resemblance, as if for imitation or simulation of an animal to some different animal, in order to serve for protection or concealment. However, in horticulture "mimicry" has often been used to describe the similarity of a portion of a flower, the whole flower or an aggregation of flowers, to another object which is commonly known. For example, many authors have attributed the similarity of the inner parts of the flower of *Peristeria elata* to a dove, the callus of *Odontoglossum grande* to a baby in a cradle, the flower of *Coeloglossum viride* to a minute frog, the flower of *Phalaenopsis* to a moth, the flower of *Oncidium papilio* to a butterfly, the inflorescence of *Bulbophyllum purpureorhachis* to a lizard, etc. These similarities are entirely happenstance.

We feel that the term "mimicry" best describes the phenomena which we intend to discuss, but also believe that we should carefully define the term in relation to our use of it. We do not apply it in the sense of similarity to another object alone. Rather, we use the term to apply only to the selective development of characteristics in the flower which tend to deceive the pollinator and cause it to approach the flower expecting to encounter food, a mate, or an enemy.

We have demonstrated in previous chapters that many orchids produce flowers which do deceive their pollinators. In some cases there is an obvious similarity between the object that is offered to the pollinator and the object which the pollinator "expects" to encounter when it arrives on the flower. For example, the flower of *Trichoceros antennifera* has a simulated fly developed from the hairy column and lip, including barred and extended side-lobes that simulate extended wings (the side-lobes appear as antennae, hence the name, but they function as false wings) (Fig. 90). This orchid is called "La Mosca" (the fly)

FIG. 90. The flower of *Trichoceros antennifera* showing its similarity to an insect.

by natives of the region where it grows. Many of the flowers of *Ophrys* have similarities to insects as is testified to by the common names applied to them, i.e., bee-orchis (*Ophrys apifera*), saw-fly orchis (*Ophrys tenthredinifera*) and the fly-orchis (*Ophrys muscifera*). In other instances the flowers of the orchid have no apparent resemblance to the object being imitated, but attract the pollinator on that basis nevertheless, indicating that the pollinator senses something not apparent to the human observer. For *O. apifera* see Fig. 87.

We have already discussed, in a round-about manner, the deception in many orchids in order to attract insects which expect food. A large portion of even higher orchids are of this type and deception is obviously basic to further development of the refinements of mimicry. A common food-deception is that of the presence of a false nectary or nectar-spot. This is usually combined with a sweet, fresh, honey-like odor which tends to attract bees and flies. Similar is the production of foetid odors coupled with colors that simulate rotten meat. These attract carrion flies. A few cases of pollen imitation occur and have been discussed above. The most striking example is that of *Calopogon*, the "grass-pink" of the eastern United States and Canada, in which the lip is erect and is covered with thick hairs which imitate—through color as well as form—a mass of closely packed stamens. Bees come to the flower to collect pollen and upon landing on the lip are thrown down onto the column by the hinged, flexible base of the lip that will not support their weight (Robertson, 1887 and Dodson, unpublished).

In discussing deception and its refinement, mimicry, we can separate the stimuli produced by the flowers into three categories: odor, optical appearance and tactility. These act on the senses of the pollinator. The three categories are commonly interdependent, i.e., appearance combines with odor to initially attract the pollinator. Occasionally the tactile sense is necessary upon landing to complete the "plot" of the deception. In some cases odor is apparently the only stimulus involved in the primary attraction and in others appearance is the sole factor. Tactility would appear to be dependent on the other two categories but is occasionally indispensable in completing the activity which lead to ultimate deposition of the pollinia. Kullenberg (1961) has a splendid discussion of stimulation in the pollination of *Ophrys*.

At present we have knowledge of two kinds of mimicry in the orchids: pseudocopulation and pseudoantagonism, with a possible third kind, pseudoparasitism, needing further investigation.

PSEUDOCOPULATION

1. *Ophrys*

Ophrys is a genus of approximately 30 species with the majority occurring in the Mediterranean region. A few species occur as far north as Sweden and Norway, to the west in England and to the east as far as the Crimea. All are terrestrial in habit. The inflorescence varies in height from six to eighteen inches and three to six flowers are produced. The species are primarily based on the characters of the lip, which is convex, velvety and strangely colored. (Fig. 87.)

The remarkable similarity to insects has long been discussed and many explanations were given for this resemblance, including (in a letter cited by Rolfe [1910]) the belief that the likeness to insects had nothing to do with pollination but served to frighten away browsing cows. Darwin wrote in a footnote that "Mr. Price has frequently witnessed attacks made upon the Bee-Orchis by a bee, similar to those of the troublesome *Apis muscorum*." Darwin also noted that he could not conjecture what this meant.

Pouyanne discovered (Correvon and Pouyanne, 1916) in Algeria that flowers of *Ophrys speculum*, offering no food whatever, attract a male wasp by imitating its females. In the course of a century many controversies had risen around this question, often as a denouncement of "nonsensical ideas of ecologists," or as tokens of unefficaciousness in nature. Arguments were especially directed against pseudonectaries in *Ophrys* which have been cited as an indication of a lack of expediency in nature.

Later Godfery and Wolff corroborated the observations and deductions from the botanical standpoint while Kullenberg (1956) analyzed the phenomenon from the zoological, physiological and chemical standpoint. Kullenberg's book (1961) with colored illustrations reads like a novel and will remain one of the classics of floral ecology.

The *Ophrys* flower (cf. p. 26) acts mainly through odors, imitating those produced by the abdominal glands of female bees or wasps which are even perceptible to man. The action on male bees or wasps, however, is but rarely species-specific. It shows some gradation in effect on different taxa, perhaps due to difference in components. Other factors assist in causing more specificity. Shape, colors (including ultraviolet reflection) and tactile stimuli by the hairs on the lip operate on the sensory organs of unsatisfied males. The same behavior as

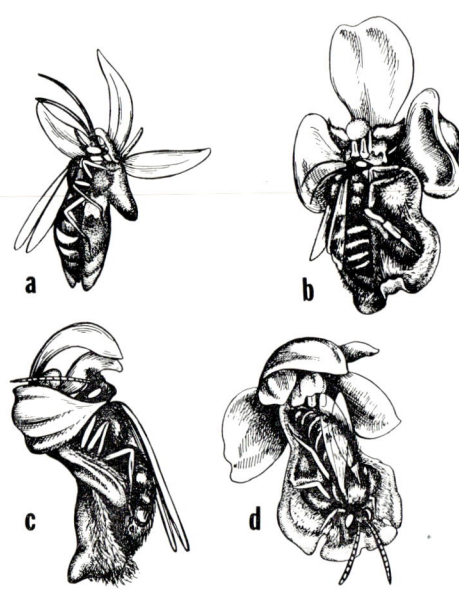

FIG. 91. Illustrations of pseudocopulation of various species of *Ophrys* by male bees and wasps (adapted from Kullenberg, 1961). a. The male wasp, *Gorytes mystaceus*, on *Ophrys insectifera*. b. The male bee, *Eucera* sp., visiting the flower of *Ophrys tenthredinifera*. c. A wasp, *Trielis ciliata*, visiting a flower of *Ophrys speculum*. d. A male bee, *Andrena maculipes*, on the flower of *Ophrys lutea*. (Drawing by P. Fawcett.)

that observed during the initial phases of copulation with female bees results. No ejection of sperm was observed. The supernormal olfactory stimulation is responsible for the long stay on the flower.

The act of pseudocopulation takes place in such a way that the pollinia are carried off and redeposited. Four genera of solitary bees and wasps appear to be the principal pollinators. The species of *Ophrys* which are pollinated by the wasps *Trielis*, *Gorytes* and the bee *Eucera* (Figs. 91a, b, c) induce the insects to attempt copulation with the apex of the lip. Those pollinated by *Andrena* (Fig. 40d) appear, for the most part, to stimulate the bee to reverse the position and copulate with the base of the lip. In the former group the pollinarium is affixed to the head of the pollinator while in the latter it is attached to the abdomen. Only the introductory behavior is necessary for pollination of the flower and the bees do not encounter structures which lead to ejection of sperm. The behavior is elicited by tactile stimulation from the hairs on the labellum but requires simultaneous and continued olfactory stimulation. The glistening pseudonectaries have a clear place in the syndrome, apparently imitating the eyes of the female bee. Metallic-blue mirrorspots similar to those found in the females enhance the effect (Fig. 92). Dimensions of the flowers in the various species of *Ophrys* help in determining specificity and success.

We list below the various species of *Ophrys*, about which we have information, and their specific (primary) pollinators (taken from Godfery, 1933 and Kullenberg, 1961). Other insects are more or less sexually attracted, including bees, beetles and flies. The sham-nectaries can mislead flies.

a. *Trielis.*

Ophrys speculum lures only males of *Trielis ciliata,* a digger wasp of the family Scoliidae, formerly known as *Scolia* or *Campso-scolia* (Fig. 91c).

b. *Gorytes.*

Ophrys muscifera is pollinated by a sphecid wasp, *Gorytes mystaceous* as discovered independently by Godfery in southern France (1921-1930) (Kullenberg found this species to be pollinated by an *Andrena* in Sweden). *Ophrys insectifera* is pollinated by the same species of *Gorytes* in Sweden (Fig. 91a).

c. *Eucera.*

Ophrys fuciflora is pollinated by *Eucera tuberculata,* an anthophorine bee. *Ophrys tenthredinifera* (Fig. 91b), *O. bombylifera* and *O. scolopax* (sensu lato) are pollinated by various species of *Eucera. Ophrys apifera* is pollinated largely by *Eucera* males in Morocco. According to Kullenberg this species has exceptionally long caudicles and the pollinia can fall out after a disturbance by some visitor. But he believes that autogamy is not the normal means of reproduction as had been previously postulated. In the English form the long caudicles perhaps are more strongly developed but the self-pollination is not really autonomous and requires some disturbance.

d. *Andrena.*

Ophrys arachnitiformis is pollinated by *Andrena trimmerana* (pollinia on the head). *Ophrys lutea* is pollinated by males of *Andrena nigro-olivacea* (Fig. 91d). Here the labellum imitates a female quite differently than in the above mentioned instances, viz., with the head directed toward the apex

FIG. 92. *Ophrys tenthredinifera,* showing the similarity to an insect. (Photo by F. Natan.)

of the labellum and the bee taking a corresponding position, receiving the pollinia at the top of the abdomen. *Ophrys fusca* is pollinated by *Andrena trimmerana, A. nigroaena* and *A. maotae*. Kullenberg did not have conclusive evidence but suggested that *O. murbeckii, O. araneifera, O. iricolor* and *O. atlantica* are pollinated by the same genus of bees.

Repeated visits to the same flower occur in *Ophrys* but they do not result in self-pollination as the pollinia do not yet fit, or at least not entirely. Simultaneous visits by two bees have a strange consequence. The stimulated second visitor tries to copulate with the first male. As with many solitary bees the insects mentioned have what zoologists describe as protandry or proterandry: the males emerge first.

When some weeks later the real females emerge the flowers are sometimes neglected, but by then the main flowering season usually is over. This is a demonstration of the orchidaceous trait of gambling—to depend on a very thin thread for survival. In such a case the biotope for plant and insect have to agree and other flowers, offering pollen and nectar to the females, must be present there. As in other cases of narrow bonds in time of appearance of flower and insect, there must also be some inborn or environmental synchronizing factor.

2. *Cryptostylis*

Edith Coleman and colleagues published parallel observations on entirely different orchids between 1929 and 1961 in the Victorian Naturalist. These orchids belong to the genus *Cryptostylis*, the "tongue-orchids" of Australia. The pollinator is the ichneumon-wasp, *Lissopimpla semipunctata*, which takes the head-up position, with the apex of the abdomen pushed in between the lip and column.

Cryptostylis has about 30 species extending from India to the South Sea Islands and forms an isolated subtribe in the subfamily Neottioideae, whereas *Ophrys* is considered as primitive in the Orchioideae (see diagram in Fig. 116).

Extensive descriptions of the pollinaton of four species of *Cryptostylis*, *C. leptochila, C. subulata, C. erecta* and *C. ovata*, in Australia were published by Coleman (1927, 1928, 1929a and b, 1930a and b). Mrs. Coleman observed numerous instances of *Lissopimpla semipunctata* visiting the flowers of *C. leptochila* (Fig. 93). The ichneumon, after backing into the stigma, bends its body into an arch with the base of the lip of the flower held by the claspers of the wasp. The dorsal side of the apex of the abdomen comes in contact with the viscidium and the pollinarium becomes cemented in place. The wasp, after a short pause, then flies on to another flower and the same behavior delivers the pollinia to the stigma. Coleman (1928) suggested an external similarity in form between the wasp and the flower but showed that the fragrance was the principal attractant.

The same wasp visits *C. subulata* and acts in a similar manner (Fig. 94) except that the different form of the lip requires that the wasp back for a considerable distance after landing on the apex of the extended lip to reach the column. The lip is pendant and concave in this species. *Cryptostylis erecta* and *C. ovata* are pollinated in a manner similar to that of *C. leptochila*. *Cryptostylis ovata* was observed by Goadby and reported upon by Coleman (1930a).

The wasp has been seen to eject seminal fluid and even preferred the flowers to the real females. Some unknown ecological or physiological barrier to hybridization appears to occur between *C. leptochila* and *C. subulata* for they occur sympatrically, and are pollinated by the same species of wasp, but no hybrids are found. In a short paper on the group Watson (1961) included fine photographs.

3. *Trichoceros*

Suspicion has long been entertained about the method of pollination of members of this genus and its allies. The simulated insect in the lip of most species of this and related genera is commonly so life-like that it appears as though it could easily fly away. Though its obvious connection to insect pollination implied that pseudocopulation might be involved, no observations were made to confirm such an assumption. Such observations were recently made and reported by Dodson (1962a).

Most of the members of *Trichoceros* and related genera occur at higher elevations in the Andes but a few extend into Central America. Six genera have been proposed in this complex: *Telipogon, Trichoceros, Stellilabium, Sodiroella, Dipteranthus* and *Cordanthera*. Only the first seem to be valid. The other three represent variants of *Stellilabium* with species discovered later bridging the generic differences. All members of the three genera, *Telipogon, Trichoceros* and *Stellilabium* have the column and lip developed in such a manner as to simulate an insect.

Trichoceros antennifera (Fig. 90) is found from Colombia to northern Peru at elevations of 2,500 to 3,000 meters, growing among low shrubs in relatively dry areas, usually on the banks of streams. In these same areas several scandent Compositae occur in abundance. These Compositae, primarily of the genus *Mikania*, produce sweet fragrances and abundant nectar to which numerous flies are attracted and on which they feed. Particularly common are flies of the family Tachinidae.

FIG. 93. Drawing of a flower of *Cryptostylis leptochila* showing the ichneumon-wasp, *Lissopimpla semipunctata*, in the proper position for pollination while the wasp attempts to copulate with the flower. (Drawing by L. Mourré.)

FIG. 94. Drawing of a flower of *Cryptostylis subulata* with the wasp, *Lissopimpla semipunctata*, attempting to copulate with the flower. (Drawing by L. Mourré.)

FIG. 95. A male fly of *Paragymnomma* sp. attempting to copulate with the flower of *Trichoceros antennifera*.

Some ten species were collected in an hour. Some days are entirely sunny and others are intermittantly cloudy. The flies are only active when the sun shines.

Female flies of this group, when ready for copulation, land on a leaf or other flat object in the sun and open and close the genital orifice when male flies pass by. This action apparently serves as a signal to the passing flies and they veer from their flight pattern and approach the females rapidly. Copulation lasts only moments.

The flowers of *Trichoceros antennifera* simulate the female flies of *Paragymnomma* sp. to a remarkable degree. The column and base of the lip are narrow, barred with yellow and red-brown and extend laterally to simulate the extended wings of a sitting fly. The blade of the lip has no particular similarity to the head and thorax of a fly but this probably is not necessary to complete the illusion. The stigma of the flower is located more or less at the apex of the "false-abdomen" of the flower and reflects sunlight, as does the genital orifice of the female fly. The viscidium, extended over the stigma on the slender rostellum, projects up through the bristles and becomes attached to the basal portion of the abdomen of the fly. The viscidium is flat and pad-like in this genus, unlike the curved hook-like viscidium in *Telipogon*. The male flies, deceived by the similarity to the female fly and stimulated by the signal from the genital orifice-like stigma, strike the flower for only a moment and then pass on to other flowers in the same area (Fig. 95). The action is sufficient, however, to pick up the pollinarium. The long slender stipe of the pollinarium bends down slightly and is forced into the stigma when the fly visits a succeeding flower.

The members of *Telipogon* are generally similar but the fly-like appearance is not as pronounced (Figs. 96-99). Usually bristles occur only on and around the column. The species appear to be quite successful within their habitats and seed pods are often encountered. Therefore it would appear that the illusion is adequate to deceive the male flies. The flowers of *Stellilabium* (Fig. 100) are even more insect-like than those of *Trichoceros*.

Though we have no observations of pollination in *Telipogon* or *Stellilabium* there seems no reason to doubt that it is based on the same principle as *Trichoceros*. The same syndrome occurs in all genera. In *Telipogon* we have found four species growing sympatrically near Loja in southern Ecuador with no evidence of hybridization. Flowers of the four species are strikingly different and no intermediates occur. If pollination mechanisms are the barrier to hybridization it indicates, for flies, an unusual degree of fidelity.

4. *Trigonidium*

Trigonidium obtusum has recently been reported to be pollinated by male bees of the genus *Trigona* (Kerr and Lopez, 1963) extending pseudocopulation to lower social bees. The bees attempted to copulate with the glandular apices of the petals (Fig. 101). The genus *Trigonidium* consists of six or eight species distributed from Mexico to southern Brazil. It is closely related to *Maxillaria*. The flowers of the various species are remarkably similar, with the sepals and petals forming a tube. The lip and column are short and the apices of each petal and the lip are swollen into a glandular, blue-gray pad.

Closely allied to *Trigonidium* are the genera *Mormolyca* and *Cyrtidium*. The flowers of these two genera are much more insect-like than *Trigonidium*, with the sepals and petals reflexed and the lip colored and shaped like an insect. The column arches over the lip and must contact the pollinator as it attempts to copulate with the lip. The mimicry is much more obvious here than in *Trigonidium*.

FIG. 96. *Telipogon* sp.

FIG. 98. *Telipogon* sp.

FIG. 97. *Telipogon* sp.

FIG. 99. Close-up view of the lip and column of the flower of *Telipogon* sp.

FIG. 100. *Stellilabium microglossum*.

A number of reports of orchid pollination are probably applicable to pseudocopulation but have not been carefully analyzed.

Coleman (1932) reported the pollination of *Diuris pedunculata* by male bees of *Halictus languinosus*. The bees force the lip of the flower back from the column in order to reach the nectar ring at the base of the lip and column. The nectar apparently acts as an intoxicant, for some bees were observed with their mandibles between the lip and column, remaining motionless for hours. They proved completely healthy and active when removed from the flower.

Fresh flowers of *D. pedunculata* were placed in a jar with three male bees and were immediately visited. Fresh flowers of *D. sulphurea* were also placed in a jar with the same bees and were not visited. Twenty male bees were collected from *D. pedunculata* but never a female. Coleman (1933) believed that both species of *Diuris* are pollinated by male bees which are stimulated in a similar manner as *Lissopimpla semipunctata* in the pollination of *Cryptostylis*. *Diuris sulphurea* is pollinated by a bee (possibly the *Paracolletes* sp. mentioned by Rayment [1932] as the pollinator of this species?) about twice as large as *Halictus languinosus*. Coleman felt that there was but one motive for the visits of the male bees to *Diuris*: "response to some mysterious attraction possessed by the orchid, partly scent, partly a resemblance to the female of their kind; but more probably to a marvelous imperceptible summons, which we humans can, as yet, only partly interpret." We do not feel that it is quite that mysterious but agree that it is marvelous.

The flowers of *D. sulphurea* have a yellow base color with dark brown markings which when seen from above give a barred effect similar to that of the bee's abdomen. The bees, when landing on the lip of the flower curve the abdomen so that its apex is extended slightly over the apex of the lip (similar to the system in *Ophrys bombylifera* in which the *Eucera* does the same while attempting copulation).

Coleman (1930a and b) indicated that she felt a similar situation, that of possible pseudocopulation, was occurring in *Caladenia barbarossae* and *C. dialata* var. *rhomboidiformis* with small bee-like insects imbedding the abdomen in the callus of the labellum of the former species. The latter species was similarly visited by a large ichneumon-fly, with a yellow banded body. Sargent (1918) reported *C. barbarossae* as pollinated by a wasp.

There seems a strong possibility that the observations mentioned above are related to the phenomena in the Western Hemisphere where only male bees of the Euglossini visit flowers of the *Catasetum* and *Stanhopea* alliances. These may be links in a chain of phenomena based on instinct-deceit by odor. Extensions of the chain into the sexual sphere may be built upon specialization of general deceit by imitative odors. Vogel (1963) feels that the attractant in *Catasetum* is part of a cycle of pseudocopulation. This may be true but we cannot agree with his reasoning that the relationship is associated with the behavior of some male bees which wait before brood cells to fecundate emerging young females. He feels that the dark apertures in the lip of many species of *Catasetum* simulate brood cells. The copulation behavior of euglossine bees would not support this idea (Dodson 1966c).

We suspect further cases of pseudocopulation such as in *Porphyroglottis maxwelliae* in Malaysia. In the combretaceous *Guiera senegalensis*, Kullenberg (1961) saw sexual attraction of a sphecid wasp *Tachysphex*. This indicates that the phenomenon is not limited to the orchids. This point is perhaps important for the phenomenon is not as limited as once thought. The development of pseudocopulation as an advanced form of mimicry has been proposed as an argument for the antiquity of the orchid family (Ames, 1937, Garay, 1960). Ames wrote: "Allowing for differences of opinion, and in this case they are delightfully negligible, the (phylogenetic) positions assigned to *Ophrys* and *Cryptostylis* indicate that pseudocopulation, no matter what future studies and discoveries may reveal with

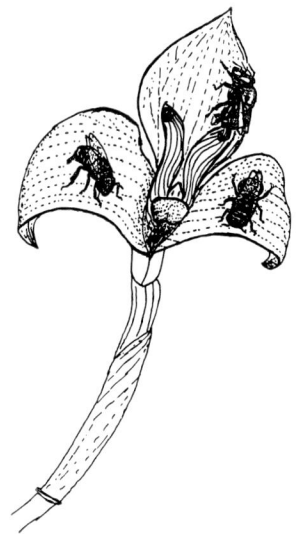

FIG. 101. Drawing of male bees of *Trigona droryana* attempting to copulate with the flower of *Trigonidium obtusum*. (Adapted from a sketch by S. F. Sakigami.)

FIG. 102. Male bee of *Bombus robustus* var. *hortulans* on a leaf surveying its territory and prepared to drive away any intruding insect.

regard to its occurrence, is a peculiarity of the lowest groups of the orchid family and therefore may be considered an ancient and long-established association." This argument seems hardly valid when we find pseudocopulation well developed in at least four very different groups of orchids, two of which are among the most advanced. In addition, primitive and advanced forms of two basically different types of insects are involved. It would appear that pseudocopulation is of relatively easy attainment when based upon mimicry and deception so prevalent throughout the family. We agree that some of the orchids involved are primitive but this does not argue for ancient derivation of the phenomena nor for the antiquity of the family.

As pointed out on p. 134, an important factor in the life cycle of the bee which makes the phenomenon of pseudocopulation more easily attainable is the earlier emergence of males. It occurs in the Euglossini. Nests which were brought in produced 20 male bees simultaneously from cells which were less than two months old (corroborated by F. Bennett in *Eulaema terminata*, in litt.). Other cells which were much older (probably at least six months) produced 70 female bees in succession over a period of a month.

Pseudocopulation, therefore, has not "fallen out of heaven" as a whole, as is often poetically stated. Deceit appears to be at the foundation of the flower-pollinator relationship in the orchids rather than nectar.

PSEUDOANTAGONISM

This category has been reported in *Oncidium* by Dodson and Frymire (1961b) and corroborated by observations of Dressler (personal communication). The likeness of some species of *Oncidium* to insects is well known. Male bees of the genus *Centris* were observed attacking the flowers of *Oncidium hyphaematicum* and *O. planilabre* in the coastal zone of Ecuador. The male bees set up territories and drive away, by attacking and striking, any other flying insects which enter their territory. The bees rest on a twig or leaf where they can survey their territory (Fig. 102). The racemes of flowers are arched and the slightest breeze causes the flowers to dance. When the flowers of an *Oncidium* located in the territory of the bee move, the bee attacks them. If the breeze continues the bee strikes flower after flower. Dressler reports the territoriality to be so pronounced that captured bees returned to the defense of their territory upon release.

The action is extremely precise. The bee does not land on the flower but merely strikes it (Pl. XIIc). The viscidium attaches to the frons of the bee, between the compound eyes, and the stipe rapidly depresses, holding the pollinia extended directly in front of the bee (Pl. XIId). Experiments with dead bees indicated that the bee must strike the flower with a margin of error of less than one millimeter in order to effect pollination. The bee rarely misses. Though, to the human eye, the flowers have no particular similarity to another insect there is a good possibility that the bee perceives quite a different object. The color combination may aid in the precision of the strike. Each of the outstretched petals of most similar species of *Oncidium* have one or two bars of color. These may act subjectively as a flight-pattern guide on the compound eyes of the bees.

This phenomenon is probably limited to certain sections of *Oncidium* and similar genera. Female *Centris* sp. was observed pollinating *Odontoglossum grande* and *Oncidium ochmatochilum* by Dodson (1965a) in Costa Rica. The bees acted in a frenzied manner but did not display the behavior observed in the males. The female bees landed on each flower and attempted to force their way into the center.

Dressler's observations were made in Panama on *Oncidium stipitatum*. He captured two species of *Centris* (males) which apparently centered their territories on the inflorescence of the orchid.

It is interesting and perhaps significant that female *Centris* are most com-

FIG. 103. Pollination of *Malpighia* by female bees of the genus *Centris*. a. Flower of *Malpighia* showing similarity to flowers of *Oncidium*. b. Female bee of *Centris* sp. clutching the dorsal petal at the stalk with her mandibles while extracting nectar from the nectaries on the sepals between the stalked petals of the flower.

FIG. 104. *Calochilus campestris*.

FIG. 105. *Polyrrhiza lindeni*. Note the flattened roots and lack of leaves on the plant.

monly encountered visiting flowers of the family Malphigiaceae which are remarkably similar in color and form to those of many species of *Oncidium* (Fig. 103).

PSEUDOPARASITISM

This is an unproven category. We only include it because it seems as logical as pseudocopulation and pseudoantagonism. There is a report by Fordham (1946) of a scoliid wasp, *Campsomeris tasmaniensis*, which made stinging movements on the hairy labellum of *Calochilus campestris* (Fig. 104). The females of this species of wasp lay their eggs on larvae of other insects and when those eggs hatch the wasp larvae consume the body of the host. Unfortunately, the sex of the pollinator was not determined but if it had a sting it was a female. But stinging and copulating movements might be confused. If the pollinators are male then it is possibly another case of pseudocopulation. In *Calochilus* imitations may be fairly common as the lip is furry, has blue spots and imitation-eyes.

Some flowers other than orchids attract pollinators on a basis similar to "pseudoparasitism." They act not on hunger, social or sexual instincts, but on oviposition. This may be deceit or lead to a cyclic symbiosis, with larvae in the postfloral parts (see van der Pijl, 1960/61, p. 412). We know of no such cases in orchids (though Darwin found fly eggs in *Cryptophoranthus* flowers), and their rapidly decaying flowers seem unfit as a substrate.

Pseudocopulation, pseudoantagonism and pseudoparasitism are similar in that they are based on deceit. We feel certain that physiologists and the diminishing group of anti-ecologists would agree that these phenomena cannot be simply relegated to "just variation, physiology or genetics."

CHAPTER 12

The Orchid Flower as a Living Whole

COMPARISON OF THE ORCHID FAMILY WITH OTHER MONOCOTYLEDONOUS PLANTS

The orchid family represents a highly advanced and terminal line of floral evolution in the monocotyledons. Several similar lines occur in both the monocotyledons and dicotyledons and the orchids are a parallel of such advanced families in the dicotyledons as Asclepiadaceae and Labiatae. In many respects the orchid family runs—in monocotyledons—parallel to the Scitamineae (the gingers and the banana family). Whereas the Scitamineae have retained the septal nectaries (nectaries within the septa of the ovary) of many of the Liliiflorae, such as Liliaceae and Iridaceae, the orchids have left this line and when offering nectar at all, present it on sepals and petals. Other members of the Liliiflorae offer nectar on the sepals but it is not certain whether we may consider the secretion of nectar on sepals in the orchids as evidence of derivation from them. Most of the relatively primitive, and many of the more advanced orchids definitely have nectaries but in many orchids they seem developed "de novo." For example, the nectar secreting glands on the lateral lobes of the lip in some of the species of *Oncidium* appear to have been developed independently.

Compared to the grasses—a highly successful line derived from the Liliiflorae—the orchids are the opposite extreme in relative diversity of flowers and seeds. In grasses, flowers follow a basic pattern with little major variation. The fine pollen is spread by wind and the seeds are large and of many types with varied means of dispersal. In orchids, the flowers are multiform. Large quantities of pollen are formed in masses which are spread by animals and the seeds are uniform and small and dispersed by wind.

1. Significance of specializations in the orchid family

It has been said that all orchids have a similar floral plan but show much variation in vegetative parts. This statement is only correct in regard to the basic plan of the orchid flower. There is probably no other plant family which demonstrates such remarkable variation in the form and functions of the basic components of the flower. They are infinitely varied and often in a progressive manner.

The vegetative parts hardly vary in function though there are vegetative variations in connection with terrestrial and epiphytic life and their various complications. The vegetative habit has been used as a basis of classification but with very little success. The various vegetative adaptations are often striking, are easy to study and tend to satisfy our thirst for explanations, whereas flowers are often set aside, as "chaotic variety" for amateurs, and as a means of classification for professional taxonomists. We know of epiphytic bulbophyllums in which the pseudobulbs are reduced to a string of minute beads and we often encounter orchids, such as species of *Camplyocentrum, Angraecum* and *Polyrrhiza* (Fig. 105) which are reduced to flat roots. We read about saprophytes with reduced roots and leaves and even about Australian subterranean orchids such as *Rhizanthella* and *Cryptanthemis*. Their flowers, on the other hand, remain fine, positive instruments with distinct relationships, both morphological and ecological. Flowering seems all important when we consider little *Porpax meirax* from the Himalayan region. We see a small, flat and nude "bulb" appressed to a tree trunk and hardly discernable, but producing one large flower, looking like a strange structure produced by the trunk of the tree. To a floral ecologist the diverse vegetative morphology of the orchids seems merely protective and rather negative in overall importance, whereas the flowers of orchids seem to produce luxury in the sexual sphere, with strong specialization toward pollinating agents. Flower dimensions may be maintained though the vegetative parts may become reduced and indistinct. It is not easy to decide what lies at the root of this onesidedness or what may be the "advantage" guiding along such a path, or the "aim" at the end.

The majority of orchid genera in the tropics lead a rather uniform vegetative life as epiphytes, especially when growing in humid forests, with a minimum of competition and a uniform macroenvironment. The biotic environment for flowers, however, provides pluriformity even there. In regard to fruits, seeds and seed dispersal, uniformity prevails.

It is true that many species of orchids have never been found with fruits. A number of botanists have considered this as proof of near extinction. Other phenomena such as the reduction of the stamens to the minimum of one and the short duration of flowers in some groups have also been indicated as proof of advancing sterility near the end of the family. The dependence on a narrow environment and on fungi (mycotrophy) have also been called decadent.

On the other hand the numerical success of the family is great. The end seems distant unless the finely adjusted overall environment is basically disturbed. "Sterility" is associated with avoidance of promiscuity and the rarity of successful pollination and fruiting appears more like the exact gambling of a long range strategist. Especially for perennials, safe in the tropical woods, a single fruiting with millions of seeds may be sufficient, notwithstanding happy-go-lucky gambling in the dispersal of seeds and difficulties in germination.

The restrictions placed on the sexual system by self-incompatibility, monophily, reduction of stamens, short duration of flowers and the gamble of placing all the pollen in one mass must have led to the extinction of many species after environmental changes, but ever again new lines of exploration into the environment were opened to a genus, as we saw in previous chapters. We also saw that the family often returned to archaic methods, superimposed on refined fixed structures, apparently contributing to the overall success of the group.

VIEWPOINTS OF BOTANISTS IN GENERAL ON POLLINATION RELATIONS

In order to indicate our lines of thought on pollination relations we will begin by stating some general viewpoints. We will briefly mention some of the adaptations of special groups of orchids which are discussed more fully in preceding pages.

We will not attempt to explain the orchid flower as a field for aesthetic forces or other idealistic concepts of form. The influence of Goethe on German botanists in this respect is not to be neglected, as we shall see. He had an aversion to sex in flowers, as postulated by Linnaeus, detesting "die ewigen Heiraten" (endless chatter on marriage). Linnaeus was often rather coarse and moreover morphologically incorrect in respect to sex in flowers. One of Goethe's followers, Velenovsky, devoted considerable space (in a fine botanical textbook) to a discourse against the concept of the flower as a "geistloser Kopulationsmechanismus" (mechanism for copulation without spirit and soul).

This trend was often supported by an anti-darwinism attitude which arose from a distinct and contrary intellectual background. The great botanist Goebel, whom we met in discussing resupination (p. 7), was the foremost proponent of this attitude. Goebel (1920) was attracted by the new physiology of his day and tried to explain morphological forms by supplanting selection-concepts with the action of physiological forces. At first approach this seems a useful attitude but we will judge to what extent this approach is sufficient after later discussion (p. 220). Goebel recognized function, but considered it as simply "Ausnutzung" (utilization) of a given form. In modern times, with most botanists limited to the laboratory, this attitude has held the field.

Nelsson (1954), whom we have to cite on some points, tried a causal explanation of forms on a pseudo-physiological basis, pitting anti-teleological physiology against ecological function. He neglected the functions of the flower, which simply cannot be neglected in an organ for pollination. In his one-sidedness he even denied (in 1954) that the likeness of *Ophrys* to insects was of any use.

The infuence of Goethe is clearly recognizable in the work of idealistic botanists like Troll (1928) and to some degree in Vogel (see p. 160). After having assembled our material for support of a Darwinian approach we shall come back to the supra-naturalistic views (p. 161).

Obviously, genetics and physiology play an important part in flower shapes. How could anything stand outside genetics and physiology and be alive? They concern, however, more the "how" than the "why," which interests us here. A possible ecological "why" should be supported independently by ecological experiments and observations.

Darwin understood why the flower as a sexual instrument was a necessity even though a sexual reproduction seems much simpler in operation. He stressed that first sexuality per se and afterwards cross-pollination brought about continuous mixing of hereditary potentials. Modern genetics has corroborated the theory that genome-recombination is the way to plasticity, survival (after changes), and progression.

When we use seemingly telelogical or anthropomorphic expressions as "birds have shaped flowers," this does not mean that we adhere to such metaphysical views. It simply avoids the necessity of repeating that factors or beings influenced each other during evolution by means of genetic processes.

EARLY ORCHIDS AND THEIR PROBABLE POLLINATION RELATIONS

Orchids are not favorable objects for fossilization, though we know a fossil, *Protorchis monorchis* from the Eocene of Monte Bolca, which might be an orchid. In that period lower wasps and bees were present though the development of higher Apidae probably started later.

We believe that the basic orchid flower is built for bee-pollination though we cannot prove it by paleontological evidence. However, only precision-insects with the right instincts for landing, penetrating, searching for hidden nectar, and for the right spatial relations could handle the intricate flowers which must be entered in a specific manner. An origin in the period when beetles were the main pollinators is unthinkable, whereas many other families (even Compositae) had their first radiation in this period. So had the basic Liliiflorae out of which orchids arose (see Grant, 1949 for a discussion of a possible bird-flower origin).

The gullet-type of the basic orchid flower (Fig. 5) is parallel to that reached in other monocotyledons such as the Zingiberaceae and in higher dicotyledons with bee-connections, such as Labiatae, Scrophulariaceae, and Acanthaceae. The Papilionaceae have a banner or flag-type flower with basic sternotriby (pollen deposition on the ventral side of the bee).

The inferior ovary of the orchid flower was obviously obtained from the liliiflorous stock, just as in the Iridaceae and Scitamineae, and is no longer ecologically significant.

1. Dispersion of pollinators in orchid genera

On page 128 we proposed a pollination-spectrum for the family. The genera *Orchis*, *Coelogyne* and the subtribes Vanillinae, Thuninae, Maxillarinae, Bletiinae, Cyrtopodiinae, Oncidiinae, Cymbidiinae, Stanhopiinae and Catasetinae remained predominantly bee-pollinated, with rising intimacy (Chapter 6). In other large groups a partial change to other pollinators took place. Many breeding systems are found in *Epidendrum, Disa, Dendrobium, Caladenia, Satyrium, Spiranthes* and *Diuris*. Others such as *Habenaria, Platanthera* and *Angraecum* seem basically changed toward moths (Chapter 7). The Pleurothallidinae, *Bulbophyllum* and *Pterostylis* are basically pollinated by flies (Chapter 9).

Butterfly-flowers are more loosely spread over some genera, foremost in *Disa, Anacamptis* and perhaps *Epidendrum*, all in part. Bird-flowers are as widely dispersed, occurring in *Elleanthus, Epidendrum, Laelia, Rodriguezia, Masdevallia, Dendrobium, Spiranthes* and probably in *Odontoglossum* and *Oncidium* (Chapter 8).

In each genus incidental deviations are possible and often lead to sufficient morphological change to give reason for recognition as separate genera. Autogamy also occurs at random in all of these groups.

Correlation was found between general primitivity of the flower in the Neottioideae (excluding the Spiranthinae) and primitivity of the wasps and lower bees which visit them. We will see later, in great detail, especially in the Disinae, that such a maze of redifferentiation, progression and regression in a young and plastic family is not bound to its taxonomic groups, and does not lend itself to the construction of new ones. We shall have occasion to warn taxonomists that such reticulate relationships should not lead to speculation on early hybridization or to supposed relationships on the basis of convergent characters and should foster distrust in loose "characters" as homologous. The discussion on the nature of non-resupination should illustrate this point—as evidenced by Ames' work (1938) (unfortunately he did not consider functions). He obtained a negative result in attempting to connect this character with taxonomy.

Mansfeld (1954) was aware of the independence of parallel characters without using floral ecology. Otherwise fine phylogenetic studies such as those of Pfitzer (1906) and Garay (1960) should in our opinion be supplemented by evidence from ecology.

FUNCTIONS OF THE FLOWER

Before we attempt to draw conclusions about the intricacies of perfection of function in the origin and further development of the family, we should analyze the functions of the flower. We will do this first by comparing, in Figure 106, a simple, generalized orchid (without special adaptations and regressions) with a much more primitive ranalian flower such as a simple member of the Magnoliaceae or Calycanthaceae.

1. Progression of development of specialization in the orchid flower

When we discuss pollination progression in general in the Orchidaceae we mean from low to high but must include to a degree the layering of subsequent reorganizations, though the latter point must wait for special consideration (e.g., Disinae and fly-flowers in Chapter 9). Because a flower has, as we saw, many functions which progress separately and because there exists no pollinator-in-general, the line of progression cannot be linear. However, we are forced to present it in this manner, planning to remedy the defects somewhat in a later scheme (p. 150).

Below, in a linear sequence, we present our idea* of the elements in the

---
* Adapted in part from similar lists previously published by other authors.

Function	Ranalian	Orchid
distant attraction	odor	color or general odor
near attraction	same	color or special odor, dissected contour
character of odor	imitating food or larval substrate	sexual or fresh, neutral odor
kind of visitors	unadapted beetles	adapted Hymenoptera
alighting	somewhere on open dish (radial) or trapped in kettle	on labellum only (zygormorphy)
guidance for entrance	none or involuntary by trap	by special color and construction of inner parts
guidance to food	none	nectar-guide, odor-guide, spur, depth-effect
specificity of visitors	by imitative odor only	odor, dimensions and placement of food
mechanical exclusion of others	none	some force or knowledge of constellation required; place of lip
food offered	none (deceit) or pollen or food bodies to be gnawed	nectar, pollen excluded
reception of pollen	by accident, on each stigma apart	centralized, common stigma at exact place in relation to the whole (zygomorphy)
distribution of pollen tubes	inside each carpel only	from part of stigma to whole ovary (unilocular)
production of pollen	diffuse from many anthers	centralized at exact place in relation to the whole (zygomorphy)
character of pollen	loose powder	one centralized pollinarium
deposition of pollen on visitor	by accident on whole animal, most eaten or lost	at specific place on visitor, by glue from rostellum; none lost
prevention of self pollination	protogyny, separation of sexes in time	herkogamy, separation in place by special part of stigma

FIG. 106. Comparison of a primitive hypothetical flower of Ranalian affinity with a generalized orchid flower.

production of a monophilous precision-instrument for cross-pollination as found in the orchids:

1. Centralization of stamens and stigma into one organ, the column, combining reception and deposition of pollen often in one visit. For exceptions see p. 52 and 154.
2. Reduction of stamen number, leaving only the originally abaxial median one; centralized pollen deposition.
3. The originally adaxial labellum was modified for procuring precise position, entry and dimensions (zygomorphy by 1, 2 and 3).
4. Resupination of labellum, bound to nototriby.
5. Pollen entirely removed from the sphere of attraction as food for bees.

6. Pollen deposited as one mass by the pollinarium, thus coupling of two different functions: a. Fertilizing the many ovules at once, b. All-or-nothing transport of the whole, with convergent contraptions for transport.
7. Primary attractant (food): No generalized fundamental nectar and often replaced by special products at specific places or returning to pure deceit or luring with narcotics and sexual stimulants.
8. Mobile or motile mechanical contraptions in traps with sensitive labellum, anther or stigma.
9. Long exposition; one visit sufficient, fast wilting afterwards.
10. Sometimes flowering synchronized in an entire area.
11. Self-pollination avoided by herkogamy (separation in space of reception and deposition by special contrivances) or physiological incompatibility.
12. Stigma as chemo-receptor or chemo-donor.
13. Development of ovules postponed until after the pollination-stimulus.
14. Endosperm abolished, together with its influences on zygotes.
15. Abandonment of sporophytic and gametophytic genetic incompatibility systems.
16. Replacement of genetic barriers by specificity of attractants, visitors and place of pollen-deposition on visitors.
17. Number of ovules adjusted to number of pollen grains deposited on visitors and flower, often in one visit.
18. In extreme cases, flower dimorphy and connation (sympetaly).
19. In highest forms dichogamy (need for two visits by pollinator) and dicliny (male and female organs in separate flowers); and some points to be treated specially.
20. Mycotrophy.
21. Smallness of seeds, random dispersal.
22. Very numerous seeds.
23. Epiphytism.

It may seem far fetched to include seeds, their germination and dispersal in our discussion of the flower, but after all the ovary is in some respects an immature organ, the beginning of a fruit with seeds. Phylogenetically seeds as as institution even antedate flowers. This is the foremost reason why some authors, such as Bernard (1909) and Ziegenspeck (1928), were less interested in floral ecology and saw physiological peculiarities as the basis for the unusual development of the orchid flower.

Mycotrophy apparently—by some correlation (as in other families with abnormal physiology)—results in smallness of seeds. The smallness leads to a large number of ovules (and consequently of seeds). Whether correlation with absence of endosperm should be included is uncertain (in other small-seeded heterotrophic plants no such correlation exists). There is some feed-back: the large number of seeds is also correlated with the lesser chance of germination, decreased by the necessity of infection by fungi, whereas small seeds might also be seen as necessitating mycotrophy. The large number of seeds necessitated a pollinarium

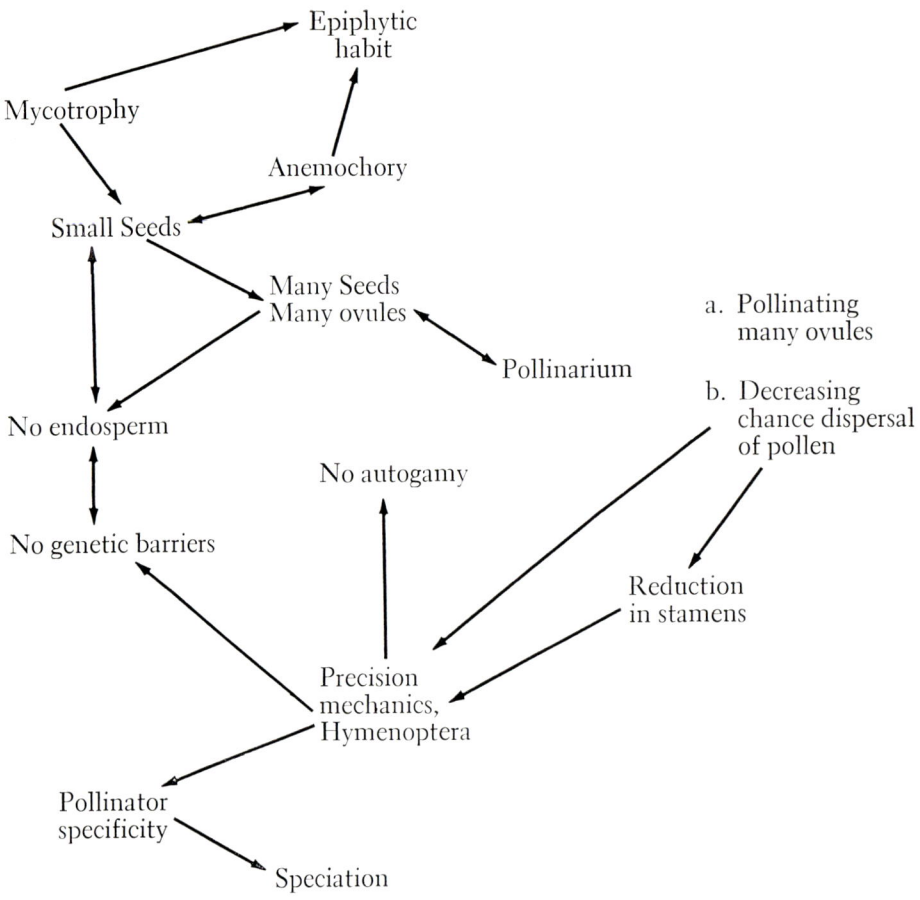

FIG. 107. Scheme of correlations between the special features of a precision-instrument for pollination as found in the orchids.

(function 6a). The coupling with function 6b (the transport of all pollen at once), led to specialization, reduction, zygomorphy and other floral-ecologic characteristics of the flower. This physiological viewpoint has the pollinarium as a turning point in common with our other views. On the other hand it explains concordance of orchid sexuality with the general preponderance of reproductive organs in heterotrophic plants. It also explains the seed characteristics, which remain otherwise accidental or secondary. Darwin considered the pollinarium as a sequence to many seeds.

We are tempted to look toward the probably ancestral Apostasioideae, which also have minute seeds, for guidance concerning the relationship between mycotrophy and the primitive orchid. Alas, we have no information on mycotrophy for this group. Does the absence of a true pollinarium here support the physiological viewpoint, that the presence of the pollinarium started other flower specializations? No, points 1-3 are already present. From the ecological viewpoint the absence of a pollinarium here is just a transitory imperfection.

Other facts unfavorable to the physiological view are: a. In orchids such as *Jimensia* (Bletilla) small seeds are not necessarily associated with mycotrophy, b. In Asclepiadaceae we find pollinia as ecological refinements in precision-flowers and not connected with special seeds. Perhaps the sequence in Ziegenspeck's range should be read in the opposite direction.

In the following scheme (Fig. 107) the correlations between the main peculiarities are expressed by lines, which often may be read in two directions. They show, in any case, how in living beings all characters are interrelated. Though linear arrangements are too simplistic, one might consider diverse lines as phyletic.

THE ORCHID FLOWER AS A CONSTRUCTIVE UNIT

1. Shape

General Shape

Shape and position of the labellum and column have already been discussed but a few additional points on the flower—or pollination unit—as a whole remain to be discussed. By pollination unit we mean the functional unit, independent of its morphological value. Usually it is the complete flower, sometimes just a part of it, sometimes a number of flowers. In the latter category we consider not a mere inflorescence, but one that is integrated into one functional unit, attracting and receiving the visitors as such.

Among pollination units in general (sometimes referred to as "blossoms") we distinguish the following types: dish, cup, bell, beaker or trumpet, brush, flag or standard, gullet, tube and prison-kettle. These types (not mere descriptions of shape) can be considered typologically and also phylogenetically in many cases. The different functions of a blossom (as indicated in Fig. 1) are spread over such types. For a discussion of this point we suggest reference to a general textbook (Faegri and van der Pijl, 1966).

The typical type in orchids is the gullet, comparable to that of the Labiatae, but formed of six separate parts. The labellum forms the lower lip, the remaining five tepals form a more or less protective upper lip. There is a tendency to part-flower formation by degradation of the five auxillary tepals and concentration on labellum plus column. This occurs in diverse ecological groups, and in *Brassavola* (Fig. 108) we see it clearly. In some fly-pollinated orchids the five tepals, or the three sepals, retain the function of visual attraction. In the small terrestrial *Corybas* (Corysanthes) *himalaica*, however, the gullet is formed by the median sepal and labellum with the other parts of the perianth being insignificant.

Aberrant Shapes

There is no advantage in repeating all of the incidental deviations in form discussed in previous chapters but it may be of importance to mention certain of the more extreme and fundamentally aberrant shapes.

Vogel (1959) analyzed new mechanisms and forms in some South African subtribes of terrestrial Orchidoideae; the Disinae and Coryciinae. We shall stress this analysis in regard to functions. In *Disa* the functions of the perianth-parts are

FIG. 108. *Brassavola cucullata*.

interchanged in comparison to the ordinary orchid flower. We are inclined to see the reduction of the labellum as primary, though the turning away of the column from it and toward the spur might also be considered as basic. This loss of functions of parts can hardly be considered as an autonomous morphological reaction. Perhaps the simple butterfly-flower of *Disa uniflora* (p. 88 and Fig. 57) demonstrates how the start of the new line can be visualized. The median sepal, resupinated toward the axis as the upper part, took the role of the labellum in regard to nectar secretion. It produced a spur, a dorsal or upper one. The ventral, paired sepals took over the function of a landing platform. The paired petals took over the function of guidance to nectar as visual honey-guides. The tip of the column (the anther plus the rostellum) bends over dorsally toward the axis and the entrance of the spur, thus resulting in sternotribic pollen deposition.

On this basis a new differentiation, accommodating other pollination classes, took place. These seem to demonstrate the never-ending adaption to new pollination-agents in orchids and also their plasticity. Sometimes new types of flowers arose, such as the standard-flower or a vertical tube-type (*Disa ferruginea*). In addition myophiles (p. 122) and even a *Cirrhopetalum*-like radial, myophilous corymb of spurless, non-resupinate flowers (*D. bivalvata*) occur.

In the related genus *Satyrium* a convergent reorganization into a new upper and lower lip has been achieved, but here the non-resupinate labellum forms the upper lip and all other perianth parts form the lower lip (the opposite of *Orchis*). The column—and this may be primary—has left its juxtaposition to the labellum and is pressed parallel and near to it, so that the normal space for visitors has disappeared. A new space is created between the column and new lower lip. The fertile side of the column, however, being turned away from this space would make pollination impossible without reorganization. A tipping-over of 210° (called ultra-resupination by Vogel) of anther and stigma now turns the sexual area toward the visitor and results in nototriby. More reorganization of the fine mechanism became necessary. As the column now covered the space of a median spur, it had to be passed to the right and left. No wonder that two spurs instead of one developed on the labellum. With the presence of these reorganizations it becomes obvious that adaptation to several different pollinators has occurred. Vogel (1959) illustrated five classes. Some of these unorchid-like forms may be neutral, polyphilous, sphingophilous or myophilous.

The subtribe Coryciinae (subtribe Disperidinae of Schlechter and used as such by Vogel) including the genera *Disperis*, *Ceratandra* and *Corycium*, shows a separate line of reconstruction, perhaps linking with types of Disinae. Here constellations are so intricate that we have to refer to Vogel's brilliant analysis. Column and erect labellum are basally fused so that the anther, rostellum and stigma had to perform strange bends and involutions to become exposed for pollination, resulting in two separate stigmas, whereas the small labellum developed strange appendages. In some species of *Ceratandra* the two side sepals form an upper lip, the median sepal plus the two side petals form a lower lip. In some species of *Corycium* and *Disperis* we find a helmet with two entrances, special pollen deposition on the feet of the visitors (perhaps the long-tongued flies mentioned), and often slide traps for bees and flies, giving precise cross-pollination on a new basis. Strata of old differentiation and precision, fixation, disorganization, reorganization, new differentiation and precision are piled on each other, with the result being a mad kaleidoscope when considered without ecological and historical analysis.

In the Coryciinae there is some analogy to simple Cypripedioideae with two exits but with one widely divided anther. But this is no reason to doubt the fundamental difference between Monandrae and Diandrae (as Adams does in Withner, 1959). It is also not a valid reason to ascribe two anthers to *Satyrium* as did Garay (1960).

The strange shapes of *Catasetum* and its allied genera form a class apart by their capriciousness, but their pollination mechanisms are all based on a single principle (Chapter 6).

Another shape which is not typical of the family is that of a flat disk, returned to by many myophilous orchids such as *Stelis*, some groups of *Pleurothallis*, probably *Malaxis* and certain species of *Paphiopedilum*.

The development of a flag-type flower in sphingophilous orchids was to be expected.

Connation

In some butterfly-pollinated orchids the gullet-type has been left behind in a different manner. The part-flower, consisting of column plus labellum, of *Epidendrum* is a result of fusion of the two organs into an erect tube, with the five tepals spatially separated underneath as a landing place.

A tube can also result from connation of other parts. In *Masdevallia* the three sepals show a tendency in this direction. The resulting shape is between a kettle and a tube, ecologically fitted to flies and birds respectively. As endlines in the development of a tube, *Physosiphon* and *Schlimia* demonstrate a more or less complete fusion. The genus *Ada* seems on the way to connation into a tube and is probably ornithophilous. Among Asiatic Dendrobiinae the genus *Cryptochilus* has the same connation of sepals. *Porpax* has a sympetalous kettle.

Among American relatives of *Masdevallia* a further refinement of connation leads to the myophilous kettle of *Cryptophoranthus*. *Pterostylis* developed such a kettle in a different tribe. Asiatic Bulbophyllinae obtained it in the curious genus *Monosepalum* and the Spiranthinae did the same in the genus *Cheirostylis*. We do not know what lies behind the fusion of the two sepals in the Cypripedioideae, *Restrepia* and several species of *Masdevallia*, but *Monomeria*—with the sepal fused at the tip—is linked with the situation in *Cirrhopetalum*. All appear to be basically myophilous.

Sympetaly in the family thus seems an independent character in different lines of adaptation with heterogenous significance. This is consistent with the generally accepted polyphyletic origin of sympetaly in the dicotyledons.

2. Aggregation

Orchid flowers are commonly organized in a raceme or a panicle. Occasionally the flowers are arranged on a spike or scape. The flowers usually open successively, each attracting visitors on its own and being visited independently, thereby spreading the total flowering over a long period.

Sometimes the flowers of the inflorescence are integrated morphologically and functionally. One approach of the pollinator is then sufficient and though it has to move to the diverse flowers by crawling or change of position, the action is comparable to the sucking on different nectaries in one flower. In this case flowering in the inflorescence may be simultaneous.

Aggregation is not basic in the family and never as complete as in Mimosaceae, Compositae, etc., where we find division of function in the heads, including centralization of nectar secretion. In orchids it seems an incidental adaptation but on the other hand not just massing of flowers which are too small. There is only loose collaboration—perhaps by common increase of odor—between the minute greenish flowers of *Chamaengis odoratissima*. In the fine spikes of species of *Dendrochilum* there is some visual collaboration and some synchrony of anthesis. The general longevity of flowers in inflorescences helps in such collaboration, even in large-flowered species of *Cymbidium*, *Vanda* and some species of *Oncidium*, etc., but there is a danger to cross-pollination by their very longevity facilitating self-pollination. Many of the members of these groups have self-incompatibility as a defense. Darwin felt that he had encountered a mechanism which makes the spike of *Spiranthes autumnalis* protandrous as a whole. Bumblebees always landed on the lower, pollen-less flowers, pollinating them, and then crawled up to younger flowers with intact pollinia, carrying their pollinia to other plants. It seems doubtful if this procedure is generally applicable. The flower itself also shows signs of protandry (late stickyness and opening of the stigma) as in *Listera*, where the stigma does not become accessible until pollinia have been removed. Müller (1873), Godfery (1918, 1933) and Daumann (1941) confirmed such ascending visits for other orchids and other families. Martens (1928) discussed them, emphasizing that the bending of pollinia is too slow to allow deposition in the next higher flower.

A narrower integration is reached in some myophilous flowers, where approach by the pollinator may be a limiting ecological factor. The species of *Bulbophyllum* grouped in the subgenus *Cirrhopetalum* (see p. 144) have flowers aggregated in a corymb—a pseudo-umbel. They flower simultaneously and form one compound, radial and dish-like unit. The same occurs in *Disa bivalvata* as previously discussed.

In the distichous-leaved species of *Notylia* the transition from a spike-like inflorescence as in *N. bicolor* to a capitate ball of flowers as in *N. xyphorius* (Fig. 109) is striking. The individual flowers structurally are nearly identical but in *N. bicolor* the flowers open somewhat in succession so that when the lowermost are open and receptive the distal ones are still buds. In *N. xyphorius* all flowers open simultaneously.

Some species of *Orchis* (in the broad sense) show condensation but rarely synchrony. In *Orchis* (*Traunsteinera*) *globosa* and other butterfly-flowers discussed on p. 90 the condensed inflorescence is globular and acts as one unit for approach and landing of the pollinator. So we find a brush-type flower system as a pollination-unit, though lack of synchronization prompts repeated visits.

In *Elleanthus* the flowers are not only crowded but also in many species are surrounded by colored bracts. Some species are synchronized in flowering and others such as *E. capitatus* (Fig. 60) have a flower-head with a jelly-like

FIG. 109. *Notylia xyphorius*.

substance through which the flowers emerge in whorls. A new whorl is open and ready for visitation each day, thereby requiring repeated visits. Some species of *Eria* belong in the same category. Their showiness, serving to attract birds, is increased by colored bracts in *E. ignea* and perhaps *E. ornata*. In some other cases additional organs assist in attracting flies. In *Satyrium pumilum* (cf. p. 122 and 152) Vogel (1959, p. 397) described how the purplish tip of a bract supplies the myophilous "lip" instead of the upturned labellum as is usual. We have discussed on p. 108 the role of a colored, flattened rachis in myophilous *Megaclinium* (Bulbophyllum) spp.

3. Heteranthy (dimorphy of flowers)

Considering the unity of function in the orchid flower it is no wonder that only rarely has it "committed division of labor." In some species of *Oncidium*—considered as members of the section *Heterantha* of *Oncidium* but composed of species of diverse origin which have apparently developed heteranthy by convergence—such as *O. heteranthum* and *O. abortivum*—we find in the basal portion of the inflorescence small reduced, sterile flowers. In the former species only the distal flower on each branch of the panicle is complete. We do not know the significance of this phenomenon.

Winkler (1906) discussed the presence of two kinds of flowers in *Vandopsis lowii* (also known as *Arachnis*, *Arachnanthe* and *Renanthera*), both fertile. The lower ones are odorless, the upper ones have a different color and emit a strong scent. Pollinators were not observed but the upper flowers may be specialized as odor-producers (cf. the sepal tip in related *Arachnis flos-aeris* on p. 25). In contrast to the lower ones they remain fresh and odorous for a long time, even after pollination, which is curious in an orchid and points to a special function.

Grammatophyllum speciosum has some larger, sterile flowers on the lower parts of the inflorescence with the lateral sepals fused and the labellum absent.

4. Longevity and Gregariousness

Orchid plants as a rule have long-lasting flowers, as long as they are not pollinated. This may, if one likes, be considered as a regulation to insure pollination. The family contains the longest-lasting flowers known (in *Grammatophyllum multiflorum* they are said to last nine months) and perhaps the shortest-lived. Of the latter, *Dendrobium* (Desmotrichum) *appendiculatum* from Java is said to be open but five minutes. Kränzlin (1910) and other authors, doubting the validity of Darwinian views and unacquainted with the rhythms of ephemeral tropical flowers, have asked of what use is flowering in such a case and have considered the phenomenon as just degeneration in these and other ephemeral orchids.

Ephemeral flowers lasting less than one day are more frequent. Some species of *Liparis, Ceratostylis, Eria, Bulbophyllum, Sarcochilus, Sobralia* and *Stelis* are examples. The short duration is not always conspicuous because of the fast sequence of anthesis. The phenomenon has a special aspect in the genera *Thrixspermum, Bromheadia* (Holttum, 1949) and in five sections of *Dendrobium* (see

Smith, 1925), as these Malaysian one-day orchids compensate for the short duration of anthesis by gregarious flowering. All plants in a region open their flowers on the same day after a period of non-flowering. In America, some species of *Sobralia* do the same. In *Sobralia* flowers apparently contain a self-digesting enzyme which is also present in the flowers of *Stanhopea*, *Gongora* and *Coryanthes*. In the latter three genera the flowers do not open until they are fully mature. We have noted that the flowers literally pop open and bees arrive almost immediately. In two to three days, the flowers suddenly begin to dissolve and even the fleshy tissue turns to a mass of gelatinous material.

When only one species demonstrates gregarious flowering in a given region, one is tempted to think of advantage of possible development of constancy by mass visits of social bees. *Apis indica*, in fact, makes sudden mass visits to *Dendrobium crumenatum* in Java with ensuing uncommonly rich fructification. *Sobralia violacea* is visited regularly in Ecuador on days of mass flowering but the rare flowers produced on alternate days are seldom visited. Sometimes other species occur sympatrically with these plants but usually have a different flowering-day. When sympatric species (as yet only investigated in cultivation) have the same latency-period, and the same flowering-day, speciation apparently is hindered. In Ecuador, sympatric *Sobralia violacea* and *S. decora* var. *aerata* tend to flower on different days but are occasionally synchronized. They are pollinated, however, by different kinds of bees.

The phenomenon has been best analyzed for *Thrixspermum arachnites* and the pigeon-orchid, *Dendrobium crumenatum* (Fig. 110). Botanists in Java, during the nineteen twenties, did considerable work on the problem as did Seifriz. Buds were found to develop continuously, but to stop at a certain phase, waiting for a

FIG. 110. *Dendrobium crumenatum*.

special stimulus leading thereby to simultaneous flowering. The stimulus is a sudden fall in temperature, usually caused by a shower after a dry spell. In *D. crumenatum* the latency-period after the stimulus is nine days. In the often cultivated *D. nobile* the same influence was later discovered.

Such a bond to a certain climatic change leading to periodicity has been found in many non-orchid flowers, where it acts primarily on the water balance of the plant. A direct flower-ecological bond with the stimulus seems out of the question there too, but the ecological consequences are still more vague.

A more diffuse influence of a dry spell on mass-flowering is visible in the giant-orchid *Grammatophyllum speciosum* which is also pollinated by social bees. We will not discuss the influence of light-intensity, photoperiodicity and thermoperiodicity.

PHYSIOLOGICAL PROCESSES IN THE FLOWER

We need to devote more attention to physiological processes. We have discussed the remarkable influence on sex-determination of physiology in the Catasetinae. Little is known about direct influence of thermonasty, nyctinasty, photonasty, on anthesis, and the orchid flower seems remarkably independent of weather. Recent experiments, using several different orchid plants, in which amounts of odor produced were measured with a gas-chromatograph indicate that much more fragrance is produced after the plants have been exposed to sunlight for several hours (Dodson, unpublished).

Thelymitras, the sun-orchids of Australia, are sensitive to radiation and close on dull, cold days. *Stelis* has forms which open and close the sepals under the opposite influence. According to Porsch (1906) the flowers open in a myophilous species at night and in a moist atmosphere on rainy days. Darwin (1877) pointed out that closed flowers reopened in water.

Rhythmic malvaceous, papilionaceous and araceous flowers, which open after stimulation by light, are known; in contrast we have no information on the induction of opening-time and odor production in nocturnal orchids and other orchids which open at specific times.

It seems superfluous to dwell here on the thigmonasty, motility and general sensivity of the labellum and anther. These processes seem limited to flowers with extreme guidance as in the Catasetinae and the sapromyophilous flowers. They have been treated in the respective chapters. The physiological treatment in the large, modern *Encyclopedia of Plant Physiology* (Vol. 17/1, 1959) by Guttenberg is outdated and incomplete.

Adams (in Withner, 1959) mentioned many instances of mobile or motile lips, some not discussed here. *Eria loheriana* and *Eulophidium maculatum* were investigated by Goebel (1920). Irritability of the column already has been discussed for *Neottia* and *Listera*.

We will not dwell extensively on influences of storage on germination of pollen or on post-pollination changes in flowers, considering these phenomena as being outside our field. The possible ecological effect of the latter was mentioned in our discussion of the functions of the column.

In most orchids, the stimulus of pollination causes development of ovules; placental proliferation does not occur until then (discovered by Crüger in 1865). This stimulation may be due to auxins, indeed present in pollinia. Even dead or non-orchid pollen may provide this stimulus (Hildebrand, 1865). The blocking of development until after a certain stimulus is not as exceptional as one might think. We have already discussed the retarded development of buds in gregarious orchids. And after all, normal ovules and carpels, though at a later phase, are also inhibited until pollination occurs. In *Paphiopedilum* and *Cypripedium*, ovules are already developed at anthesis and are even provided with a macrospore-mother cell. In the primitive orchid *Apostasia* we found that the ovules are also small and numerous but do not show retardation. Flowers of a species from New Guinea which had recently opened already had an embryo-sac mother-cell and sometimes even tetrads were present. The ovary of this genus is usually described as trilocular but in reality is unilocular with unvascularized parietal placentas which often fuse centrally. All six vascular bundles lie in the peripheral pericarp. These comments also apply to members of the genus *Phragmopedium*.

Müller (1868) demonstrated extremely rapid toxic effects after self-pollination for *Rodriguezia* (Burlingtonia), *Gomezia*, *Oncidium* and species of *Notylia* where the column and the pollinia destroy each other. In *Bulbophyllum lobbii* one can cause closing of the flower in this manner within a few hours. We recommend *Angraecum eburneum* for a demonstration of swellings around the stigma after pollination. Winkler (1906) found that among many kinds of foreign pollen only that of *Cattleya labiata* had a rapid toxic effect on *Phalaeonopsis violacea*. It was due to a water-soluble thermolabile substance.

This phenomenon cannot be considered as only one more mechanism in the same class as herkogamy, unisexuality, heterostyly, etc., promoting cross-pollination above self-pollination. It is more like self-incompatibility, and prevents not only self-fertilization, but goes further, as it prevents in a radical way all further pollination and its consequences. The phenomenon is not limited to the orchids. In cacao, self-pollination leads to abnormal development of the ovules and to shedding of the ovaries in some varieties. Laibach (1930) supplemented older observations of Fittings in this field, demonstrating the chemical influence of slight lesions of the stigma on such changes, including wilting and swelling in the column which were not followed by seed setting. He proved that substances from pollen do not act directly but steer secondary substances from the column itself. Just removal or displacement of pollinia or the mere separation of the viscid disc from the rostellum may initiate changes. Premature fading of the flower in *Vanda* may be caused by removal of the anther, pollination or exposure to ethylene gas (Akamine, 1963). Duncan and Shubert (1947) worked on *Cymbidium* in this connection. The chemical side of integration in the orchid flower is well demonstrated by these experiments. Changes after normal cross-pollination by such specific biochemical processes are familiar to any plant cultivator. In some cases (e.g., *Phalaenopsis* and *Zygopetalum*) the perianth persists in some form after fertilization.

The precise correlation between odor production and the unvisited, undisturbed state of the flower is clear in species of *Catasetum* and *Cycnoches* where the odor stops shortly after ejection of the pollinarium and in female flowers after pollination as shown by Dodson (1962b) and Vogel (1962).

THEORETICAL CONSIDERATIONS

Now that we have more material at our disposal, theoretical considerations seem in order. Almost without exception, motile elements in the flower are involved in fly-flowers. These are a means of guiding unadapted visitors in flowers which are based on systems too precise for the behavior of such insects. In one of the exceptions, the Catasetinae, it is a refinement enabling an unusually precise type of flower to be pollinated by "intoxicated" bees. Motile lips in *Arachnanthe* and *Eria loheriana* should be studied.

We consider parallelisms in the different genera as ecologically determined, not as genetically homologous or proof of a particular descent. Taxonomists should handle them with discretion. Other points of view are frequent. One of these is that such an apparent maze-relationship in the family should be used as a basis for phyletic taxonomy, or even that it is proof of early hybridization to a large extent.

Another view has been applied by Good (1956) to other families with the same parallelisms, i.e., that a limited number of floral possibilities is continuously recombined as in a kaleidoscope. Differentiative development is without direction, regardless of function, as an autonomous impulse free from the environment. We consider this view as ostrich-reasoning. It is disproved by clearly directed development as soon as we open our eyes to the function and to the steering forces in the environment. This is not meant to deny the existence of interior forces but we believe that the emphasis should lie elsewhere.

We now move to more general questions. There has been resistance to unbased teleology, often leading to denial of the holistic-functional approach to the flower in general. In Chapter 2 (p. 12) and p. 145 of this chapter we discussed Nelsson's physiological approach and Troll's idealistic concepts with immaterial "Gestalten" as supposed sufficient basis. Both of these authors practically deny the influence of the environment and any major influence of natural selection. For Troll (1928) this is even more surprising as he himself pointed to the simularities between different myophilous flowers, inflorescences and leaf-traps.

Werth (1956) wrote a book on floral ecology in which the growing refinements of flowers were also considered as autonomous and lying beyond the sphere of selection. He admitted that the narrow relationship between fly-traps could not be explained on this basis and made for this field the mental leap into the sudden recognition of a finalistic will in creation.

Vogel, whose fine work on orchids we have often cited, is influenced by two more or less opposite tendencies, viz., idealistic and static supranatural ideas, and the recognition of phylogeny and the ecological significance of the flower-insect bond, the structural syndrome of which he called "Stil" (Style). According to him, flower and insect are both contained in one holistic, intrinsic "plan" (he mentioned this in his general book [1954] but did not come back to it in his book on orchid pollination [1959]). His argument is that the intricate mechanisms cannot be the product of mechanistic selection on parts, so that a co-adaptation of higher nature behind the parts must be assumed. We will not argue the point that the selection theory has left separate characters as sole material. Stebbins (1951) urged that one characteristic may be incidental and neutral but that the combination procedures selective advantages. We have other objections, however. Formerly (van der Pijl, 1960/61) one of us remarked that the Cactus-Euphorbia convergence is clearly the consequence of common adaptation to a desert climate. Anemophilous flowers have adapted to the common wind. Abiotic factors then also should be placed in the "plan." But in fly-traps the higher unity of plan behind flower and insect seems strange. Here the flower only profits and progresses, whereas the flies are passive, static, deceived and clearly the suffering party, as most pollinators in primitive beetle-flowers (see van der Pijl, 1960/61).

We should, just as in human sociology, not be too provincial in our thinking and mentally bound to recent times, and should not start with the latest, balanced relations of social bees as "friends" of higher flowers and project this back into history as eternal and basic.

Goebel (1920) tried an escape into physiology, deriving movements, positions and reductions in flower parts as a repetition of unfolding movements, whereas the function is just "Ausnützung" (utilization). He ridiculed many old ecological, functional explanations of structures, often however, on insufficient grounds. Later investigation shows a clear advantage of such ridiculed devices as the non-resupination of labellae, the movements in *Bulbophyllum* and *Pterostylis*, the tails, etc. As one instance where he considers resemblance between flowers as just accidental, defying Darwinists to find a solution, we cite his chapter on window-flowers. In his Figure 40, he illustrates flowers of *Ceropegia* and *Cryptophoranthus*, stating that this is, in both, just incomplete opening by failure of petal tips to separate. This is undoubtedly true, but it is not the whole truth. We now know that this character is based on common fly-pollination and also occurs in some species of *Bulbophyllum* and in *Satyrium bicallosum* as well as in such non-orchid flowers as *Hydnora, Sterculia, Abroma, Aristolochia* and many Annonaceae. We now even understand the likeness of sympetalous Annonaceae and *Aristolochia*.

CHAPTER 13
Speciation and Natural Hybridization

Since the primary theme of this book is the discussion of the orchid flower, its functions, pollination, evolution, etc., we feel that it is important to introduce speciation (the formation of new and distinct species) and natural hybridization. These phenomena are often indicated as exaggerated in the orchids and perhaps rightly so. An extended discussion of these and allied subjects, however, is not essential to the general theme of the book and we therefore suggest the books by Anderson (1953), Stebbins (1951), Grant (1963) and Mayr (1963) for more complete treatments.

SPECIATION

The presence of numerous and diverse kinds of pollinators available for orchid pollination probably has been of particular importance in the development of the numerous species encountered in the family. The intrinsic characteristics of the Orchidaceae have made it possible for various members of the family to adapt to a major portion of the insects and birds which are efficient pollinators. These characteristics have also led to the "improvement of efficiency" of those pollinators which are not generally effective—by means of special adaptations. Many of these special adaptations are based on deceit of the pollinator.

The development of adaptations for specific pollination is highly important in speciation in evolutionarily advanced flowering plants (Grant, 1949, Straw, 1956, Sprague, 1962).

A group in which the species are promiscuously pollinated by several genera of bees, for instance, will have less opportunity to develop pollination mechanisms as effective mechanical barriers to hybridization. These groups must depend upon genetic, ecological or spatial barriers to achieve isolation. On the other hand, a plastic group like the orchids—with special characteristics that attract particular species as pollinators—has an opportunity for the development of pollination mechanisms which preclude natural crossing between otherwise compatible plants.

The development of barriers to hybridization by adaptation to specific pollinators need not affect genetic compatibility between groups. Genetic incompatibility is more commonly associated with populations which have been spatially separate for some time. If, within a group of orchids, adaptations arise to specific pollinators which are fundamentally different, the gross structure of the flower may change radically. Thus a group which is separated from another on the basis of distinct pollination mechanisms may be morphologically dissimilar and appear to be worthy of generic or subtribal distinction on the basis of classic taxonomic criteria. Genetically, however, they may remain compatible and the occasional hybrid may result either in a new species, blurring of the differences between two entities through introgression (the accumulation of genetic material in one species through hybridization with another), or in a long-lived individual which when introduced into the limited collections in herbaria of tropical orchids can cause difficulties for plant taxonomists.

For example, in the genus *Oncidium*, the section containing *O. papilio* and its allies—in respect to cytology and morphology of the plant—is most closely allied to the *Odontoglossum grande* alliance. However, probably due to adaptation to another kind of pollinator, the flowers have become sufficiently different from the latter group to warrant separation. Oddly enough, the adaptive differences (lip at right angles to the column) placed them within the concept of the genus *Oncidium* as it is recognized at the present time.

One kind of speciation, documented by Dodson (1962a), based on adaptation of species to pollinators which differ primarily in size—but which are morphologically and behaviorally similar—can result in very rapid development of species. The example used was *Stanhopea* and the term "leap-frog speciation" was applied. The system revolves on adaptation to one species of pollinator followed by adaptation to another and then returns to the former or an even different species and so on. Each adaptation requires rapid, but minor, morphological adjustments in the flower. When this operates progressively the consequence is a series of slightly different species (any of which can be sympatric) all based on the same pollination mechanism but taking advantage of different pollinators. Since (cf. p. 44) there are several species of the larger size pollinators (*Eulaema* and *Euplusia*) and several of the smaller (*Euglossa*), each of which can be attracted to the exclusion of the other, the end result is the development of a plethora of sympatric micro-species.

In the case of *Stanhopea* such speciation has apparently been quite rapid as indicated by the lack of change in the vegetative characteristics of the plants. It is not possible to separate the species merely on the basis of vegetative characteristics. Nearly all species are restricted to similar environmental conditions with few invasions of different habitats. When these phenomena are combined with relatively easy spatial isolation in the mountain cloud-forests which are divided by ridgelines and valleys, it is little wonder that we find many micro-species in the more advanced section of the genus.

A similar situation is probably occurring in the genus *Catasetum* and we have definite evidence that *Cycnoches* has developed two distinctive subgenera based on the two types of pollinators (Dodson and Frymire, 1961b). The *Cycnoches* with similar male and female flowers are pollinated by species of *Eulaema*, whereas most of the heteromorphic species are pollinated by species of *Euglossa* (Pl. IV and V and p. 64).

1. Concurrent speciation of orchid and pollinator

The complex floral mechanisms of certain orchids have been cited in discussions of evolution where it has been pointed out that the "orchids and the insects have wandered the paths of evolution hand in hand." These comments have indicated that the development of a particular complexity on the part of an orchid would elicit a compensating complexity on the part of its pollinator. We do not support these views. To a limited degree such could be true in other flowering plants which have been in existence over a long period but we feel that the orchids have not affected their pollinators to a noticeable degree. Most of the pollinators of orchids known at present have probably developed their extreme or unique characteristics as adaptations to other much older plant groups. For example, the extremely long-tongued bees, the Euglossini, may have developed their tongue length in response to the deep nectar tubes of early Apocynaceae, Zingiberaceae or Marantaceae. The idea of the moth, *Xanthopan morgani* f. *praedicta* evolving an extremely long proboscis in response to the long nectary of *Angraecum sesquipedale* is often attributed to Darwin but at no point did Darwin imply such a connection. It would seem that orchids have been quite facile at adapting to advantageous characteristics already present in existing pollinators.

2. Autogamy

In one of the hybrid swarms involving *Oncidium pusillum* and *O. pumilo*, discussed on p. 167, a particular type of hybrid was especially frequent and varied only slightly (Fig. 111). This kind of hybrid was found to be autogamous. Autogamy may be significant in the rapid establishment of some hybrid combinations and extensive populations may be developed quite rapidly.

When considered from the standpoint of evolution, and particularly selection, autogamy can be extremely important. If within a population of a normally cross-pollinated species a plant occurs which is genetically modified so as to become self-pollinated, and its progeny retain this ability, this type incidentally or temporally may have a great selective advantage. This would be particularly true in orchid species which do not have a high percentage of flowers pollinated as in many species of *Encyclia* and *Oncidium*.

3. The epiphytic habit

The rapid evolution of the orchid family, which has resulted in the production of numerous and diverse species can be attributed in part to the epiphytic habit. The epiphytic habitat would seem to be in a constant state of change, particularly in the rainforests where the macroclimate may seem uniform. In these forests seldom are two of the same species of tree found in close proximity and many species grow rapidly. There is constant renewal of different types of trees so that the composition of a forest may change with growing trees reaching a different layer. This change continually sets up new types of habitats for epiphytic plants and allows for differently adapted genotypes. Thus the epiphytic populations too, are subject to succession, and may be completely changed in a relatively short time. Space is usually available on any given tree for more epiphytes than are actually found. Some of the available space may be unusuable for existing species, but provides an unused habitat which is open for new genotypes.

The characteristics of many of the epiphytic tropical orchids (e.g., complexes of closely related species, highly variable populations, taxonomically difficult groups, hybrid swarms, species showing introgressive hybridization and many species of a genus within an area) can be regarded as expressions of a dynamic rate of evolution and an active continual exploitation of varied habitats. Many of the terrestrial members of the family found in the temperate zones exhibit characteristics associated with stable habitats, and thus lower morphological variability and few species per genus in a given area though visitor specificity declines as a barrier to hybridization. Certainly regions, such as the Andes, the volcanic mountains of Central America, the Himalayas and the Pacific Islands, where great and rapid changes in ecology have occurred, contain the bulk of orchid species, as well as the major portion of the highly variable complexes within the species.

The type of habitat is thus a factor permitting or prohibiting hybridization and its effects on plant species. The ecological conditions (vegetative) for the tropical orchids are such as to facilitate the results of hybridization, thereby acting to increase variation and heterozygosity. We feel that these phenomena have strongly influenced the evolutionary patterns of this group.

NATURAL HYBRIDIZATION

It would appear that many of the tropical orchids have differentiated very rapidly (as a result of isolation, selection and the development of such barriers to hybridization as pollinator specificity) with little change occurring at the chromosomal level. When rare chance hybridization occurs between species which are morphologically quite distinct but genetically compatible, the result can be the production of fertile hybrids. These fertile hybrids are often morphologically quite different from either parent and several things can happen to them including extinction as a result of failure to encounter a hospitable environment or pollinator. When self-pollination (or sibling crosses) occurs among such hybrids, however, extremely variable complexes or new species may result.

The rapid evolution of the orchids and their characteristically extreme patterns of variation have doubtless been facilitated by some of the intrinsic features of the family itself. The production of enormous numbers of ovules, the transfer of pollen as compact masses, the natural long life of the individual, the light, wind-borne seed easily distributed for long distances, and the absence of endosperm from the seeds may have greatly affected the course of evolution in the family.

With the great numbers of ovules and pollen grains produced in an orchid flower the possibilities of a few fertile seed being produced in a nearly sterile hybrid are greatly improved. A high incompatibility between orchid species could be circumvented in this manner, whereas a great number of pollinations would be required to produce a fertile hybrid in plants which produce relatively few seed. The complete lack of endosperm in the orchid seed may be an extremely important factor in allowing interspecific crosses which might not be possible in other plant groups where the endosperm occasionally prohibits the growth of a physiologically incompatible hybrid embryo. The hybrid, once formed, may reproduce despite partial sterility for the same reasons, namely, the great output of gametes and the absence of an endosperm barrier. Orchid plants are usually long-lived perennials, a circumstance which also provides nearly sterile hybrids with a greater chance of reproduction.

Orchid seed is extremely light and easily distributed by wind and it readily may be carried for great distances. When seedlings are established after relatively long-distance dispersal, they may develop a new population which is isolated from the parent population and is free to evolve in the new situation without genetic ties to the parent species. On the other hand, a seedling may well be established within the range of a genetically compatible species. In such a case hybridization may occur and may profoundly affect the host species.

The extreme ecological preferences exhibited by many orchid species, coupled with reproductive isolation mechanisms such as insect pollinator specificity, probably have been factors in the tremendous burst of evolution exhibited by the orchid family. This pollinator specificity fits well with the general life-cycle of the orchid, i.e., long life, relatively uncommon pollination—but with copious seed production when fertilization takes place—and the richness of the insect fauna in tropical regions where the family is best developed.

1. Effects of hybridization when it occurs

Often the most subtle effect of hybridization is the introgression of genic material from one species into another, causing variability within one or both species. This is a common and well studied effect. The importance of this type of hybridization on evolutionary processes has been well documented by Anderson (1953), Stebbins (1951) and others. Briefly, its importance lies in the possibility of entirely foreign adaptive systems being made available to a previously stabilized species. This allows for reshuffling of different types of adaptive systems within populations, so that selection is provided with segregating blocks of genic materials which, after recombination, could accommodate some individuals to different habitats.

One case of natural hybridization in orchids, studied intensively by Dodson (unpublished) in Ecuador, is that of *Oncidium pusillum* and *O. pumilio*, which have produced hybrid swarms as a result of disturbance of the *O. pumilio* habitat by man. *Oncidium pusillum* (Fig. 112), on the Amazon side of Ecuador, grows in shady locations on lianas overhanging streams, while *O. pumilio* (Fig. 113) grows in the tops of guava trees where it is exposed to direct sunlight. The pruning and cultivation of the wild trees in order to achieve a better harvest of their fruit has changed the conditions so that the lower parts of the tree experienced partial shade. These conditions are hospitable for hybrids between the two species of *Oncidium* and they occur in great abundance. The hybrids vary considerably but little backcrossing with the parental population occurs. Similar hybrids are to be found throughout tropical America wherever *O. pusillum* and

FIG. 112. *Oncidium pusillum*.

FIG. 111. Autogamous hybrid between *Oncidium pusillum* and *O. pumilio*.

FIG. 113. *Oncidium pumilio*.

O. pumilio are sympatric and the guava trees are cultivated by man. These hybrids were named *O. glossomystax* by H. G. Reichenbach f.

An example of introgression in orchids which was studied at the same time was that of the terrestrial genus *Cranichis* in the Andes of central Ecuador. A variable population of *Cranichis ciliata* was found to result from introgression of genic material from *C. cucullata* as a result of habitat disturbance. *Cranichis ciliata* grows in dense shade while *C. cucullata* grows in full sun in boggy meadows. The cutting of the trees and the consequent invasion by thorn scrub provides a habitat for hybrids between the two species. The hybrids have backcrossed with and introgressed into the population of *C. ciliata*, causing great variability. Backcrossing to *C. cucullata* was not encountered, probably because that species grows in the habitat which was not disturbed. A pure population of *C. ciliata* at a different locality demonstrated little variation.

A different effect of hybridization is the direct production of a new species. In plants in general this effect is most often associated with an increase in chromosome number to form allopolyploids, which are fertile and immediately isolated genetically from the parental species. This situation is well documented in a number of instances, such as *Galeopsis tetrahit* (Muntzing, 1930a and b) and *Brassica napus* (Nagahuru, 1935), however, it has not yet been reported for orchids. It is also possible for a new species to be derived without allopolyploidy although this requires special circumstances. If the hybrid itself is strongly selected for, due perhaps to adaptibility to a distinct niche not open to either parent, or in the case of orchids, being selected for by an available insect pollinator which is not utilized by either parent, the hybrid could conceivably become established as a distinct population. Such a case is reported in *Ophrys*, i.e., *O. murbeckii*, in Algeria and has been well documented by Stebbins and Ferlan (1956).

Natural hybrids between sympatric compatible species—either of the same genus or allied genera—are rather common in the orchids. For the most part, however, their effect on the parental species appears limited, perhaps indicating the difficulties involved in breaking physiological and ecological barriers to hybridization. An interesting situation occurs in *Stanhopea* where hybridization occasionally occurs between the primitive *S. ecornuta* and advanced species such as *S. graveolens*. The result is a hybrid which is strikingly different from any other *Stanhopea* and has been named *S. lewisae* by Ames. It is not pollinated and only occurs as an occasional artifact, encountered rarely in nature.

Figure 114 demonstrates natural hybrids which have been reported between species of European orchids (mainly composed from Keller and van Soo, 1930-1940, and Godfery, 1927). Though they are abundant they have not seriously affected the population system of the species. In the figure the species are organized according to their basic pollinators and clearly demonstrate the importance of ecological classes which sometimes override generic limits. Hybrids, except those from the mixed class, have occurred within classes or between border cases.

In tropical regions the primary effect of such hybrids seems to be confusion of taxonomists working with the group. Collectors readily pick them up in the field because they differ from species previously encountered. The result, in the

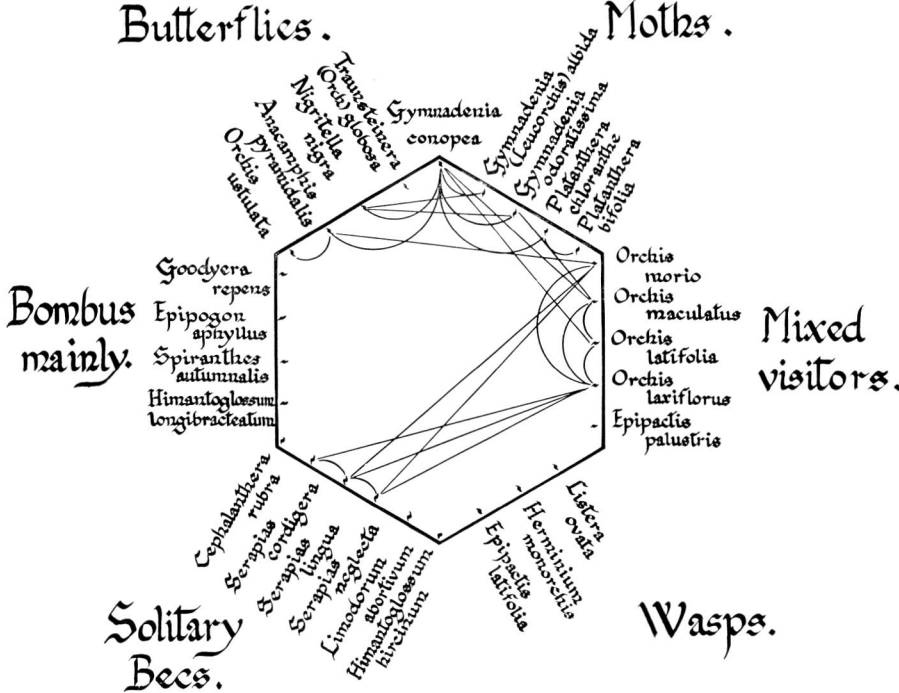

FIG. 114. Diagram of relationships between European orchids arranged according to their pollinators. Lines indicate reported hybrids. (Also see p. 79 on *Bombus*.)

normally limited herbarium collections, gives the appearance of highly variable species to the taxonomist doing superficial work.

2. Barriers to hybridization

A number of factors can contribute to the hindrance of hybridization. These factors may be considered as consisting of two classes: those which act as barriers to hybridization from outside the plant and those from within the plant. These barriers are normally considered to consist of spatial and physiological barriers. Spatial barriers imply that two plants (or plant populations) are too far apart for hybridization to take place. Physiological barriers encompass such phenomena as ecological isolation of plants, mechanical isolation of flowers by means of pollinators and distinct flower seasons, all of which act as external barriers. Internal barriers consist of interspecific sterility (genic or chromosomal), incompatibility factors prohibiting fertilization, hybrid inviability in the F_1 or further generations, and failure of the hybrid to flower.

Examples of vegetative ecological isolation in sympatric populations are: growth of one species in the sun and the other in the shade, strict preferences for acid or basic soils, or in the epiphytic orchids a preference for a particular position on a tree or a kind of tree as a substrate. Hybrids are often unable to encounter an intermediate environment and do not survive unless disturbance produces a hybrid habitat. Isolation of populations by different blooming seasons is common in orchids.

Mechanical isolation (sexual) of species is of more interest to us for it involves their pollination phenomena. Most of the more advanced orchids appear to be pollinated by particular species of insects. This specificity is accomplished by a combination of pollination mechanism and attractant. Many of the bees and quite probably the flies and moths are attracted to certain fragrances and not to others, as we have seen (p. 75).

Other barriers to gene exchange, in addition to spatial, ecological and mechanical barriers, of course, operate within the family. It has long been recognized that genetic incompatibilities within species as well as between species occur here. These phenomena were probably first noted by Scott (1864), who attempted to produce hybrids in *Oncidium*. The same types of barriers were also found in numerous species crossed within this large genus by Dodson (1957). In addition to the barriers mentioned above, great differences in chromosome numbers within the genera tend to act as barriers (Dodson l.c.). In the hybrids between west-European orchids discussed on p. 169 we should point out that some botanists (Heslop-Harrison [1955]) consider two subgenera of the old genus *Orchis*, viz., *Orchis* and *Dactylorchis* to be separated by a ploidy-barrier. The subgenus *Orchis* has $2n = 42$ while the subgenus *Dactylorchis* has $2n = 40$ or 80. They doubt the existence of hybrids between the two, though (see Fig. 114) in the literature *Orchis laxiflora* has been reported as hybridizing with *Dactylorchis* (*Orchis*) *latifolia* and *O. coriophora* with *D. latifolia*.

In many cases, however, chromosome number differences have proven to be only a partial barrier. The unpublished work of W. W. G. Moir of Honolulu, Hawaii, has shown that even supposed subtribal differences may not be sufficient to preclude hybridization. In his work, he has made as many as 50 attempts to achieve a particular cross, and he has shown that numerous attempts were necessary to achieve success in many cases. This was particularly so where he has attempted to use hybrids, produced from parents with different chromosome numbers, in the production of further hybrids. He has had success even there, however. Other workers have accomplished similar results.

Obviously in small populations this low fertility is important, but in large populations of long-lived plants, wherein each seed-pod produces a large quantity of seed, a fertility rate of 1 to 100,000 could have an effect on gene flow over long periods of time. Consequently, hybrid incompatibility and sterility can be only relative terms.

3. Breakdown of barriers

The breaking down of barriers to hybridization is commonly associated with changes in the ecological habitat. Occasionally it simply involves sufficient climatic change for previously isolated populations to migrate together. Natural phenomena such as landslides, falling of large trees in the jungle, fires and floods, commonly change the habitat so that hybrids between ecologically separated sympatric types can survive. The activities of man have had a greater effect in this respect than natural phenomena. Road building through mountains and jungles, clearing and cultivation of forest lands, and the large scale changes necessary to provide grazing land for man's domestic animals have made profound changes in natural habitats. In orchids this has provided sufficiently changed habitats for natural hybrids to succeed as well as, and in some cases better than, natural species.

The occasional migration of effective but not selective pollinators into a zone where other pollinators maintain a barrier system could easily result in hybrids. When species have adapted to different specific pollinators and have become stable, distinguishable taxa, a third pollinator entering the picture can initiate large scale hybridization. Our evidence is inconclusive for documentation of this situation but is worth citing at this point. In southern Ecuador two color forms of *Epidendrum secundum* grow side by side on rock faces and seldom is an intermediate form found. It appears that these two forms are pollinated by two different hummingbirds and the birds are specifically attracted by the different colors. They apparently do not make a mistake often even though the two flowers are nearly identical in respect to form. In northern Ecuador a bewildering hybrid swarm occurs, with the two color forms of *E. secundum* as parents. The whole complex seems to be pollinated and sustained by a third hummingbird which does not occur in southern Ecuador. Such a situation may help explain a number of instances in which two species of orchid grow side by side and are distinct over large areas but in a few localized spots seem to hybridize and result in taxonomic difficulties for the botanist studying them.

CLASSIFICATION IN THE ORCHIDS

It seems important at this point to discuss briefly the taxonomic situation in the Orchidaceae to indicate the kinds of difficulties involved in their classification. These difficulties often reflect the evolutionary status of a particular group. Those groups of plants which are taxonomically difficult are often the groups in which evolution is active, as opposed to clearly defined groups which are evolutionarily static. Orchids have long been known as one of the "problem groups," in which great taxonomic difficulties are encountered, and many questions remain unanswered. There has been a general tendency in recent years simply to rework the same herbarium material without undertaking the necessary field work and study of living materials to find out what is actually occurring in living populations. Many of the botanists who have done taxonomic work in the family have seen very few living populations of tropical orchids. These same botanists tend to feel that it is "elegant" to dabble at random through the family, describing species based on few specimens, with little knowledge of the relationships of allied species. Such work is less than useful. Specialization in particular groups with the same amount of effort expended usually results in usable treatments which reflect natural phenomena.

As with Gramineae, the higher categories within the Orchidaceae have had a long history of changes and revisions due to confusion. Much of the difficulty has been encountered at the generic level. For example, in the subtribes Oncidiinae, Epidendrinae, Pleurothallidinae and the Sarcanthinae, some of the genera are, at best, genera of convenience. Many of these genera were described and delineated before much botanical exploration had been undertaken in the tropics, and subsequently many generic concepts were bridged by newly collected species. The resulting confusion, rather than leading to deep thought on the matter, was resolved either by placing the species in the genus with which they shared some "key" feature, or by describing them as new genera. In many cases, such single features as number of divisions in the pollinia, the presence or absence of a foot on the column or formation of spurs from the lip or sepals were the sole characters arbitrarily used to divide higher groups within the family. Very often these characters are found to intergrade and to be of little significance in indicating relationships. The tendency has been to shuffle these problem groups back and forth or set up new categories for them, rather than to reexamine the significance of the original character chosen. With the advent of extensive horticultural hybridization, the close genetic relationships of many groups previously thought to be widely separate, on the basis of such criteria as mentioned above, have become evident and the taxonomic situation has deteriorated. It has been found that many species from previously delineated genera are quite interfertile. However, the fact that hybrids can be made in the greenhouse should not necessarily be used as a criterion for the destruction of taxa which are genuinely distinct on another basis.

The point here is not so much that the generic concepts were erroneous from the start, though it is obvious in some cases that they were, but that the problems involve the nature of the genera themselves. Although barriers to interspecific or intergeneric hybridization are numerous, they are often in the nature of geographical, ecological, and mechanical isolation rather than in strictly intrinsic genetic incompatibility. For instance, nearly all members of the *Epidendrum* alliance have a diploid chromosome number of 40 and many can be hybridized in cultivation. Many of the members of the Oncidiinae have either 28 or 56 somatic chromosomes and can be hybridized within their respective genome levels. The most important single isolating factor within orchids would appear to be simple spatial isolation of populations, although in many cases where compatible genera are sympatric the isolation is mechanical or ecological.

Species problems abound in the Orchidaceae, but seem to follow the same pattern as the difficulties found at the generic level. Species complexes which are taxonomically very difficult are found throughout the problem genera and only a great deal of field and laboratory study will ever resolve them. In general it might be said that in this family the species is more natural than the genus. This would be true in the much publicized "problem genera." Many of the genera are, however, quite natural and involve little or no difficulty for botanists.

APPENDIX

I. SYNOPSIS OF TAXONOMIC RELATIONS IN THE ORCHIDS

We have used many examples and discussed many genera in this book. We therefore feel that a means of placing these genera in focus with respect to their relationships to each other, and to those of higher taxa, is necessary for clarity.

For many years the classification system of Schlechter was accepted as either a natural one or at least a usable one. It did have many faults and a general discontent with the system led to the nearly simultaneous publication of two papers on the subject. Those papers (Dressler and Dodson, 1960 and Garay, 1960) reviewed the problems and the new knowledge and proposed new classification systems. Neither system was proposed as an end product or suggested as perfect. They were produced quite independently and by workers using somewhat dissimilar approaches. The differences reflect the approaches used.

For the purposes of our discussion here, we will not attempt to propose any new system but will draw heavily from Dressler and Dodson, 1960 and Dressler, 1960a and b.

By compiling our latest impressions, with the kind assistance of Dr. Dressler, we present the following classification system. As examples within the subtribes we have included only genera which we have mentioned in the text of the book and those which are basic and commonly known for each subtribe. The groups are arranged in a systematic sequence, so that closely related groups are listed together as far as possible. We have also added a brief characterization of each of the higher categories of subfamily and tribe (in cases where only one tribe occurs in a subfamily the tribe is not characterized).

I. SUBFAMILY APOSTASIOIDEAE
   Perianth essentially regular, lip never deeply saccate; fertile anthers 2 or 3, elongate; style slender.
   TRIBE APOSTASIEAE: *Apostasia, Neuwiedia.*

II. SUBFAMILY CYPRIPEDIOIDEAE
   Perianth irregular with a deeply saccate lip; fertile anthers 2, subglobose; a conspicuous, flattened median staminode present; style relatively thick.
   TRIBE CYPRIPEDIEAE: *Cypripedium, Paphiopedilum, Phragmopedium, Selenipedium.*

III. SUBFAMILY NEOTTIOIDEAE
   Fertile anther 1, more or less erect, often dorsal, pollinia 2-4, soft and mealy; stems without corms or other thickenings, leaves not jointed at base.

   TRIBE NEOTTIEAE
Subtribe Limodorinae:	*Cephalanthera, Epipactis, Limodorum.*
Subtribe Chloraeinae:	*Acianthus, Caladenia, Calochilus, Chloraea, Corybas, Thelymitra.*
Subtribe Rhizanthellinae:	*Cryptanthemis, Rhizanthella.*
Subtribe Pterostylidinae:	*Caleana, Drakaea, Pterostylis.*
Subtribe Neottiinae:	*Listera, Neottia.*
Subtribe Diuridinae:	*Diuris, Orthoceras.*
Subtribe Cryptostylidinae:	*Coilochilus, Cryptostylis.*
Subtribe Prasophyllinae:	*Microtis, Prasophyllum.*
Subtribe Spiranthinae:	*Anoectochilus, Cheirostylis, Erythrodes, Goodyera, Haemaria, Macodes, Ponthevia, Prescottia, Spiranthes, Stenoptera, Tropidia, Zeuxine.*

IV. SUBFAMILY ORCHIDOIDEAE
   Fertile anther 1, erect or reclinate (rarely incumbent), persistent, usually broadly joined to the column, pollinia in soft masses, caudicles arising from the base of the pollinia.

   TRIBE ORCHIDAE
Subtribe Epipogiinae:	*Epipogium, Stereosandra.*
Subtribe Orchidinae:	*Anacamptis, Bartholina, Bonatea, Coeloglossum, Galeorchis, Gymnadenia, Habenaria, Herminium, Himantoglossum, Nigritella, Ophrys, Orchis, Platanthera, Serapias, Stenoglottis.*
Subtribe Disinae:	*Disa, Satyrium.*
Subtribe Corycinae:	*Ceratandra, Corycium, Disperis.*

V. SUBFAMILY EPIDENDROIDEAE
   Fertile anther 1, often incumbent, pollinia 2-12, usually hard, waxy,

sometimes mealy, without caudicles or these terminal; leaves often jointed at the base.

TRIBE GASTRODIEAE
Pollinia mealy, 2 or 4; plants saprophytic or green; leaves (if present) more or less fleshy (except in *Nervilia*, with fan-shaped leaves), not jointed at the base.

SUBTRIBE VANILLINAE:	*Epistephium, Galeola, Vanilla.*
SUBTRIBE GASTRODIINAE:	*Didymoplexis, Gastrodia.*
SUBTRIBE POGONIINAE:	*Cleistes, Isotria, Nervillia, Pogonia, Triphora.*

TRIBE EPIDENDREAE
Pollinia mealy to compact and hard 2-12, usually club-shaped or laterally flattened (except in *Coelogyne* and some species of *Polystachya*); viscidium present (usually more or less liquid) or absent; stipe rarely present (in *Polystachya*); leaves usually jointed at the base.

SUBTRIBE SOBRALIINAE:	*Elleanthus, Isochilus, Palmorchis, Sobralia.*
SUBTRIBE THUNIINAE:	*Arundina, Thunia.*
SUBTRIBE ARETHUSINAE:	*Arethusia, Calopogon, Bletilla.*
SUBTRIBE BLETIINAE:	*Acanthephippium, Bletia, Bothriochilus, Calanthe, Chysis, Coelia, Phajus, Plocoglottis, Spathoglottis.*
SUBTRIBE COELOGYNINAE:	*Coelogyne, Dendrochilum, Panisea, Pholidota, Pleione.*
SUBTRIBE EPIDENDRINAE:	*Barkeria, Brassavola, Broughtonia, Cattleya, Encyclia, Epidendrum, Hexisea, Laelia, Scaphyglottis, Schomburgkia, Sophronitis.*
SUBTRIBE ERIINAE: (or Old World Epidendrinae)	*Appendicula, Ceratostylis, Cryptochilus, Eria, Glomera, Neobenthamia, Podochilus, Polystachya, Porpax, Sepalosiphon.*
SUBTRIBE PLEUROTHALLIDINAE:	*Cryptophoranthus, Lepanthes, Masdevallia, Physosiphon, Pleurothallis, Restrepia, Scaphosepalum, Stelis.*
SUBTRIBE ADRORHIZINAE:	*Adrorhizon, Josephia.*
SUBTRIBE THELASIINAE:	*Phreatia, Thelasis.*
SUBTRIBE RIDLEYELLINAE:	*Ridleyella.*

TRIBE MALAXIDEAE
Pollinia 2-4, completely naked, without caudicles of any sort; viscidia or stipes (usually double) rarely present.

SUBTRIBE MALAXIDINAE:	*Liparis, Malaxis, Oberonia.*
SUBTRIBE DENDROBIINAE:	*Bulbophyllum, Dendrobium, Monosepalum.*

SUBTRIBE GENYORCHIDINAE: *Drymoda, Genyorchis, Ione, Monomeria.*
SUBTRIBE THECOSTELINAE: *Thecostele.*

TRIBE VANDEAE

Pollinia 2-4, dorsoventrally flattened if 4; viscidium normally always present; stipe often present.

SUBTRIBE CYMBIDIINAE: *Ansellia, Cymbidium, Grammatophyllum, Lissochilus, Porphyroglottis, Tipularia.*

SUBTRIBE CYRTOPODIINAE: *Aplectrum, Corallorhiza, Cyrtopodium, Eulophia, Eulophidium, Eulophiella, Galeandra, Govenia.*

SUBTRIBE CATASETINAE: *Catasetum, Cycnoches, Mormodes.*

SUBTRIBE VANDINAE: *Aerides, Angraecum, Arachnanthe,*
(Sarcanthinae) *Arachnis, Camplyocentrum, Chaemaeangis, Dendrophylax, Luisia, Phalaenopsis, Renanthera, Sarcochilus, Stauropsis, Taeniophyllum, Thrixspermum, Trichoglottis, Vanda, Vandopsis.*

SUBTRIBE STANHOPEINAE: *Acineta, Cirrhaea, Coeliopsis, Coryanthes, Gongora, Houlletia, Kegeliella, Lacaena, Peristeria, Polycycnis, Schlimia, Sievekingia, Stanhopea.*

SUBTRIBE ZYGOPETALINAE: *Aganisia, Chondroryncha, Cochleanthes, Huntleya, Kefersteinia, Pescatorea, Warrea, Zygopetalum.*

SUBTRIBE LYCASTINAE: *Anguloa, Bifrenaria, Lycaste.*

SUBTRIBE MAXILLARIINAE: *Centropetalum, Cyrtidium, Maxillaria, Mormolyca, Pachyphyllum, Trigonidium, Xylobium.*

SUBTRIBE ORNITHOCEPHALINAE: *Dichaea, Ornithocephalus, Stellilabium, Telipogon, Trichoceros.*

SUBTRIBE ONCIDIINAE: *Ada, Aspasia, Brassia, Cochlioda, Comparettia, Gomesa, Leochilus, Lockhartia, Miltonia, Notylia, Odontoglossum, Oncidium, Pterostemma, Rodriguezia, Trichocentrum, Trichopilia.*

In Figure 115 we compare the major components of this system with those of Bentham and Hooker (taken primarily from Lindley) and Schlechter (adapted from Pfitzer). There is a remarkable similarity between our system and that of

BENTHAM AND HOOKER (based on Lindley)	SCHLECHTER (based on Pfitzer)	SYSTEM USED HERE (Dressler and Dodson)
	(Apostasiaceae)	Subfamily Apostasioideae
Tribe Cypripedieae	Subfamily Diandrae Tribe Cyprepediloideae	Subfamily Cypripedioideae

Tribe Neottieae
  Subtribe Limodoreae
    Spirantheae
    Vanilleae
    Arethuseae
    etc.
	Subfamily Monandrae
	  Tribe Polychondreae
	    Subtribe Cephalanthereae
	      Sprirantheae
	      Cranichideae
	      Physureae
	      Vanilleae
	      Sobralieae
	      Bletilleae
	      etc.
		Subfamily Neottioideae
		  Tribe Neottieae
		    Subtribe Limodorinae
		      Spiranthinae
		      etc.

Tribe Ophrydeae
  Subtribe Habenarieae
    Diseae
    Corycieae
	Tribe Ophrydoideae
	  Subtribe Habenarieae
	    Plantanthereae
	    Diseae
	    Satyrieae
	    Diserideae
		Subfamily Orchidoideae
		  Tribe Orchidae
		    Subtribe Orchidinae
		      Disinae
		      Coryciinae
		      etc.

Tribe Epidendreae
  Subtribe Bletieae
    Laelieae
  (Tribe Malaxideae Lindl.)
    Malaxieae
    Liparieae
    Dendrobieae
Tribe Vandeae
  Subtribe Eulophieae
    Cymbidieae
    Cyrtopodieae
    Sarcantheae
    Stanhopieae
    Oncidieae
	Tribe Kerosphaereae
	  Subtribe Phajeae
	    Pleurothalideae
	    Laelieae
	    Ponereae
	    Liparideae
	    Dendrobieae
	    Bulbophylleae
	    Polystachyeae
	    Cymbidieae
	    Cyrtopodieae
	    Cataseteae
	    Gongoreae
	    Maxillareae
	    Trichocentreae
	    Cochliodeae
	    Trichopilieae
	    Comparettieae
	    Dichaeieae
	    Lockhartieae
	    Telipogonieae
	    Notylieae
	    Saundersieae
	    Oncidieae
	    Ornithocephaleae
	    Sarcantheae
	    etc.
		Subfamily Epidendroideae
		  Tribe Gastrodieae
		    Subtribe Vanillinae
		    etc.
		  Tribe Epidendreae
		    Subtribe Arethusinae
		      Sobraliinae
		      Bletiinae
		      Epidendrinae
		      Pleurothallidinae
		      etc.
		  Tribe Malaxideae
		    Subtribe Malaxadinae
		      Dendrobiinae
		      etc.
		  Tribe Vandeae
		    Subtribe Cymbidiinae
		      Cyrtopediinae
		      Catasetinae
		      Vandinae
		      Stanhopeinae
		      Zygopetalinae
		      Lycastinae
		      Maxillariinae
		      Ornithocephalinae
		      Oncidiinae

FIG. 115. Comparison of orchid classification systems of Bentham and Hooker (based on Lindley's system), Schlechter (based on Pfitzer's system), and the system used here (based on the system of Dressler and Dodson).

Bentham and Hooker, the primary difference being the shifting of the Vanillinae, Arethusinae and the Sobraliinae from the Neottieae, to the Epidendroideae. In our opinion, these groups have closer relationships with the latter group than with the former. The system of Schlechter, in attempting to be natural, was split into an overabundance of inconsistant subtribes based on minor morphological differences (which in many instances were simple results of adaptation to a different type of pollinator from that of the well known groups).

Any natural system of classification is at least three dimensional and therefore impossible to depict accurately on two-dimensional paper; however, in order to give a pictorial idea of relationships we substitute in Fig. 116 an explanatory diagram. It approaches an expression of actual relationships as they exist in nature. It is also designed to make it quickly possible to place a particular genus referred to in the text—after reference to its tribal position—in relation to the other higher taxa in the family.

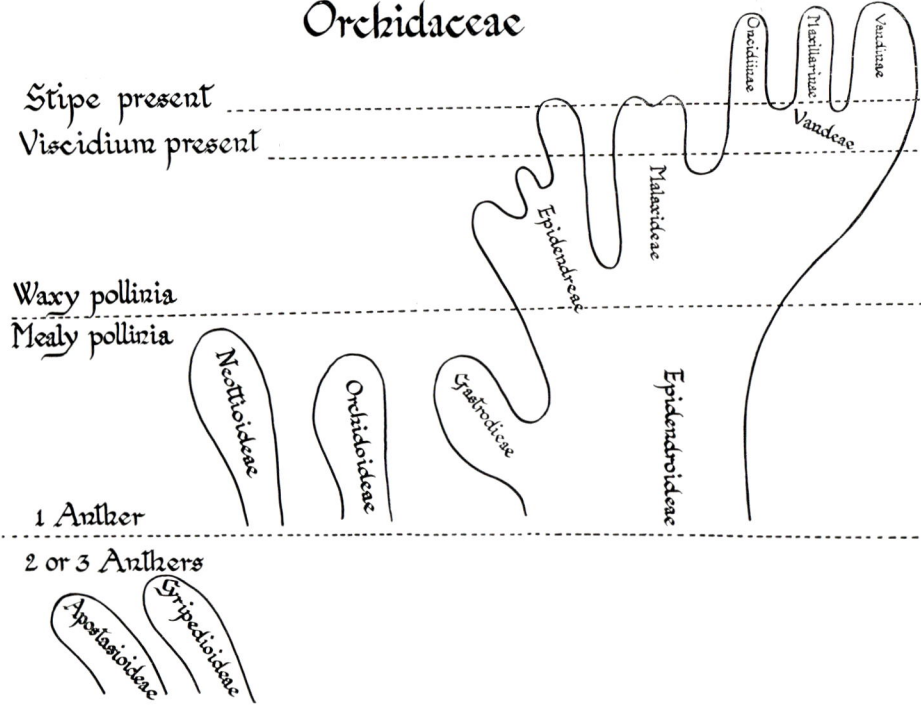

FIG. 116. Diagram showing our concept of the relationships between the higher categories of the Orchidaceae. As the groups become more advanced, more complex structures, which aid in pollination, appear in the flowers.

II. LIST OF ORCHIDS AND THEIR KNOWN POLLINATORS

ORCHID	POLLINATOR	KIND OF ANIMAL	OBSERVER
ACINETA			
A. barkeri	Euplusia concava	Bee	Grant (Pers. Comm.)
A. chrysantha	Euplusia concava	Bee	Dodson (1965a)
A. superba	Euplusia concava	Bee	Dressler (1966)
ANACAMPTIS (see Orchis)			
ANGULOA			
A. clowesii	Eulaema boliviensis	Bee	Dodson (1966)
A. ruckeri	Eulaema cingulata	Bee	R. Wilson (Pers. Comm.)
ARUNDINA			
A. speciosa	Xylocopa sp.	Bee	van der Pijl (1954)
ASPASIA			
A. psitticina	Eulaema cingulata	Bee	Dodson & Frymire (1961b) (as A. epidendroides)
	Eulaema polychroma	Bee	Dodson & Frymire (1961b)
BARKERIA			
B. lindleyana	Xylocopa tabaniformis	Bee	Dodson (1965a)
	*Auglochlora sp.	Bee	Dodson (1965a)
	*Euglossa sp.	Bee	Dodson (1965a)
	*Skippers (4 spp.)	Skipper	Dodson (1965a)
BLETIA			
B. catenulata	Xylocopa tricuspidifera	Bee	Bennett, D. (Pers. Comm.)
B. purpurea	Euglossa hemichlora	Bee	Dodson & Frymire (1961b)
	Melipona sp.	Bee	Dodson & Frymire (1961b)
	Thygater sp.	Bee	Dodson & Frymire (1961b)
	*Papilio sp.	Butterfly	Dodson & Frymire (1961b)
	*Skippers (3 spp.)	Skipper	Dodson & Frymire (1961b)
BONATEA			
B. speciosa	Pyrgus elmo	Butterfly	Darwin (1877)
BRASSAVOLA			
B. digbyana	sphingid	Moth	Fuchs (Pers. Comm.)
BRASSIA			
B. aff. antherotes	Campsomeris columba	Wasp	Dodson (Unpubl.)
B. ochroleuca	Pepsis gloriosa	Wasp	Dressler (Pers. Comm.)
BROMHEADIA			
B. alticola	Xylocopa sp.	Bee	Ridley (1890)
B. aporoides	Xylocopa sp.	Bee	Ridley (1890)
B. palustris	Xylocopa sp.	Bee	Ridley (1890)
BULBOPHYLLUM			
B. macranthum		Fly	Ridley (1890)
B. striatellum		Fly	Ridley (1890)
CALADENIA			
C. alba			Fitz-Gerald (1882)
C. barbarossae	Halictus sp.	Bee	Coleman (1930)
		Wasp	Coleman (1930), Sargent (1907 & 1918)
C. deformis	Halictus subinclinans	Bee	Rogers (1931)
C. dialata var. rhomboidiformis		Wasp	Coleman (1930)
C. dimorpha		Fly	Rogers (1931)
CALOCHILUS			
C. campestris	Campsomeris tasmaniensis	Wasp	Fordham (1946)

*Nonpollinating visitors.

ORCHID	POLLINATOR	KIND OF ANIMAL	OBSERVER
CALOPOGON			
C. barbatus	Auglochlora festiva	Bee	Robertson (1887) (as C. parviflorus)
	Auglochlora sp.	Bee	Robertson (1887)
	Halictus sp.	Bee	Robertson (1887)
C. pulchellus	Xylocopa micans	Bee	Dodson (Unpubl.)
CALYPSO			
C. borealis	Bombus sp.	Bee	Loew in Knuth (not well-defined)
CATASETUM			
C. barbatum	Euglossa cordata	Bee	Dodson & Dressler (Unpubl.)
C. bicolor	Euglossa cordata	Bee	Dressler (1966)
	Euglossa sp. (RLD 2)	Bee	Dressler (1966)
	Euglossa sp. (RLD 58)	Bee	Dressler (1966)
C. cernuum	Euplusia violacea	Bee	Hoehne (1933)
C. costatum	Euglossa sp.	Bee	Ostlund (Notes)
C. dilectum	Euglossa sp.	Bee	Lankester (1960)
C. discolor	Eulaema cingulata	Bee	Dressler (Pers. Comm.)
C. eburneum	Eulaema cingulata	Bee	Dodson & Frymire (1961b) (as C. fragrans)
C. fimbriatum	Euplusia auriceps	Bee	Dressler (Pers. Comm.)
C. hookeri	Euglossa cordata	Bee	Dressler & Dodson (Unpubl.)
C. integerrimum	Eulaema cingulata	Bee	Pollard (Pers. Comm.) D. O. Allen (Unpubl.)
	Eulaema polychroma	Bee	Pollard (Pers. Comm.) D. O. Allen (Unpubl.)
C. luridum	Euglossa cordata	Bee	Dressler (Pers. Comm.)
C. macrocarpum	*Euglossa imperialis	Bee	Ducke (1902), Dressler (Pers. Comm.)
	Eulaema cingulata	Bee	Ducke (1902), Crüger (1865), Dressler (Pers. Comm.)
	Eulaema meriana	Bee	Ducke (1902),
	Eulaema bennettii	Bee	F. Bennett (Pers. Comm.)
	Eulaema nigrita	Bee	Dressler (Pers. Comm.)
C. macroglossum	Eulaema bomboides	Bee	Dodson & Frymire (1961b)
	Eulaema cingulata	Bee	Dodson & Frymire (1961b)
	Eulaema polychroma	Bee	Dodson & Frymire (1961b)
	Eulaema speciosa	Bee	Dodson & Frymire (1961b)
C. maculatum (C. oerstedii)	Eulaema cingulata	Bee	Allen (1952), Dodson (1965a)
	Eulaema polychroma	Bee	Allen (1952), Dodson (1965a)
C. platyglossum	Eulaema cingulata	Bee	Dodson & Frymire (1961b)
	Eulaema bomboides	Bee	Dodson & Frymire (1961b)
	Eulaema polychroma	Bee	Dodson & Frymire (1961b)
C. reichenbachianum	Euglossa sp.	Bee	Dressler (Pers. Comm.)
C. russellianum	Eulaema cingulata	Bee	Dodson (1965a)
C. saccatum	Eulaema cingulata	Bee	Dodson (1965a)
	*Euglossa ignita	Bee	Dodson (1965a)
	*Euglossa augaspis (Moure mss.)	Bee	Dodson (1965a)
C. tabulare	Eulaema cingulata	Bee	Dodson (Unpubl.)
C. viridiflavum	Eulaema cingulata	Bee	Dressler (Dodson 1965a)
C. warczewitzii	Eulaema meriana (large form)	Bee	Dodson & Dressler (Unpubl.)
	Eulaema nigrita	Bee	
CATTLEYA			
C. luteola	Melipona flavipennis	Bee	Dodson (Unpubl.)
C. maxima	Eulaema polychroma	Bee	Dodson & Frymire (1961b)
C. Mendellii	Eulaema cingulata	Bee	Dodson (Unpubl.)
C. warszewiczii	Eulaema polychroma	Bee	Dodson (Unpubl.)
	Eulaema cingulata	Bee	Dodson (Unpubl.)
	Xylocopa aff. viridis	Bee	Dodson (1965a)

ORCHID	POLLINATOR	KIND OF ANIMAL	OBSERVER
CEPHALANTHERA			
C. ensifolia	Halictus sp.	Bee	Godfery (1933)
	Dolerus sp.	Wasp	Godfery (1933)
C. grandiflora	Andrena sp.	Bee	Godfery (1933)
	Halictus sp.	Bee	Godfery (1933)
C. rubra	Heriades sp.	Bee	Evans (1934)
	Eucera sp.	Bee	Evans (1934)
CHONDRORYNCHA			
C. sp. (Panama)	Eulaema speciosa	Bee	Dodson & Dressler (Unpubl.)
CIRRHAEA			
C. sp.	Euplusia violacea	Bee	Hoehne (1933)
CIRRHOPETALUM			
C. psittacoides		Fly	Ridley (1890)
C. aff. pulchrum		Fly	Ridley (1890)
C. sp.		Fly	Ridley (1890)
COCHLEANTHES			
C. aromatica	Eulaema seabrae	Bee	Dodson (1965a)
C. sp. (Ecuador)	Eulaema meriana	Bee	Dodson (1965a)
COCHLIODA			
C. vulcanica	Undet. hummingbird	Bird	Dodson (1965a)
	Undet. butterfly	Butterfly	Dodson (1965a)
COELIOPSIS			
C. hyacinthosma	Eulaema cingulata	Bee	Dodson & Dressler (Unpubl.)
	Eulaema meriana	Bee	Dodson & Dressler (Unpubl.)
	Euplusia schmidtiana	Bee	Dodson & Dressler (Unpubl.)
	Euplusia sp.	Bee	Dodson & Dressler (Unpubl.)
	*Euglossa dodsoni	Bee	Dodson & Dressler (Unpubl.)
	*Euglossa sp. (RLD 2)	Bee	Dodson & Dressler (Unpubl.)
COELOGLOSSUM			
C. viride	Tenthredopsis sp.	Wasp	Godfery (1933)
	Cryptus sp.	Wasp	Silen (1906a)
	Tipula sp.	Mosquito	Silen (1906a)
	Cantharis sp.	Beetle	Silen (1906a)
COMPARETTIA			
C. falcata	Amazalia tzacatl	Bird	Dodson (1965a)
CORALLORHIZA			
C. innata	Syrphus cinctellus	Fly	Silen (1906b)
CORYANTHES			
C. elegantium (C. wolfii)	Euglossa hemichlora	Bee	Dodson (1965d)
C. leucocorys	Eulaema meriana	Bee	Dodson (1965d)
	*Euglossa ignita	Bee	Dodson (1965d)
C. macrantha	Eulaema cingulata	Bee	F. Bennett (Pers. Comm.) Dodson (1965a)
	Eulaema basalis	Bee	F. Bennett (Pers. Comm.)
C. maculata	Euglossa azureoviridis	Bee	Dressler (1966)
C. rodriguezii	Euplusia superba	Bee	Dodson (1965a)
	*Eulaema meriana	Bee	Dodson (Unpubl.)
C. speciosa	Euglossa cordata	Bee	Allen (1952)
C. aff. speciosa	Euglossa alleni	Bee	Dodson & Dressler (Unpubl.)
C. trifoliata	Euglossa ignita	Bee	Dodson (1965a)
	Euglossa mixta	Bee	Dodson (Unpubl.)
CORYBAS (Corysanthes)			
C. sp.		Fly	Thompson (1927)
CRYPTOSTYLIS			
C. erecta	Lissopimpla semipunctata	Wasp	Coleman (1929)
C. lepitochila	Lissopimpla semipunctata	Wasp	Coleman (1927)

ORCHID	POLLINATOR	KIND OF ANIMAL	OBSERVER
C. ovata	Lissopimpla semipunctata	Wasp	Coleman (1930a)
C. subulata	Lissopimpla semipunctata	Wasp	Coleman (1930b)
CYCNOCHES			
C. aureum	Eulaema nigrita	Bee	Dressler (Dodson 1965a)
	*Euglossa sp. (RLD 2)	Bee	Dressler (1966)
	*Euglossa sp. (RLD 58)	Bee	Dressler (1966)
	*Euglossa sp. (RLD 96)	Bee	Dressler (1966)
C. egertonianum (type form)	Euglossa ignita	Bee	Dressler (1966)
C. cf. egertonianum ("species 1" of Dressler 1966)	Euglossa cyanura	Bee	Dressler (1966)
C. cf. egertonianum ("species 2" of Dressler 1966)	Euglossa sp. (RLD 2)	Bee	Dressler (1966)
C. cf. egertonianum ("species 3" of Dressler 1966)	Euglossa hansoni	Bee	Dressler (1966)
C. lehmannii	Eulaema cingulata	Bee	Dodson & Frymire (1961a)
C. pentadactylon	Euplusia superba	Bee	Dodson (1965a)
C. peruviana	Euglossa hemichlora	Bee	Dodson & Frymire (1961a) (as C. egertonianum)
C. ventricosum	Eulaema cingulata	Bee	Dodson (1965a)
C. ventricosum var. warscewiczii	Eulaema cingulata	Bee	Allen (1952), Dressler (1966)
CYMBIDIUM			
C. aloifolium	Vespa cincta	Wasp	Ridley (1894)
	Xylocopa sp.	Bee	Ridley (1894)
C. finlaysonianum	Apis dorsata	Bee	Burkill (1919)
CYPRIPEDIUM			
C. arietinum	Megachile sp.	Bee	Irwin (Pers. Comm.)
C. calceolus	Andrena spp. (5)	Bee	Müller (1873)
C. parviflorum	Ceratina sp.	Bee	Robertson (1928)
	Zaodontomerus sp.	Bee	Guignard (1886)
CYRTOPODIUM			
C. punctatum	Euglossa hemichlora	Bee	Dodson (1962a)
DENDROBIUM			
D. crumenatum	Apis indica	Bee	V. Leeuwen (1934)
	Apis dorsata	Bee	Burkill (1919)
D. linguiforme	Syrphis viridiceps	Fly	Gilbert (1958)
	Tinnid wasps	Wasp	Gilbert (1958)
D. lawesii		Bird	Slade (1962)
D. secundum	Cyrtostomus pectoralis	Bird	Burkill (1919)
D. superbum	Apis dorsata	Bee	Burkill (1919)
	Apis indica	Bee	Burkill (1919)
DICHAEA			
D. panamensis	Euglossa cordata	Bee	Dressler (1966)
DISA			
D. cornuta		Fly	Vogel (1954)
D. draconis	Pangonia sp.	Bee-fly	Vogel (1954)
D. lugens		Fly	Vogel (1954)
D. uniflora	Meneris sp.	Butterfly	Marboth (1915)
DISPERIS			
D. polygonoides		Bee-fly	Vogel (1954)
DIURIS			
D. pedunculata	Halictus languinosus	Bee	Coleman (1932)
D. sulphurea	*Halictus languinosus	Bee	Rayment (1932)
	Paracolletes sp.	Bee	Rayment (1932)

ORCHID	POLLINATOR	KIND OF ANIMAL	OBSERVER
ELLEANTHUS			
E. arpophyllostachys	Ocreatus underwoodii	Bird	Dodson (1965a)
E. aurantiacus	Undet. hummingbird	Bird	Dodson (1962a)
E. aureus	Undet. hummingbird	Bird	Dodson (1962a)
E. capitatus	Undet. hummingbird	Bird	Dodson (1962a)
E. hallii	Undet. hummingbird	Bird	Dodson (1965a)
E. hymenophorus	Amazalia tzacatl	Bird	Dodson (1965a)
E. rosea	Undet. hummingbird	Bird	Dodson (1965a)
ENCYCLIA			
E. crassilabia	Xylocopa frontalis	Bee	Dodson (1965)
E. pentotis	Campsomeris columba	Wasp	Dodson (Unpubl.)
EPIDENDRUM			
E. cf. acuminatum	Xylocopa frontalis	Bee	Dodson (1965a)
E. cnemidophorum	Amazalia tzacatl	Bird	Dodson (1965a)
E. difforme	Amastus acona	Moth	Dodson & Frymire (1961a)
E. fimbriatum		Fly	Dodson (1962a)
E. latilabium	Amastus acona	Moth	Dodson (1965a)
E. paniculatum	Heliconia sp.	Butterfly	Dodson (Unpubl.)
E. pseudepidendrum	Hummingbird	Bird	Dodson (Unpubl.)
E. radicans (as E. ibaguense)	Papilio sp.	Butterfly	Dodson (1965a)
E. secundum	Papilio polyxenes var. americus	Butterfly	Dodson (1962a & 1965a)
	Urbanus proteus	Skipper	Dodson & Frymire (1961b)
	Amazalia sp.	Bird	Dodson (1962a)
EPIPACTIS			
E. gigantea	Syrphus sp.	Fly	Grant (Pers. Comm.)
E. latifolia	Vespa sylvestris	Wasp	Darwin (1877) a.o.
		Fly	Darwin (1877) a.o.
E. palustris	Apis mellifera	Bee	Darwin (1877) a.o.
	Sarcophaga carnosa	Fly	Darwin (1877) a.o.
	Coelopa frigida	Fly	Darwin (1877) a.o.
	Crabro brevis	Wasp	Darwin (1877) a.o.
E. viridiflora	Vespa diabolica	Wasp	Porter (1896)
EPIPOGIUM			
E. aphyllus	Bombus lucorum (dubious?)	Bee	Rohrbach (1866)
EULOPHIA			
E. horsfallii	Xylocopa sp.	Bee	Kullenberg (1961)
GASTRODIA			
G. javanica		Fly	Holttum (1953)
GOMEZA			
G. sp.		Bee	F. Müller (1897)
GONGORA			
G. armeniaca	Euglossa cf. viridissima	Bee	Dodson (1965a)
G. armeniaca var. bicornuta	Euglossa dodsoni	Bee	Dodson (1965a)
G. bufonia	Euplusia violacea	Bee	Hoehne (1933)
G. grossa	Euglossa hemichlora	Bee	Dodson (1962a)
	Euglossa nigropilosa	Bee	Dodson (1965a)
G. quinquenervis (Palmar, Costa Rica)	Euglossa cordata	Bee	Allen (1955)
G. quinquenervis (Tilaran, Costa Rica)	Euglossa cordata	Bee	Dodson & Dressler (Unpubl.)
G. quinquenervis (Panama)	Euglossa cordata	Bee	Dressler (1966)
	Euglossa orichalcea	Bee	Dressler (1966)
	Euglossi townsendii	Bee	Dressler (1966)
	Euglossa sp. (RLD 2)	Bee	Dressler (1966)
	Euglossa sp. (RLD 58)	Bee	Dressler (1966)
G. quinquenervis (Quevedo, Ecuador)	Euglossa cf. variabilis	Bee	Dodson (1962a)

ORCHID	POLLINATOR	KIND OF ANIMAL	OBSERVER
G. quinquenervis (Iquitos, Peru)	Euglossa ignita	Bee	Dodson (1962a)
	Euglossa augaspis (Moure mss.)	Bee	Dodson (1962a)
	Euglossa decorata	Bee	Dodson (1962a)
	Euglossa cordata	Bee	Dodson (1962a)
G. sp. (Golfito, Costa Rica)	Euglossa ignita	Bee	Dressler (1966), Dodson (Unpubl.)
	Euglossa dodsoni	Bee	Dressler (Pers. Comm.), Dodson (Unpubl.)
G. sp. ("Guanacaste red" of Dressler 1966)	Euglossa viridissima (KU 5)	Bee	Dressler (1966)
G. sp. ("species 1" of Dressler 1966)	Euglossa gorgonensis	Bee	Dressler (1966)
	*Euglossa asarophora	Bee	Dressler (1966)
	Euglossa sp. (RLD 151)	Bee	Dressler (1966)
	*Euglossa sp. (RLD 177)	Bee	Dressler (1966)
G. sp. ("yellow lip" of Dressler 1966) (Turrialba, C.R.)	Euglossa gorgonensis	Bee	Dressler (1966)
	Euglossa hansoni	Bee	Dressler (1966)
	Euglossa sp. (RLD 85)	Bee	Dressler (1966)
	*Eulaema cingulata	Bee	Dressler (1966)
	*Eulaema nigrifacies	Bee	Dressler (1966)
	*Eulaema polychroma	Bee	Dressler (1966)
	*Eulaema speciosa	Bee	Dressler (1966)
G. tricolor	Euglossa cyanura	Bee	Dressler (1966)
	*Exaerete smaragdina	Bee	Dressler (1966)
G. unicolor	Euglossa purpurea	Bee	Dressler (1966)
GOODYERA			
G. repens	Bombus pratorum	Bee	Müller (1881)
GRAMMATOPHYLLUM			
G. speciosum	Apis dorsata	Bee	Ridley (1905)
	Vespa cincta	Wasp	Ridley (1905)
GYMNADENIA			
G. conopsea	Plusia chrysiles	Moth	Darwin (1877)
	Plusia gamma	Moth	Darwin (1877)
	Anaites plagiata	Moth	Darwin (1877)
	Triphaena pronuba	Moth	Darwin (1877)
	Macroglossa stellatarum	Moth	Fritsch (1913)
		Butterflies	H. Müller (1881)
	Zygaena filipendula	Butterflies	Ziegenspeck (1928)
HABENARIA (see also Platanthera)			
H. bifolia (as Platanthera bifolia)	Hadena dentata	Moth	Darwin (1877)
	Plusia aureum	Moth	Darwin (1877)
	Deilkphila sp.	Moth	Ziegenspeck (1928)
	Agrotis segetum	Moth	Darwin (1877)
	Agrotis plagiata	Moth	Darwin (1877)
	Cucullia umbratica	Moth	Darwin (1877)
	Macroglossa sp.	Moth	Ziegenspeck (1928)
	Nisioniades sp.	Moth	
	Sphinx pinastri	Moth	Silen (1906b)
H. leucophaea	Chaerocampa sp.	Moth	Robertson (1928)
H. orbiculata	Sphinx drupiferanum	Moth	Sargent (1894)
H. polyphylla	Hippotion celerio	Moth	Vogel (1954)
HAEMARIA			
H. discolor	Plesioneura asmara	Butterfly	Ridley (1896)
HERMINIUM			
H. monorchis	Tetrastichus diaphantus	Wasp	Darwin (1877), Müller (1881)
	Malthodes brevicollis	Beetle	Darwin (1877), Müller (1881)
HIMANTOGLOSSUM			
H. hircinum	Andrena carbonaria	Bee	Schmid (1911)
H. longibracteatum	Bombus sp.	Bee	Evans (1934)
	Apis sp.	Bee	Evans (1934)
	Xylocopa sp.	Bee	Evans (1934)
HOULLETIA			

ORCHID	POLLINATOR	KIND OF ANIMAL	OBSERVER
H. brocklehurstiana	Euglossa sp. (RLD-BR 7)	Bee	Dressler (1966)
HUNTLEYA			
H. meleagris	Eulaema meriana	Bee	Dodson (1965a)
ISOCHILUS			
I. carnosiflorus	Amazalia tzacatl	Bird	Dodson (1965a)
KEFERSTEINIA			
K. graminea	Eulaema polyzona	Bee	Dodson (1965)
K. sp.	Euglossa sp. (RLD 206)	Bee	Dressler (1966)
	Eulaema speciosa	Bee	Dressler (1966)
KEGELIELLA			
K. nigropilosa	Euplusia concava	Bee	Dressler (1966)
LACAENA			
L. bicolor	Euplusia cf. caerulescens	Bee	D. O. Allen (Unpubl.)
L. spectabilis	Euglossa sp. (RLD 161)		Dodson & Dressler (Unpubl.)
LAELIA			
L. milleri	Undet. hummingbird	Bird	Dodson (Unpubl.)
LEOCHILUS			
L. sp. (Panama)	Pachdynerus nassidens	Wasp	Dressler (Pers. Comm.)
LIMODORUM			
L. abortivum	Anthidium septemdentatum	Bee	Godfery (1933)
	Various bees	Bee	Godfery (1933)
LIPARIS			
L. liliifolia	Hylemyia juvinalis	Fly	Robertson (1928)
	Hopidea sp.	Bug	Robertson (1928)
LISTERA			
L. ovata	Ophinoninae	Wasp	Sprengel (1793), Darwin (1877), Ziegenspeck (1928), Kirchner 1922, 1925), Schremmer (1961), and many others.
L. cordata	Tipula subnodicornus	Crane fly	Silen (1906a)
	Microgaster sp.	Wasp	Silen (1906a)
LOCKHARTIA			
L. oerstedii	Eulaema meriana	Bee	Dodson (Unpubl.)
LYCASTE			
L. aromatica	Euglossa viridissima	Bee	Ostlund (notes), Pollard (Pers. Comm.)
L. consobrina	Euglossa viridissima	Bee	Pollard (Pers. Comm.)
L. xytriophora	Euglossa cf. variabilis	Bee	Dodson (1962a)
MASDEVALLIA			
M. erythrochaete	Drosphila sp.	Fly	Dodson (1965a)
M. fractiflexa	Undet. flies	Fly	Dodson (1962a)
M. rosea	Undet. hummingbird	Bird	Dodson (1962a)
MAXILLARIA			
M. fletcheriana	Bombus volucellioides	Bee	Dodson (1965a)
M. furstenbergae	Melipona eburnea	Bee	Dodson (1962a)
M. grandiflora	Eulaema cingulata	Bee	Dodson & Frymire (1961b)
M. reichenheimiana	Trigona testacea	Bee	Dodson (1965a)
	Trigona amalthea	Bee	Dodson (1965a)
M. sanderiana	Eulaema Cingulata	Bee	Dodson (1962a)
M. sp.	Pantrope insignis	Bird	Dodson (1965a)
MILTONIA			
M. endresii	Ptiloglossa ducalis	Bee	Dodson (1965a)
MORMODES			
M. atropurpurea	Euglossa championi	Bee	Dressler (1966)
	Euglossa mixta	Bee	Dressler (1966)
	Euglossa sp. (RLD 85)	Bee	Dressler (1966)

ORCHID	POLLINATOR	KIND OF ANIMAL	OBSERVER
M. cf. buccinator	Euglossa hemichlora	Bee	Dodson (1962a)
M. cartonii	Euglossa cordata	Bee	Dressler (1966), Allen (1955) (as M. igneum)
	Euglossa mixta	Bee	Dressler (Unpubl.)
M. colossus	Euglossa mixta	Bee	Dressler (1966)
	Euglossa asarophora	Bee	Dressler (1966)
	Euglossa sp. (RLD 161)	Bee	Dodson & Dressler (Unpubl.)
	*Eulaema cingulata	Bee	Dressler (1966)
	*Eulaema meriana	Bee	Dressler (1966)
	Eulaema nigrita	Bee	Dodson & Dressler (Unpubl.)
M. flavidum	Euglossa viridissima	Bee	Dressler (1966)
M. igneum	Euglossa igniventris	Bee	Dressler (1966)
	Euglossa mixta	Bee	Dressler (1966)
M. lineatum	Euglossa viridissima	Bee	Pollard (Pers. Comm.)
M. maculatum	Euglossa viridissima	Bee	Pollard (Pers. Comm.)
M. powellii	Euglossa sp. (RLD 2)	Bee	Dressler (1966)
M. uncia	Euglossa sp.	Bee	Ostlund (in notes)
NIGRITELLA			
N. nigra		Butterfly	Müller (1874)
	Laucania spp.	Butterfly	Godfery (1931)
	Zygaena spp.	Butterfly	Godfery (1931)
NOTYLIA			
N. cf. barkeri (Panama)	Euglossa sp. (RLD 2)	Bee	Dressler (1966)
N. buchtenii	Euglossa augaspis (Moure mss.)	Bee	Dodson (1965a)
	*Euglossa ignita	Bee	Dodson (1965a)
N. cf. buchtenii	Euglossa ignita	Bee	Dodson (1965a)
N. panamensis	Euglossa hemichlora	Bee	Dressler (1966)
N. pentachne	Euglossa cingulata	Bee	Dressler (Pers. Comm.)
N. sp. (aff. barkeri) (Costa Rica)	Euglossa ignita	Bee	Dressler (1966)
	Euglossa hansoni	Bee	Dressler (1966)
	Euglossa sp. (RLD 2)	Bee	Dressler (1966)
	*Euglossa sp. (RLD 117)	Bee	Dressler (1966)
N. xyphorius	Euplusia surinamensis	Bee	Dodson & Frymire (1961b)
N. wulschlegeliana	Euplusia surinamensis	Bee	Dressler & Dodson (Unpubl.)
ODONTOGLOSSUM			
O. grande	Centris sp.	Bee	Dodson (1965a)
O. kegeljani	Bombus hortulans var. robusta	Bee	Dodson (1962a)
ONCIDIUM			
O. hyphaematicum	Centris buchwaldii	Bee	Dodson & Frymire (1961a)
O. lanceanum	Centris sp.	Bee	Dodson (1965a)
O. macranthum	Bombus hortulans var. robusta	Bee	Dodson (1962a)
	Centris sp.	Bee	Dodson (1965a)
O. ochmatochilum	Centris sp.	Bee	Dodson (1965a)
O. onustum	Xylocopa cf. transitoria	Bee	Dodson & Frymire (1961a)
O. planilabre	Centris geminata	Bee	Dodson & Frymire (1961a)
O. stipitatum	Centris sp.	Bee	Dressler (Dodson 1965a)
OPHRYS			
O. apifera	Eucera nigrilabris	Bee	Kullenberg (1961)
	Tetralonia lucasi	Bee	Kullenberg (1961)
	T. sp.	Bee	Kullenberg (1961)
O. araneifera	Andrena nigroaenea	Bee	Kullenberg (1961)
	A. ocatula	Bee	Kullenberg (1961)
	Gorytes mystaceus	Wasp	Kullenberg (1961)
O. bombylifera	Eucera nigrilabris	Bee	Kullenberg (1961)
O. fusca	Andrena trimmerana	Bee	Stebbins and Ferlan (1956)
	Andrena nigroaenea	Bee	Stebbins and Ferlan (1956)
	Andrena fulvicrus	Bee	Stebbins and Ferlan (1956)
O. insectifera	Gorytes mystaceus	Wasp	Kullenberg (1961)
	Gorytes campestris	Wasp	Kullenberg (1961)

ORCHID	POLLINATOR	KIND OF ANIMAL	OBSERVER
O. lutea	Andrena seneciones	Bee	Stebbins and Ferlan (1956)
O. murbeckii	Andrena nigro-olivacea	Bee	Stebbins and Ferlan (1956)
O. muscifera	Gorytes mystaceous	Wasp	Kullenberg (1961)
O. scolopax	Eucera nigrilabris	Bee	Kullenberg (1961)
O. speculum	Trielis ciliata	Wasp	Kullenberg (1961) & Pouyanne (1916)
O. tenthredinifera	Eucera nigrilabris	Bee	Kullenberg (1961) & Schremmer (1961)
	Tetralonia sp.	Bee	Kullenberg (1961) & Schremmer (1961)
ORCHIS[1]			
O. (Leucorchis) albida		Moth	Fritsch (1913)
O. (Traunsteinera) globosa		Butterfly	Godfery (1931)
O. latifolia		Mixed	(In text)
O. maculata		Mixed	(In text)
O. mascula	Bombus muscorum	Bee	Darwin (1877)
	Bombus spp. (4)	Bee	Darwin (1877)
	Apis mellifera	Bee	Darwin (1877)
	Eucera longicornis	Bee	Darwin (1877)
	Osmia rufa	Bee	Darwin (1877)
	Xylocopa violacea	Bee	Darwin (1877)
	Empis livida	Fly	Darwin (1877)
	Empis pennipes	Fly	Darwin (1877)
	Strangalia atra	Beetle	Darwin (1877)
O. militaris	Andrena sp.	Bee	Godfery (1933)
O. morio	Anthophora acervorum	Bee	Evans (1934)
	Apathus rupestris	Bee	Godfery (1918)
O. purpurea	Andrena sp.	Bee	Godfery (1933)
O. (Anacamptis) pyramidalis	Acontia luctuosa	Butterfly	Darwin (1877)
	Caradrina blanda	Moth	Darwin (1877)
	Caradrina alsines	Moth	Darwin (1877)
	Arge galathea	Moth	Darwin (1877)
	Anthrocera filipendulae	Butterfly	Darwin (1877)
	Anthrocera trifolii	Butterfly	Darwin (1877)
	Agrotis cataleuca	Moth	Darwin (1877)
	Eubolia mensuraria	Moth	Darwin (1877)
	Euclidia glyphica	Moth	Darwin (1877)
	Hadena dentina	Moth	Darwin (1877)
	Heliothis marginata	Moth	Darwin (1877)
	Hesperia sylvanus	Skipper	Darwin (1877)
	Hesperia linea	Skipper	Darwin (1877)
	Leucania lithargyria	Moth	Darwin (1877)
	Lithosia complana	Moth	Darwin (1877)
	Lycaena phalaeas	Butterfly	Darwin (1877)
	Melanippe rivaria	Moth	Darwin (1877)
	Polyommatus alexis	Butterfly	Darwin (1877)
	Spilodes palealis	Moth	Darwin (1877)
	Spilodes cinctalis	Moth	Darwin (1877)
	Syrichthus alveolus	Skipper	Darwin (1877)
	Toxocampa pastinum	Moth	Darwin (1877)
	Xylophasia sublustris	Moth	Darwin (1877)
O. spectabilis	Bombus separatus	Bee	Robertson (1928)
	Bombus americanorum	Bee	Robertson (1928)

[1] Many other pollinators of members of this genus have been reported in European literature. We primarily cite the basic observations of Darwin, Müller and Robertson and therefore adhere to their nomenclature here.

ORCHID	POLLINATOR	KIND OF ANIMAL	OBSERVER
ORNITHOCEPHALUS			
O. avicula	Paratetrapedia testacea	Bee	Dodson (1965a)
O. bicornis	Paratetrapedia calcarata	Bee	Dressler (Pers. Comm.)
O. cf. patentilobus	Paratetrapedia testacea	Bee	Dodson (1965a)
O. powellii	Paratetrapedia calcarata	Bee	Dressler (Pers. Comm.)
PAPHINIA			
P. clausula	Euglossa gorgonensis	Bee	Dressler (1966)
(P. cristata var. modiglianiana)	Euglossa hansoni	Bee	Dressler (1966)
	Euglossa asarophora	Bee	Dressler (1966)
	Euglossa orichalcea	Bee	Dressler (1966)

ORCHID	POLLINATOR	KIND OF ANIMAL	OBSERVER
PERISTERIA			
P. elata	Euplusia concava	Bee	Dressler (1966)
	*Euglossa sp. (RLD 96)	Bee	Dressler (1966)
P. pendula	Euglossa ignita	Bee	Dodson (1965a)
	Euglossa mixta	Bee	Dodson (1965a)
	*Eulaema meriana	Bee	Dodson (1965a)
P. sp. (Panama)	Euglossa cordata	Bee	Dressler (1966)
	Euglossa dodsoni	Bee	Dressler (1966)
	Euglossa dressleri	Bee	Dressler (1966)
	Euglossa igniventris	Bee	Dressler (1966)
	Euglossa imperialis	Bee	Dressler (1966)
	Euglossa sp. (RLD 2)	Bee	Dressler (1966)
	Euglossa sp. (RLD 51)	Bee	Dressler (1966)
	Euglossa sp. (RLD 85)	Bee	Dressler (1966)
	Euglossa sp. (RLD 110)	Bee	Dressler (1966)
	Euglossa sp. (RLD 161)	Bee	Dressler (1966)
	Euglossa sp. (RLD 206)	Bee	Dressler (1966)
	Euglossa sp. (RLD 330)	Bee	Dressler (1966)
	*Eulaema nigrifaces	Bee	Dressler (1966)
	*Eulaema nigrita	Bee	Dressler (1966)
	*Eulaema meriana	Bee	Dressler (1966)
	*Euplusia schmidtiana	Bee	Dressler (1966)
PESCATORIA			
P. wallisii	Eulaema polychroma	Bee	Dodson & Frymire (1961a)
PHALAENOPSIS			
P. amabilis	Xylocopa sp.	Bee	Pers. Comm. to L. van der Pijl
PHAJUS			
P. tankervilliae	Xylocopa sp.	Bee	van der Pjil (1954)
PHRAGMOPEDIUM			
P. longifolium var. hartwegii	Chlerogella sp.	Bee	Dodson (1965a)
	Chaenohalictus sp.	Bee	Dodson (1965a)
	Syrphus sp.	Fly	Dodson (1965a)
PLATANTHERA (see also Habenaria)			
P. blumei	Agrotis nigrum	Moth	van Leeuwen (1933)
P. chlorantha	Hadenia sp.	Moth	Darwin (1877)
	Plusia sp.	Moth	Darwin (1877)
	Cuculliagu sp.	Moth	Darwin (1877)
P. ciliaris		Moth	Knuth III
P. fimbriata		Moth	Knuth III
P. suzannae		Moth	Knuth III
PLATYCLINIS			
P. longifolia	Rhynchophours sp.	Beetle	Ridley (1896)
PLEUROTHALLIS			
P. eumecocaulon	Lacodrosophila sp.	Fly	Dodson (1965a)
P. monocardia	Lycoria sp.	Fly	Dodson (1962a)
P. ruscifolia	Lacodrosophila sp.	Fly	Dodson (1965a)
P. xanthochlora	Drosophila sp.	Fly	Dodson (1962a)
PLOCOGLOTTIS			
P. foetida		Fly	Ridley (1896)
POLYCYCNIS			
P. gratiosa	Euglossa sp. (RLD 177)	Bee	Dressler (1966)
PRASOPHYLLUM			
P. archeri	Claviceps flavipes	Fly	Garnet (1940)
	Oscinosoma subpilosa	Fly	Garnet (1940)
P. dispectans	Oscinosoma subpilosa	Fly	Garnet (1940)
P. gracilis	Trogoderma adelaidae	Beetle	Rogers (1913)
P. morrisii	Oscinosoma subpilosa	Fly	Garnet (1940)

ORCHID	POLLINATOR	KIND OF ANIMAL	OBSERVER
P. mülleri	Ametalla spinolae	Beetle	Coleman (1933)
P. nigricans	Oscinosoma subpilosa	Fly	Garnet (1940)
PTEROSTEMMA (reported as unnamed genus)			
P. sp.	Euplusia surinamensis	Bee	Dodson & Frymire (1961b)
PTEROSTYLIS			
P. nutans	Psychodid flies	Fly	Hyett (1960)
P. spindens	Mycetophilid flies	Fly	Sargent (1909)
RODRIGUEZIA			
R. leeana	Euglossa nigropilosa	Bee	Dodson (1965a)
R. secunda	Undet. hummingbird	Bird	Dodson (1965a)
SATYRIUM			
S. pumilum		Fly	Vogel (1954)
S. saxicolum		Fly	Vogel (1954)
SCHLIMIA			
S. trifida	Euplusia cf. purpurata	Bee	Dodson (Unpubl.)
	*Euglossa townsendii	Bee	Dodson (Unpubl.)
SCHOMBURGKIA			
S. crispa (S. moyobambae)	Trigona nigrior	Bee	Dodson (1965a)
S. lyonsii	Xylocopa sp.	Bee	F. Bennett (Pers. Comm.)
S. splendida	Xylocopa lachnea	Bee	Dodson (Unpubl.)
SERAPIAS			
S. cordigera	Ceratina albilabris	Bee	Darwin (1877) Moggridge (1865)
S. sp.	Osmia sp.	Bee	Godfery (1928)
	Anthidium sp.	Bee	Godfery (1928)
SIEVEKINGIA			
S. fimbriata	Euglossa sp. (RLD 117)	Bee	Dressler (1966)
	Euglossa sp. (RLD 120)	Bee	Dressler (1966)
	*Euglossa mixta	Bee	Dressler (1966)
	*Euglossa sp. (RLD 51)	Bee	Dressler (1966)
S. jenmanii	Euglossa nigropilosa	Bee	Dodson (1965a)
S. suavis	Euglossa dodsoni	Bee	Dressler (1966)
	*Euglossa townsendii	Bee	Dressler (1966)
SOBRALIA			
S. amabilis	Pantrope insignis	Bird	Dodson (1965a)
S. decora	Euglossa viridissima	Bee	Dressler (Pers. Comm.)
S. leucoxantha	Eulaema speciosa	Bee	Dodson (1965a)
S. rosea	Bombus morio	Bee	Dodson (1965a)
	Eulaema polyzona	Bee	Dodson (1965a)
	Euplusia ornata	Bee	Dodson (1965a)
S. sessilis	Euglossa cordata	Bee	Ducke (1902)
S. violacea	Bombus morio	Bee	Dodson (1965a)
	Bombus hortulans var. robusta	Bee	Dodson (Unpubl.)
	Xylocopa frontalis	Bee	Dodson (1962a)
	Xylocopa cf. transitoria	Bee	Dodson (1965a)
	Euplusia surinamensis	Bee	Dodson (1962a)
	Eulaema cingulata	Bee	Dodson (1962a)
	Eulaema polychroma	Bee	Dodson (1962a)
	Eulaema speciosa	Bee	Dodson (1965a)
	Epicharis rustica	Bee	Dodson (1965a)
S. aff. weberbaueriana	Eulaema polychroma	Bee	Dodson (Unpubl.)
SPIRANTHES			
S. autumnalis	Bombus sp. (not confirmed)	Bee	Darwin (1877)
S. gracilis	Bombus americanorum	Bee	Robertson (1928)
	Megachile brevis	Bee	Robertson (1928)
	Calliopsis andreniformis	Bee	Robertson (1928)
S. romanzoffiana	Halictus sp.	Bee	Godfery (1933)
	Chlorhalictus sp.	Bee	Godfery (1933)

ORCHID	POLLINATOR	KIND OF ANIMAL	OBSERVER
S. sinensis	Halictus sp.	Bee	Coleman (1934a)
STANHOPEA			
S. candida (S. randii)	Englossa ignita	Bee	Dodson (1965a)
	Eulaema meriana	Bee	Dodson (1965a)
S. cirrhata	Euglossa cf. ignita	Bee	Dressler (1966)
S. connata	Eulaema speciosa	Bee	Dodson (1965a)
	*Euglossa nigropilosa	Bee	Dodson (1965a)
S. costaricensis	Eulaema seabrae	Bee	Dodson (1965a)
S. ecornuta	Euglossa nigropilosa	Bee	Dodson (1965a)
	*Eulaema meriana	Bee	Dodson (1965a)
S. florida	Euplusia schmidtiana	Bee	Dressler (1966)
	Eulaema seabrae	Bee	Dodson (Unpubl.)
	*Eulaema nigrita	Bee	Dressler (1966)
S. gibbosa	Eulaema meriana	Bee	Dodson (1965a)
S. grandiflora	Eulaema meriana	Bee	Dressler (Pers. Comm.)
	Euglossa ignita	Bee	Ducke (1902)
S. aff. jenishiana	Eulaema bomboides	Bee	Dodson & Frymire (1961a)
S. oculata	Eulaema cingulata	Bee	Heller (Pers. Comm.)
S. reichenbachiana	Eulaema leucopyga	Bee	Dodson (Unpubl.)
S. saccata	Euglossa viridissima	Bee	Dressler, Schwartz, Pollard (Pers. Comm.)
S. tigrina	Euglossa viridissima	Bee	Friese (1899)
S. tricornis	Eulaema meriana	Bee	Dodson & Frymire (1961a)
S. wardii	Eulaema polychroma	Bee	Dodson (1965a)
S. warscewicziana	Euplusia macroglossa	Bee	Dodson (1965a)
STELIS			
S. aemula	Bradysia sp. (Sciaridae)	Fly	Dodson (Unpubl.)
S. sp.		Fly	Dodson (1965a)
TRICHOCENTRUM			
T. panamensis	Euglossa cordata	Bee	Dressler (Pers. Comm.)
T. tigrinum	Eulaema cingulata	Bee	Dodson (1962a)
TRICHOCEROS			
T. antennifera	Paragymnomma sp.	Fly	Dodson (1962a)
TRICHOPILIA			
T. rostrata	Euglossa hemichlora	Bee	Dodson (1962a)
TRIGONIDIUM			
T. obtusum	Trigona droryana	Bee	Kerr & Lopez (1963)
VANDA			
V. teres	Xylocopa latipes	Bee	van der Pijl (1954)
V. tricolor	Xylocopa sp.	Bee	Holttum (1953)
VANILLA			
V. planifolia	Melipona beechii	Bee	(Assumed in literature without author)
XYLOBIUM			
X. latilabium	Trigona amalthea	Bee	Dodson (1965a)
X. variegatum	Trigona cf. amalthea	Bee	Dodson (Unpubl.)
ZYGOPETALUM			
Z. rhombilabium	Eulaema cingulata	Bee	Dodson (1965a)
ZYGOSEPALUM			
Z. labiosum	Eulaema meriana	Bee	Dressler (Pers. Comm.)

LITERATURE CITED

Akamine, E. 1963. Ethylene production in fading Vanda orchid blossoms. Science 143: 1217-1218.
Allen, P. A. 1951. Pollination of Coryanthes speciosa. American Orch. Soc. Bull. 19: 528.
———. 1952. The swan orchids, a revision of the genus Cycnoches. Orch. Journ. 1: 226.
———. 1954. Pollination in Gongora maculata. Ceiba 4: 121-124.
Ames, O. 1937. Pollination of orchids through pseudocopulation. Bot. Mus. Leafl. Harv. Univ. 51: 1-30.
———. 1938. Resupination as a diagnostic character in the Orchidaceae. Bot. Mus. Leafl. Harv. Univ. 6: 145-183.
Anderson, E. 1953. Introgressive Hybridization. Biol. Rev. 28: 280-307.
Beck, G. 1912. Die Futterschuppen der Blüten von Vanilla planifolia. Sitz. Ber. K. Akad. Wiss. Wien. M-N. Kl. 121: 509-521.
———. 1914. Die Pollennachahmung in den Blüten der Orchideen-Gattung Eria. Sitz. Ber. Akad. Wiss. Wien. M-N. Kl. 123: 1033-1046.
Bernard, N. 1909. l'Evolution dans la symbiose. Ann. Sci. Nat. 9^9: 1-196.
Bolus, H. 1893. Icones Orchidacearum Austro-africanarum Extratropicum. Vol. 1. pt. 1. London.
Burkill, I. H. 1919. Some notes on the pollination of flowers in the Botanic Gardens, Singapore, and other parts of the Malay Peninsula. Str. Sett. Gard. Bull. Singapore 2: 165-176.
Coleman, E. 1927. Pollination of the orchid Cryptostylis leptochila. Vict. Nat. 44: 20-22.
———. 1928. Pollination of Cryptostylis leptochila. Vict. Nat. 44: 333-340.
———. 1929a. Pollination of an Australian orchid, Cryptostylis leptochila. Journ. Bot. 67: 97-00.
———. 1929b. Pollination of Cryptostylis subulata (Labill) Rchb. f. Vict. Nat. 46: 62-66.
———. 1930a. Pollination of some West Australian orchids. Vict. Nat. 46: 203-206.
———. 1930b. Pollination of Cryptostylis erecta R. Br. Vict. Nat. 46: 236-238.
———. 1932. Pollination of Diuris pedunculata. Vict. Nat. 49: 179-186.
———. 1933. Pollination of orchids genus Prasophyllum. Vict. Nat. 49: 214-221.
———. 1934a Further notes on the pollination of Spiranthes sinensis. Vict. Nat. 50: 61-64.
———. 1934b. Pollination of Peterostylis acuminata and P. falcata. Vict. Nat. 50: 248-252.
———. 1937. Pollination of Prasophyllum parviflorum. Vict. Nat. 51: 101-107.

Correvon, H. and A. Pouyanne. 1916. Un curieux cas de mimétisme chez les Ophrydées. Journ. Soc. Nat. d'Hortic. de France 4^{17}: 29-31, 41-42.

Crüger, H. 1865. A few notes on the fecundation of orchids and their morphology. Jour. Linn. Soc. London, Bot. 8: 129-135.

Darwin, C. 1862 and 1877. The fertilisation of orchids by insects. 1st and 2nd ed. London.

Daumann, E. 1941. Die anbohrbaren Gewebe und rudimentären Nektarien in der Blütenregion. Beitr. Bot. Centr. bl. 61: 11-82.

Delpino, F. 1873. Ulteriori Osservasione, etc. Atti Soc. Ital. Sci. 16: 200-.

Dexter, J. S. 1913. Mosquitos pollinating orchids. Science II: 37-867.

Dodson, C. H. 1957. Studies in Oncidium: III, Chromosome numbers in Oncidium and allied genera. American Orch. Soc. Bull. 26: 323-330.

—————. 1962a. The importance of pollination in the evolution of the orchids of tropical America. American Orch. Soc. Bull. 31: 525-534, 641-649, 731-735.

—————. 1962b. Pollination and variation in the subtribe Catasetinae. Ann. Missouri Bot. Gard. 49: 35-56.

—————. 1965a. Agentes de polinización y su influencia sobre la evolución en la familia Orquidacea. Univ. Nac. Amazonia Peruana.

—————. 1965b. Studies in orchid pollination: The genus Coryanthes. American Orch. Soc. Bull. 34: 680-687.

—————. 1966a. Studies in orchid pollination: Cypripedium, Phragmopedium and their allies. American Orch. Soc. Bull. 35: 125-128.

—————. 1966b. Studies in orchid pollination: the genus Anguloa. American Orch. Soc Bull. 35: 624-627.

—————. 1966c. Ethology of some Euglossine Bees. Journ. Kansas Ent. Soc. XX: mss.

Dodson, C. H. and G. P. Frymire. 1961a. Preliminary studies in the genus Stanhopea. Ann. Missouri Bot. Gard. 48: 137-172.

—————. 1961b. Natural pollination of orchids. Missouri Bot. Gard. Bull. 49: 133-139.

Dodson, C. H. and H. G. Hills. 1966. Gas chromatography of orchid fragrances. American Orch. Soc. Bull. 35: 720-725.

Dressler, R. L. 1960a. Nomenclatural notes on the Orchidaceae I. Taxon 9^7: 213-214.

—————. 1960b. On the evolution of the Orchidaceae. American Orch. Soc. Bull. 29: 759-760.

—————. 1966. Observations on orchids and euglossine bees in Panama and Costa Rica. Mss. (in press).

Dressler, R. L. and C. H. Dodson. 1960. Classification and phylogeny in the Orchidaceae. Ann. Missouri Bot. Gard. 47: 25-68.

Ducke, A. 1902. As especies Paraenses do gênero Euglossa Latr. Bol. Mus. Paranense 3: 1-19.

Duncan, R. E. and C. K. Schubert. 1947. Dislodgement of anthers in Cymbidium. American Orch. Soc. Bull. 16: 208-210.

Evans, 1934. (Letter to Poulton read at Entomological Society of London meeting.) Proc. R. Ent. Soc. 9: 82-83.

Faegri, K. and L. van der Pijl. 1966. Principles of pollination ecology. Pergamon.

Fordham, F. 1946. Pollination of Calochilus campestris. Vict. Nat. 62: 199-201.

Friese, K. 1899. Monographie der Bienengattung Euglossa. Termeszetrajzi Fuzetek 22: 136.

Frisch, K. von. 1947. Duftgelenkte Bienen im Dienste der Landwirtschaft und Gärtnerei. Springer—Wien.

—————. 1962. Dialects in the language of bees. Sci. Amer. 207^2: 78-87.

Fritsch, K. 1933. Beobachtungen über blütenbesuchende Insekten in Steirmark, 1913. Sitzungsber. Akad. Wien I, 142: 19-40.

Garay, L. A. 1960. On the origin of the Orchidaceae. Bot. Mus. Leafl. Harv. Univ. 19: 57-96.

Garnet, J. R. 1940. Observations on the pollination of orchids. Vict. Nat. 56: 191-197.

Gellert, M. 1923. Anatomische Studien über den Bau der Orchideenblüte. Fedde Rep. Beih. 25: 1-65.

Ghose, H. V. 1955. Wirtschaftliche und giftige Orchideen. Die Orchidee. 6: 53-55.

Gilbert, P. A. 1958. Denrobium linguiforme Sw.—Australian Dendrobiums. American Orch. Soc. Bull. 27: 472-475.

Godfery, M. J. 1918. Notes on Orchis mascula and O. morio. Journ. Bot. 56: 193-197.

—————. 1922. Notes on the fertilization of orchids. Journ. Bot. 60: 359-361.

—————. 1927. Natural orchid hybrids. Genetica. 9: 19-38.

—————. 1928. Letters to Poulton. Proc. R. Entom. Soc. London 3: 36, 60.

———. 1931. The pollination of Coeloglossum, Nigritella, Serapias, etc. Journ. Bot. 59: 129-130.
———. 1933. Monograph and Iconograph of native British orchids. Cambridge Univ.
Goebel, K. 1920. Die Entfaltungsbewegungen der Pflanzen. Jena.
Good, R. 1956. Features of evolution in the flowering plants. Longmans, London—N.Y.
Grant, V. 1949. Pollination systems as isolating mechanisms in Angiosperms. Evolution 3: 82-97.
———. 1950. The protection of ovules in flowering plants. Evolution 4: 179-201.
———. 1961. The diversity of pollination systems in the phlox family. Recent Advances in Botany. Univ. Toronto press.
———. 1963. Origin of Adaptations. Columbia Univ.
Gray, A. 1862-63. Fertilization of orchids. American Jour. Sci. 34: 420-429, 36: 292-294.
Guttenberg, H. 1915. Anatomisch-physiologische Studien an den Blüten von Catasetum und Cycnoches. Jahrb. wiss. Bot. 56: 374-415.
———. 1928. Studien an den Blüten Orchideen—Gattung Mormodes. Jahrb. wiss. Bot. 68: 135-148.
———. 1959. Encyclopedia of plant physiology. Springer, Berlin.
Hagerup, O. 1947. The spontaneous formation of haploid, polyploid and aneuploid embryos in some orchids. K. Dansk. Vid. Selsk. Biol. Med. 20: No. 15.
———. 1951. Pollination in the Faroes—in spite of rain and poverty of insects. K. Dansk. Vid. Selsk. Biol. Med. 18, No. 15.
Heimans, E. and J. P. Thysse. 1907. In de Duinen. Amsterdam.
Heslop-Harrison, J. 1955. Orchid hybrids in North Down. Irish Naturl. Journ. 11: 1-4.
Hildebrand, F. 1865. Bastardierungsversuche an Orchideen. Bot. Ztschr. 23: 245-249.
Hoehne, F. C. 1933. Contribuiçao para o conhecimento do gênero Catasetum especialmente hermaphroditismo e trimorphismo das suas flores. Bol. Agric. Brazil 133-196.
Holttum, R. E. 1949. Gregarious flowering of the terrestrial orchid Bromheadia finlaysoniana. Gdns. Bull. Singapore. 12: 295-302.
———. 1953. A revised flora of Malaya, I. Orchids. Gvt. Pr. Singapore.
Hurst, C. C. 1896. Notes on some curiosities of orchid breeding. Jour. Roy. Hort. Soc. 21: 442-486.
———. 1925. Experiments in genetics. Cambridge Univ. Press.
Hyett, J. 1960. Pollination of the nodding greenhood. Vict. Nat. 76: 240-241.
Isle, D. 1928. Über den Farbensinn der Tagfalter. Z. vergl. Physiol. 8.
Janse, J. M. 1886. Imitierte Pollenkörner bei Maxillaria spec. Ber. D. Bot. Ges. 4: 227-283.
Jost, L. 1929. Über die Blüte von Mormodes. Ber. D. Bot. Ges. 47: 515-522.
Keller, G. and R. van Soo. 1930-1940. Monographie der Orchideen Europas und des Mittelmeergebietes. II Fedde Rep. Spec. Nov.
Kerr, W. E. and C. R. Lopez. 1963. Biologia da reproduçao de Trigona (Plebeia) Droryana F. Smith. Rev. Brasil Biol. 22: 335-341.
Kirchner, O. von. 1922. Über Selbstbestäubung bei den Orchideen. Flora 115: 103-129.
———. 1952. Über die sogenannten Pollenblumen und die Ausbeutestoffe der Blüten. Flora 118/119: 312-330.
Knoll, F. 1858. Über den Schleudervorgang der männlichen Catasetum-Blüte. Berichte D. Bot. Ges. 71: 337-348.
Knuth, P. and E. Loew. 1898-1905. Handbuch der Blütenbiologie, I-III Leipzig. (English translation—Handbook of flower pollination. Oxford 1906).
Kränzlin, F. 1910. Orchidaceae in Das Pflanzenreich IV.
Kullenberg, B. 1956. Field experiments with chemical sexual attractants on aculeate Hymenoptera males. Zool. Bidrag. Upsala 31: 253-352.
———. 1961. Studies in Ophrys pollination. Almquist-Upsala.
Laibach, F. 1930. Untersuchungen über die Postfloration tropischer Orchideen. Planta 9: 341-387.
Lankester, C. H. 1960. A reminiscence and its cause. Orch. Rev. 68: 354.
Leavitt, R. 1901. Notes on the embryology of some New England Orchids. Rhodora 3: 61-63, 202-205.
Leeuwen, W. W. Docters van. 1933. Biology of plants and animals occurring in the higher parts of Mount Panggrango-Gedeh in West-Java. Verh. K. Akad. Wet. Amsterdam 2: No. 31.
———. 1937. The biology of Epipogium roseum. Blumea Suppl. I: 57-65.

Linsley, E. G. 1958. The ecology of solitary bees. Hilgardia 27: 543-599.

Mansfeld, R. 1954. Über die Verteilung der Merkmale innerhalb der Orchidaceae-Monandrae. Flora 142: 65-80.

Martens, L. 1926. L'Autogamie chez l'Orchis et chez quelques autres Orchidées. Bull. Soc. R. Bot. Belg. 59: 69-88.

———. 1928. A propos de la pollination de l'Epipactis. Bull. Soc. Bot. Belg. 50: 109-111.

Mayr, E. 1963. Animal species and evolution. Harvard Univ. Press.

Michener, C. 1954. Bees of Panama. Bull. American Mus. Nat. Hist. 104: 1-175.

Moggridge, J. T. 1865. Observations on some orchids of the south of France. Journ. Linn. Soc. London 8: 256-258.

Molisch, H. 1930. Neues über die Orchideenblüte. Ztschr. f. Bot. 22: 593-605.

Moure, J. S. 1950. Contribuiçao para o conhecimento do gênero Eulaema Lepeletier (Hymen.-Apoidea). Dusenia 1: 181-200.

Müller, F. 1868. Über Befruchtungserscheinungen bei Orchideen. Bot. Ztschr. 26: 629-631.

Müller, H. 1873. Die Befruchtung der Blumen durch Insekten. Englemann-Leipzig.

———. 1881. Die Alpenblumen. Leipzig.

———. 1883. The fertilization of flowers (English translation). MacMillan, London.

Muntzing, A. 1930a. Outlines to a genetic monograph of Galeopsis. Hereditas 13: 185-341.

———. 1930b. Über Chromosomenvermehrung in Galeopsis—Kreuzungen und ihre phylogenetische Bedeutung. Heredits 14: 153-172.

Nagahuru, U. 1935. Genome analysis in Brassica with special reference to the experimental formation of B. napus and peculiar mode of fertilization. Japanese Journ. Bot. 7: 389-452.

Nelsson, E. 1954. Gesetzmässigkeiten der Gestaltwandlung im Blütenbereich. Chernex-Montreux.

Nuernberg, E. L. 1956. Gibt es bei Orchideen einen Photoperiodismus? Die Orchideen 7: 13-16.

Oliver, F. W. 1888. On the sensitive labellum of Masdevallia muscosa. Ann. Bot. 1: 237-253.

Pearson, J. F. W. 1933. Studies on the ecological relations of bees in the Chicago region. Ecol. Monogr. 3: 373-442.

Percival, W. S. 1965. Floral Biology. Pergamon, London/New York.

Pfitzer, E. 1906. On the phylogeny of orchids. Rep. 3rd Int. Conf. Genetics Ed. Hortic. Soc. 476-481. London.

Pijl, L. van der. 1954. Xylocopa and flowers in the tropics, I, II, III. Proc. K. Ned Akad. Wet. Amsterd. C 57: 413-424, 541-562.

———. 1955. Some remarks on myrmecophytes. Phytomorph. 5: 190-199.

———. 1960/61. Ecological aspects of flower evolution, I, II. Evloution. 24: 403-416. 25: 44-59.

Pohl, F. 1927. Die anatomischen Grundlagen für die Gleitfallenfunktion von Stanhopea tigrina and S. oculata. Jahrb. f. Wiss. Bot. 66: 556-577.

———. 1935. Zwei Bulbophyllum Arten mit besonders bemerkungswert gebauten Gleit- und Klemmfallenblumen. Beih. Bot. Centr. bl. 53: 501-518.

Popov, V. V. 1956. Bees, their relations to melitophilous plants and the problems of the alfalfa pollination. Abstracted from Rev. Ent. USSR. 35: 582-598.

Porter, E. W. 1896. Note on the pollination of Epipactis viridiflora. Bot. Gaz. 22: 250.

Porsch, O. 1905. Beiträge zur "histologischen" Blütenbiologie, I. Österr. Bot. Ztschr. 55: 165-173, 227-235, 253-260.

———. 1906a. Beiträge zur "histologischen" Blütenbiologie, II. id. 56: 41-47, 83-95, 125-143, 176-185.

———. 1906b. Orchidaceae in Erg. Bot. Exped. K. Akad. nach Süd Brasilien, I. Wien

———. 1908. Neuere Untersuchungen über die Insektenanlockungsmittel der Orchideenblüte. Mitteilungen Naturw. Ver. Steierm. 45: 346-370.

———. 1926. Vogelblütige Orchideen I. Biol. Gener. 2: 107-136.

———. 1955. Zur Biologie der Cataseum-Blüte. Österr. Bot. Ztschr. 102: 117-157.

Rayment, T. 1932. Two orchids and a bee. Vict. Nat. 49: 140.

Richards, O. W. 1931. Insects fertilizing Orchis maculata L. near Oxford. Proc. R. Ent. Soc. London, A. 6: 59.

Ridley, H. N. 1890a. The genus Bromheadia. Linn. Journ. 28: 331-339.

———. 1890b. On the method of fertilization in Bulbophyllum macranthum and allied orchids. Ann. Bot. 4: 327-336.
———. 1896. Orchideae and Apostasiaceae of the Malay Peninsula. Journ. Linn. Soc. Bot. 32: 213-416.
———. 1905. On the fertilization of Grammatophyllum. Roy. Asiatic Soc. Str. Br. 44: 228-229.
Robertson, C. 1887. Fertilization of Calopogon parviflorus. Bot. Gaz. 12: 288-291.
———. 1893. Flowers and insects X. Bot. Gaz. 18: 47-54.
———. 1928. Flowers and Insects. List of visitors to 453 flowers. Carlinville, Ill.
Rogers, R. S. 1931. Pollination of Caladenia deformis. Trans. Roy. Soc. S. Australia 55: 143-146.
Rohrbach, P. 1866. Über den Blütenbau und die Befruchtung von Epipogium gmelini. Preisschrift. Göttingen.
Rolfe, R. A. 1887. The genus Cryptophoranthus or window bearing orchids. Gard. Chron. 692-693.
———. 1909-1912. The evolution of the Orchidaceae. Orch. Rev. 17-20.
———. 1910. The bee-orchis. Orch. Rev. 10: 261.
Ruschi, A. 1949. A Polinizaçao realizada pelo Trocholideos, a sua area de alimentaçao e a repovoamento. Bol. Mus. Biol. Sta. Teresa 2: 1-51.
Sargent, O. H. 1907. Pollination of Caladenia barbarossae. Journ. Nat. Hist. Soc. W. Australia. 4: 6.
———. 1909. Notes on the life-history of Pterostylis. Ann. Bot. 23: 265-274.
———. 1918. Fragments on the flower biology of West Australian plants. Ann. Bot. 33: 215-231.
———. 1934. Pollination in Pterostylis. Vict. Nat. 51: 82.
Schlechter, H. 1927. Die Orchideen (2nd ed.) Parey, Berlin.
Schmid, G. 1912. Zur Ökologie der Blüte von Himantoglossum. Berlin. Deuts. Bot. Ges. 30: 464-469.
Schremmer, F. 1961. Bemerkenswerte Wechselbeziehungen zwischen Orchideenblüten und Insekten. Natur und Volk 91: 52-61.
Scott, J. 1864. On the individual sterility and cross-impregnation of certain species of Oncidium. Journ. Linn. Soc. 8: 162.
Silen, F. 1906a. Blombiologisk iakttagelser i Killila Lappmark. Meddel. Soc. pro Fauna et Flora Fenn. 31: 80-99.
———. 1906b. Blombiologisk iakttagelser i sodra Finland. l.c. 32: 120-139.
Slade, H. 1962. Some attractive Dendrobiums from New Guinea. American Orch. Soc. Bull. 31: 993-996.
Smith, J. J. 1925. Ephemeral orchids. Ann. Jard. Bot. Buitenzorg 35: 50-70.
Sprague, E. 1962. Pollination and evolution in Pedicularis (Scrophulariaceae) Aliso 5: 181-209.
Sprengel, C. 1793. Das entdeckte Geheimnis der Natur.
Stebbins, G. L. 1951. Variation and evolution in plants. Columbia, N.Y.
Stebbins, G. L. and L. Ferlan. 1956. Population variability, hybridization and introgression in some species of Ophrys. Evolution 10: 32-46.
Steiner, G. 1948. Fallenversuche zur Kennzeichnung des Verhaltens von Schmeissfliegen. Ztschr. Vergl. Physiol. 31: 1-38.
Straw, R. W. 1955. Hybridization, homogamy and sympatric speciation. Evolution 9: 441-444.
———. 1956. Adaptive morphology of the Penstemon flower. Phytomorph. 6: 112-119.
Suessenguth, K. 1923. Über Pseudogamie bei Zygopetalum mackayi. Ber. D. Bot. Ges. 41: 16-23.
Thomson, G. M. 1927. The pollination of New Zealand flowers by birds and insects. Trans. Proc. New Zealand Inst. 57: 106-125.
Troll, W. 1928. Organisation und Gestalt im Bereich der Blüte. Springer, Berlin.
Vogel, G. 1958. Verhaltungsphysiologische Untersuchungen über den Weibchenbesprung des Stubenfliegen-Männchens. Ztschr. Tierpsychol. 14: 309-323.
Vogel, S. 1954. Blütenbiologische Typen als Elemente der Sippengliederung. Fischer, Jena.
———. 1959. Organographie der Blüten Kapländischer Ophrydeen I, II. Abh. Math-Nat. Kl. Ak. Wiss. Mainz. 6, 7.
———. 1962. Duftdrüsen im Dienste der Bestäubung, über Bau und Funktion der Osmophoren 10: 601-763.

———. 1963. Das sexuelle Anlockungsprinzip der Catasetinen- und Stanhopeen-Blüte und die wahre Funktion ihres sogenannten Futtergewebes. Österr. Bot. Zeitschr. 110: 308-337.

Vries. J. F. de. 1953. On the flowering of Phalaenopsis schillerianum. Ann. Bogor. 1: 61-76.

Watson, I. M. 1961. Tongue-orchids and ichneumonids. Vict. Nat. 78: 32-35.

Werth, E. 1911. Das Perzeptionsorgan der Pterostylisblüte. Ber. D. Bot. Ges. 31: 728-738.

———. 1956. Bau und Leben der Blumen. Enke, Stuttgart.

Winkler, H. 1906. Über den Blütendimorphismus von Rhenanthera lowii. Ann. Jard. Bot Buitenzorg 20: 1-12.

Withner, C. L. 1959. The orchids. Ronald.

Ziegenspeck, H. 1928. Orchidaceae, in Kirchner-Loew-Schroeter, Lebensgeschichte der Blütenpflanzen M.-Europas. Stuttgart.

GLOSSARY

ABDOMEN. In insects, the posterior division of the body.
ACROTONY. Pollinia united at their apex with the rostellum.
ADAPTATION. The process by which an organism becomes fitted to its environment; a structure or habit fitted for some special circumstance.
AGGREGATION. Gathering of organs (or complete flowers) into a cluster.
ALLOGAMY. Cross-fertilization.
ALLOPOLYPLOIDY. More than two sets of chromosomes derived from different species by hybridization.
ANEMOPHILY. Plant pollination by agency of wind.
ANTENNAE. Slender appendages on each side of the column of some species of Catasetum; the "trigger" which sets off the pollen throwing mechanism (sometimes called a cirrhus).
ANTHER. The pollen bearing structure of a flower (see also stamen).
ANTHESIS. Stage at which a flowerbud opens.
APOGAMY. Reproduction without intervention of male cells.
APOMIXIS. Reproduction and development from unfertilized egg cells or other cells.
APPENDICLE. A term used by older authors equivalent to the caudicle.
AURICLE. A small lateral outgrowth on the column of Habenaria and allied genera, possibly a sterile anther.
AUTOGAMY. Self-pollinating, without the aid of insects or other pollinating agents (see also cleistogamous).
BASITONY. Pollinia united at their base with rostellum.
BLADE. The expanded part of a leaf or petal.
BRACT. A small, leaf-life or scale-like structure at the base of the flower (below the pedicel in orchids).
BURSICLE. A sac-like covering over the viscidium in some genera of the Habenaria group.
CALLUS. A crest or fleshy outgrowth of the lip, as in many species of Oncidium and its allies.
CANTHAROPHILY. Pollination by beetles.
CARPEL. A leaf-like structure which bears the ovules and seeds.
CAUDICLE. A portion of the pollinium which is usually slender and is composed of viscin with some pollen grains; often confused with the stipe (also occasionally called the appendage).
CHEMORECEPTION. Detection of a chemical stimulus usually through special organs (chemoreceptors).

CLAW. The narrow basal portion of a lip or petal.
CLEISTOGAMY. Where flowers are self-pollinated without opening; a form of autogamy.
COLUMN. The central portion of the orchid flower, which is formed by the partial or complete union of the male and female parts (stamens and styles). (Also called gynandrium, gynostegium or gynostemium.)
COLUMN FOOT. A ventral extension of the the base of the column which has the lip attached at its tip.
COLUMN WING. A lateral projection on each side of the column, as in Oncidium; these may represent sterile anthers.
CONNATION. United or joined parts of leaves, sepals or petals, etc., said of like structures.
CONSTANCY. Behavior of pollinating agents in which particular kinds of flowers are constantly visited on a learned basis for a short period.
CO-POLLINATOR. Where more than one kind of pollinator acts effectively in the pollination of a plant.
CORYMB. A broad, flat-topped indeterminate inflorescence with the outer flowers opening first.
CUTICLE. Outer covering over cells of epidermis.
DEHISCENCE. The spontaneous opening of an organ or structure along certain lines or in a definite direction.
DIANDRAE. The group of orchids having two fertile anthers; the Cypripedium alliance.
DICHOGAMY. Maturing of sexual elements at different times ensuring cross-pollination.
DICLINY. Stamens and pistil in separate flowers.
DIMORPHY. Having two different forms.
DORSAL. Referring to the upper side.
DORSUM. The back or upper surface of an animal.
DYSTROPHIC. Feeding which results in damage to the flower without pollination resulting.
EGG CELL. The female gamete which develops into the embryo.
EMBRYO. A young organism in early stages of development.
ENDOSPERM. The nutritive tissue of certain seeds.
EPHEMERAL. Short-lived plant or flower.
EPICHILE. The terminal portion of the lip in Stanhopea and related genera.
EXTRA-FLORAL NECTARIES. Nectaries produced outside the flowers or on bracts or leaves.
FALSE NECTARIES. Structures simulating nectaries, which do not secrete nectar, or simply color spots simulating nectaries.
FIDELITY. An extension of constancy where the pollinator visits many different flowers in its rounds but is especially attracted to certain narrowly adapted types.
FILAMENT. The slender, sterile portion of the stamen which bears the anther, forming a part of the column in the orchid flower.
FLAG-TYPE LABELLUM. A broad showy labellum held erect.
FRENICLE. A fold of the caudicle supposed by some authors to be of tapetal origin.
FRONS. Forehead or comparable structure in insects.
GALEA. A helmet-shaped petal or combination of tepals.
GAMETES. Sex cells.
GENOME. The normal haploid set of chromosomes of an organism.
GENOTYPE. Genetic constitution of an individual; group of individuals which have the same genetic constitution.
GULLET-TYPE. Attractive parts of the flower divided into upper and lower lips. In orchids a spacious tubular lip.
GYNOECIUM. The female organs of a flower.
HERKOGAMY. A condition in which self-fertilization is impossible due to spatial separation.
HETERANTHY. Having different types of flowers produced on the same inflorescence.
HETEROSTYLY. Having unlike or unequal styles.
HETEROTROPHY. Receiving nourishment from organic substances.
HYDROPHILY. Pollinated through the agency of water.
HYPOCHILE. Basal portion of the lip in Stanhopea and allied genera.
INTROGRESSION. Passing of genetic material from one population to another through hybridization (also called Introgressive Hybridization).
INTRORSE. Turned inward or toward the axis.

ISTHMUS. The narrow middle portion of the lip in orchids which have a wide gap between the lateral lobes and the mid-lobe.
KETTLE-FLOWER. A flower in which the perianth is swollen at the base to form a kettle-shaped cavity, often employed in trap-flowers.
LABELLUM. A petal formed into a lip.
LAMINA. The broad flattened portion of a lip, petal or leaf.
LANTERN-TYPE FLOWER. A flower with the apices of the petals or sepals joined, leaving only narrow slits for entrance of the pollinator.
LARVA. A development phase which becomes self-sustaining and independent before it has assumed the characteristic features of the adult; in the larval stage.
LATERAL. To either side of a vertical line drawn through the center of the flower, as in "lateral sepal."
LIMB. The flat expanded portion of the lip, as opposed to the throat or claw.
LIP. One of the three petals which is usually larger and differently shaped than the other two (also called the labellum).
MELITTOPHILY. Bee-pollination.
MENTUM. A chin-like extension at the base of the flower associated with the column foot.
MESOCHILE. The middle portion of the lip in Stanhopea and related genera.
METATHORAX. Posterior segment of the thorax of an insect.
MIMICRY. An adaptation leading to a close external resemblance, for imitation or simulation, in order to serve for protection or deception.
MONANDRAE. The group of orchids having only one anther.
MONOPHILOUS. A flower which attracts only one kind of pollinator.
MONOTROPIC. A pollinator which visits only one kind of flower for its subsistence.
MYCOTROPHY. Symbiotic relationship between plants and fungi.
MYOPHILY. Fly-pollination (also spelled Myiophily).
NECTAR-GUIDE. Markings or structures on petals or lip of a flower which lead the pollinator to the nectar or to the center of the flower.
NECTARIES. Nectar producing structures.
NECTAR-TUBE. Tube derived from the sepals, petals or lip which leads to the nectar (in many orchids no nectar is produced in the nectar-tube).
NOTOTRIBY. Flowers which have the anthers arranged so as to deposit pollen on the back of the pollinator.
NYCTINASTY. Movement at night.
OLIGOTROPIC. A pollinator which visits only related kinds of plants.
ORNITHOPHILY. Bird-pollination.
ORTHOGENIC. Evolution in a definite direction conditioned internally.
OSCILLATORS. Appendages such as hairs which move in the breeze and attract certain kinds of pollinators.
OSMOPHORE. Specialized odor secreting organs located in sepals, petals or lip.
OUTCROSS. A cross to an individual of a different strain, variety or type.
OVARY. The part of the flower which develops into the fruit.
OVIPOSITOR. A specialized structure in female insects for placing eggs.
OVULE. The structure which develops into the seed.
PANICLE. A branched inflorescence.
PARTHENOGENETIC. Plants developed from egg cell without fertilization by pollen.
PEDICEL. The stem which supports an individual flower, usually jointed at the base. (This word has also been used to designate the stipe of the pollinarium.)
PEDUNCLE. The stem of an inflorescence or solitary flower.
PERIANTH. A collective term for sepals and petals or tepals.
PERIODICITY. The fulfillment of functions at regular intervals.
PETAL. Colored, leaf-like flower parts, forming part of a corolla.
PHALAENOPHILY. Moth-pollination.
PHOTONASTY. Response to variation in illumination.
PISTIL. The female or seed-bearing element of a flower, composed of one or more carpels, usually divided into ovary, style and stigma.
PISTILLATE. Bearing pistils or female reproductive organs.

PLACENTA. Ovule-bearing part of the carpel.

PLOIDY-BARRIER. Barrier to hybridization resulting from the incompatibility of quantitatively different genome levels.

POLLEN. One-celled spores borne in the anthers; these develop the male gametes or sperm nuclei.

POLLEN-TUBE. A tubular process developed from pollen grains after attachment to the stigma and growing towards the ovule; represents part of the male gametophyte.

POLLINARIUM. The complete set of pollinia with associated parts, such as viscidium and stipe, if present.

POLLINIA. Compact masses of pollen in the orchids and asclepiads; the anther may contain 2-12 pollinia.

POLLINATION MECHANISM. Morphological arrangements in flowers which guide the pollinator to deposit the pollen properly; often acting to exclude certain potential pollinators.

POLLINATION SPECTRUM: The total kinds of pollinators to which a group of plants has become adapted and their relative frequency.

POLYPHYLETIC. Having origin from several lines of descent.

POLYTROPIC. A pollinator which visits many kinds of plants.

PROBOSCIS. In insects, the development of the mouthparts into a tube for sucking.

PROMISCUITY. Pollination by many kinds of agents.

PROTANDROUS. Where male elements of the flower mature or are shed before female elements reach maturity.

PROTHORAX. Anterior segment of the thorax of an insect.

PSEUDOANTAGONISM. Where flowers achieve pollination by deceiving male insects actively defending their territories through imitation of other flying insects.

PSEUDOCOPULATION. A situation where male insects are attracted to a flower on the basis of sexual instincts and attempt to copulate with the flower.

PSEUDOPARASITISM. Where parasitic flies and wasps are deceived and lay eggs on a flower, believing it to be the normal prey.

PSEUDOPOLLEN. Structures developed on the lip of the flower which deceive the pollinator by imitating structures from which the insect would normally collect pollen.

PSEUDOPREY. See pseudoparasitism.

PSYCHOPHILY. Butterfly-pollination.

RACEME. A simple, elongated, indeterminate inflorescence with pedicellate or stalked flowers.

RECOMBINATION. The rearrangement of genes after sexual processes.

RESUPINATION. Twisting or bending so that the part of the flower which is uppermost in the bud (the lip) is on the lower side when the flower matures.

ROSTELLUM. A portion of the stigma which is specialized to take part in the pollen transfer from one flower to another; the tissue which separates the anther and the functional stigma.

SALVIA-TYPE ANTHER. Stamens balanced on a fulcrum so that the anthers depress and touch the pollinator on the dorsum when pushed against.

SAPROMYOPHILY. Pollination by carrion flies.

SCAPE. In plants, a leafless peduncle arising from the ground bearing one to several flowers. In insects, a structure formed by the basal segments of the antennae.

SCUTELLUM. In insects, the posterior part of the dorsal segments of the thorax.

SECTILE. The condition in which soft, granular pollinia are subdivided into small packets interconnected by elastic threads.

SELF-COMPATIBLE. A plant which can produce seed as a result of self-fertilization of ovaries with its own pollen.

SELF-INCOMPATIBLE. A plant or clone incapable of being fertilized by its own pollen.

SELF-POLLINATION. Transference of pollen-grains from anthers to stigma of the same flower or of the same clone.

SEPAL. The outermost, usually green, leaf-like elements in a flower.

SEPTUM. A partition separating two cavities, as in the ovary of many flowers.

SLIDE-FLOWER. Flower developed to be pollinated by insects which fall or slide through as in Stanhopea or Gongora.

SPECIATION. The evolution of species; species formation.

SPHINGOPHILY. Pollination by Sphinx moths.

SPIKE. Inflorescence with sessile flowers along the axis.

SPUR. A slender, tubular or sac-like projection from a flower part; usually containing a nectary; commonly found at the base of the lip.

STAMEN. The male or pollen-bearing element of a flower usually composed of a filament and an anther.

STAMINODE. A vestigial body in some flowers derived from a metamorphosed stamen.

STERNOTRIBY. Anthers of the flower arranged to place pollen on the ventral surface of the abdomen of an insect.

STERNUM. The ventral sclerites of the thoracic segments in insects.

STIGMA. The terminal, receptive portion of the pistil.

STIPE. A non-viscid band or strap of tissue derived from the column which connects the pollinia to the viscidium.

STYLE. The slender portion of the pistil between the ovary and the stigma; forms part of the column in orchids.

SYMPATRIC. Having the same or overlapping areas of geographical distribution (the opposite of allopatric).

SYNDROME. A group of concomitant symptoms; e.g., pollination syndrome—characters which as a group act to attract a particular class of pollinators.

SYNSEPALUM. Organ composed of fused or united sepals.

TABULA-INFRASTIGMATICA. A flat pad located on the column below the stigma in the genus Oncidium.

TAILS. Elongate sepals or petals in such orchid flowers as Masdevallia and Brassia.

TARSI. Distal segments of leg.

TELEOLOGY. The doctrine of adaptation to a definite purpose and that evolution is purposive.

THECA. Structure serving as a protective covering for an organ.

THERMONASTY. Reactions to variations of temperature.

THIGMONASTY. Reaction to contact.

THORAX. In insects, the body region between head and abdomen.

THROAT. Referring to the lip of an orchid flower and in particular to the beginning of the tubular portion.

TRAP-FLOWER. A flower which traps and retains for a specific period the insects which pollinate it.

VENTRAL. The portion or surface turned toward the axis in plants or toward the ground in animals.

VERSATILE. Referring to anthers which are attached so as to swing freely.

VIBRATORS. Hairs or pieces of tissue which move freely with the slightest breeze, thereby attracting flies as pollinators.

VISCIDIUM. A viscid part of the rostellum which is removed with the pollinia as a unit and serves to attach the pollinia to the pollinator.

VISCIN. An elastic or somewhat viscid material which binds together the pollen grains in the pollinia and caudicles.

ZYGOMORPHIC. A flower which can be divided into equal halves along one plane only; bilaterally symmetrical.

ZYGOTE. Cell formed by the union of two gametes or reproductive cells.

INDEX

Illustrations are indicated by asterisks.

Acianthus, 120
Acineta, 68
    A. barkeri, 68
    A. chrysantha, 68
    A. superba, 68
acrotony, 16
Ada, 96, 154
aggregation, 154
Agrotis, 85
Alemania,
    A. punicea, 96
Amastus,
    A. acona, 86*, 87
Amazalia, 95
Ametalla, 121, 123
Anacamptis,
    A. pyramidalis, 90
Anaites, 84
andine forms, 100
Andrena, 23, 36, 39, 40, 132
    A. carbonaria, 39
    A. maculipes, 132*
    A. maotae, 134
    A. nigro-olivacea, 133
    A. trimmerana, 133
Angraecum, 9, 12, 23, 84
    A. eburneum, 8*, 12, 84
    A. sesquipedale, 84, 85*
Andrenidae, 36
Anguloa, 76, 100
    A. clowesii, 76, 115*
    A. ruckeri, 76

antennae, 51
ant-guard, 42
ant-pollination, 123
anther, 5, 15
Anthidium, 36, 39
Anthophora, 79
Anthophorinae, 36
Apathes,
    A. rupestris, 79
Apidae, 36
Apinae, 36
Apis, 31, 34, 36, 76, 90
    A. dorsata, 78
    A. florea, 78
    A. indica, 78, 157
    A. mellifera, 43, 70
Apoidea, 35
apomixis, 127
Apostasioideae, 4, 10, 15, 17, 21, 150, 159
appendicle, 16
Arachnis,
    A. flos-aeris, 25
Arundina
    A. speciosa, 42, 124
attraction, 21
Auglochlora, 40, 78
auricle, 18
autogamy, 124, 159, 165

Barkeria,
    B. lindleyana, 43, 44*
Barlia, 39

barriers (to hybridization)
  34, 73, 134, 164, 166, 170
Bartholina, 86
basitony, 16
bee-flies, 88
bee-flowers, 29, 33
bee-orchid, 130
bees (taxa), 35
beetle-pollination, 31, 121, 123, 146
bird-pollination, 11, 30, 91
Bletia,
  B. catenulata, 43
  B. purpurea, 41, 127
Bombus, 34, 36, 37, 43, 78, 80, 90
  B. americanorum, 78, 79
  B. hortensis, 79
  B. lucorum, 78
  B. morio, 81
  B. robustus var hortulans, 80*, 116*, 140*
  B. separatus, 79
  B. volucellioides, 81
Bombus (distribution), 80
Bonatea, 86
Bradysia, 108*
Brassavola, 21, 27, 84
  B. digbyana, 28*, 87
  B. cucullata, 152*
  B. nodosa, 28*
Brassia
  B. antherotes, 38*
breakdown of barriers, 171
Bromheadia, 156
  B. alticola, 42
  B. aporoides, 42
  B. palustris, 42
brush-type flower, 90, 155
Bulbophyllum, 104
  B. arachnites, 106
  B. barbigerum, 106, 107*
  B. campanulatum, 108
  B. cupreum, 108
  B. emiliorum, 106
  B. fritillariiflorum, 107
  B. grandiflorum, 106
  B. ipanemensis, 107
  B. lobbii, 106*, 108
  B. lupeniorum 119
  B. macranthum, 106, 108
  B. medusae, 106, 107*
  B. ornatissimum, 106, 107*
  B. psittacoides, 106
  B. singaporeanum, 106
bumblebee, 34
bursicle, 16
butterflies, 30, 83, 87

Caenohalictus, 40
Caladenia, 15

C. barbarossae, 38, 139
C. deformis, 50
C. dialata, 139
Calanthe, 126
Caleana, 120
callus, 24, 64
Calochilus, 18
  C. campestris, 38, 142*
Calopogon, 23, 130
  C. barbatus, 40, 43
  C. parviflorus, 40
  C. pulchellus, 40, 41*, 43
Calypso,
  C. borealis, 123
Campsomeris,
  C. columba, 38*
  C. tasmaniesis, 142
cantharophily, 31, 123
cantharis, 37
carpenter bee, 36
Catasetinae, 51, 52
Catasetum, 12, 49, 52, 63
  C. barbatum, 63
  C. bicolor, 63
  C. cernuum, 63
  C. costatum, 63
  C. dilectum, 53
  C. eburneum, 52*
  C. fimbriatum, 63
  C. hookeri, 63
  C. integerrimum, 63
  C. macrocarpum, 63
  C. macroglossum, 49, 53*, 63
  C. maculatum, 63
  C. oerstedii, 63
  C. platyglossum, 57*, 58*, 63
  C. russellianum, 53*
  C. saccatum, 63
  C. tabulare, 63
  C. viridiflavum, 63
Cattleya, 16, 21, 43, 48, 96, 126
  C. aurantiaca, 96, 98*, 124
  C. luteola, 77, 81, 117*
  C. maxima, 23, 47, 48, 56*
  C. medelii, 48
  C. skinneri, 96
  C. warszewiczii, 43, 48, 57
Cattleya hybrids, 49
caudicle, 5, 6, 16*
Centridini, 36
Centris, 41, 44, 55*, 81, 141*
  C. geminata, 118*
Cephalanthera, 15, 16, 18, 36
  C. ensifolia, 37
  C. grandiflora, 39, 124
  C. rubra, 39
Ceratandra, 8, 9, 153
  C. atrata, 25

206

Ceratina,
  C. albilabris, 39
Chamaeorchis, 37
chemoreceptors, 49
Chlerogella, 40*
Chloropidae, 121
chromosome level, 166, 169, 170, 172
Chrysomelidae, 121
Cirrhaea, 72
Cirrhopetalum, 107
classification, 171, 175
cleistogamy, 124
Cochleanthes,
  C. aromatica, 47, 56*
Cochlioda,
  C. rosea, 97*
  C. vulcanica, 89, 95
Coeliopsis,
  C. hyacinthosma, 67, 61*
Coeloglossum,
  C. viride, 37, 122
Coelogyne, 43
  C. lawrenciana, 77
Coerebidae, 92
Coleman, E, 40, 121, 134
Colletidae, 36, 81
color, 24
column, 5, 15, 17
column foot, 5
Comparettia,
  C. falcata, 95, 96*
compatibility, 124, 164
concurrent speciation, 165
connation, 119, 153
constancy of bees, 31, 157
convergence, 108, 109, 112, 156, 160, 161
Coryanthes, 72, 100
  C. albo-rosea, 73
  C. bicalcarata, 73, 114*
  C. leucocorys, 73, 114*
  C. macrantha, 72, 73
  C. maculata, 73
  C. rodriguezii, 73, 113*
  C. speciosa, 72, 75*
  C. trifoliata, 73, 113*
  C. wolfii, 75
Corybas, 120
  C. himalaica, 151
Coryciinae, 151
Corycium, 153
Corysanthes, 120, 151
Crabro, 37
Cranichis,
  C. ciliata, 168
  C. cucullata, 168
Crüger, 51, 72, 75
Cryptanthemis, 126

Cryptochilus, 154
  C. sanguinea, 96
Cryptophoranthus, 108*, 161
Cryptostylis, 12, 38, 134
  C. erecta, 134
  C. leptochila, 134, 135*
  C. ovata, 134
  C. subulata, 134, 135*
Cryptus, 36, 37
Culicidae, 120
Cycnoches, 8, 17, 64, 165
  C. aureum, 60*
  C. egertonianum, 52, 59*, 61*, 65
  C. lehmanii, 59*, 64
  C. pentadactylon, 65
  C. ventricosum, 65
  C. warszewiczii, 20*, 64
Cymbidium, 16, 24, 43, 159
  C. aloifolium, 43
  C. devonianum, 50
  C. finlaysoniaium, 78
Cypripedioideae, 10, 23, 103
Cypripedium, 40, 103*, 104, 159
  C. arietinum, 40*
  C. calceolus, 23, 40
  C. spectabile, 40
Cyrtidium 137
Cyrtopodium, 51
Cyrtostomus, 95

Dactylorchis, 79
Darwin, i, 17, 22, 51, 66, 67, 79, 84, 89, 90,
    119, 123, 124, 131, 146, 150, 154, 163
Deilephila, 85
Delpino, 28, 79, 104
Dendrobium, 22, 25, 156
  D. apendiculatum, 156
  D. crumenatum, 78, 157*
  D. flammula, 95
  D. hasseltii, 95
  D. lawesii, 95, 98*
  D. linguiforme, 122
  D. nobile, 157
  D. roseum, 95
  D. secundum, 95
  D. sophronitis, 95
  D. superbum, 78
Dendrochilum, 154
  D. longifolia, 123
deposition of pollen, 17, 149
diagram of flower, 15
dichogamy, 18, 52, 67
dicliny, 52
digger wasps, 35, 37, 132
Disa, 12, 25, 86, 88, 94, 151
  D. bivalvata, 124, 152
  D. cornuta, 122

D. *crassicornis*, 88
D. *draconis*, 88
D. *ferruginea*, 94
D. *fragrans*, 86
D. *lugens*, 25, 122
D. *macrantha*, 86
D. *polygonoides*, 88
D. *porrecta*, 94
D. *racemosa*, 88
D. *uniflora*, 12, 88*, 152
D. *zeyheri*, 94
Disinae, 151
disk-shape, 153
Disperis, 89, 153
Diuris, 17, 22
D. *pedunculata*, 25, 40, 138
D. *sulphurea*, 138
Drakaea, 120
Drepanididae, 92

Elleanthus, 155
E. *arpophyllostachys*, 95
E. *aurantiacus*, 95
E. *aureus*, 95, 96, 99*
E. *capitatus*, 93*, 94, 155
E. *hallii*, 95
E. *hymenophorus*, 95*
E. *rosea*, 95
emergence of male bees, 133, 141
Empis, 86, 122
Encyclia, (see also Epidendrum) 27, 44
E. *crassilabia*, 43*
E. *cochleata*, 127
E. *pentotis*, 38*
endosperm, 149, 166
ephemeral flowers, 156
epichile, 13, 73
Epidendrum (see also Encyclia) 27, 30, 86, 89
E. *acuminatum*, 43
E. *arachnoglossum*, 86
E. *ardens*, 99*, 100
E. *ciliare*, 86
E. *difforme*, 86*, 87
E. *ibaguense*, 92*
E. *fimbriatum*, 121*, 122
E. *latilabre*, 87
E. *nocturnum*, 26, 127
E. *paniculatum*, 117*
E. *pfavii*, 95
E. *pseudepidendrum*, 95
E. *purpurascens*, 86
E. *radicans*, 89
E. *scabrum*, 100
E. *secundum*, 89, 171
Epipactis, 22, 37
E. *latifolia*, 37, 124
E. *palustris*, 37

E. *rubiginosa*, 37
E. *viridiflora*, 37
epiphytic habit, 144, 165
Epipogium,
E. *aphyllum*, 12, 78
E. *roseum*, 79
Eria, 22, 156
E. *ignea*, 96, 156
E. *loheriana*, 158
E. *monostachya*, 22
E. *ornata*, 156
E. *paniculata*, 22
E. *vulpina*, 24
Eristalis, 80, 122
Eucera, 39, 132*, 133
E. *tuberculata*, 133
E. *longicornis*, 36
Euglossa, 24, 34, 44, 45, 71
E. *augaspis*, 57
E. *azureovirdis*, 73
E. *championi*, 66
E. *cordata*, 63, 66, 73, 75*, 114*
E. *dodsoni*, 71, 112*
E. *gorgonensis*, 69
E. *hemichlora*, 34, 61*, 66*, 74*
E. *ignita*, 61*, 62*, 70, 73, 111*, 113*, 114*
E. *nigropilosa*, 65, 68, 70, 72
E. *purpurata*, 69
E. *purpurea*, 62
E. *townsendii*, 51
E. *viridissima*, 65, 66, 70, 73, 111, 112
Euglossini, 34, 36, 44, 140
Eulaema, 45, 49, 50, 69
E. *basalis*, 73
E. *boliviensis*, 76, 115*
E. *bomboides*, 53*, 70
E. *cingulata*, 46*, 48*, 50*, 52*, 53*, 55*, 57*, 59*, 67, 73
E. *leucopyga*, 71
E. *meriana*, 61*, 66, 67, 70, 71*, 111*
E. *nigrita*, 60, 65, 68
E. *polychroma*, 53*, 55*, 56*, 57*, 63, 71
E. *seabrae*, 56*, 70*
E. *speciosa*, 70, 111*
Eulophia,
E. *horsfallii*, 24, 42, 78
Euplusia, 45
E. *auriceps*, 63
E. *combinata*, 63
E. *concava*, 68, 69
E. *macroglossa*, 74*
E. *purpurata*, 49*, 69
E. *schmidtiana*, 67, 69
E. *superba*, 65, 73, 113*
E. *surinamensis*, 45*, 48*, 50*
E. *violacea*, 63, 72
extrafloral nectar, 22, 42

farnesol, 26
fidelity, 33
flag-type, 11, 12, 84, 152, 153
food-hairs, 23
fly-flowers, 30, 101, 161
frenicle, 16
frog-pollination, 123

Galea, 119
Gastrodia,
    G. javanica, 122
Gaultheria, 99*
generic hybrids, 170
genome-recombination, 146
gnats, 120
Goebel, 145, 158, 161
Goethe, 145
Gongora, 8, 10, 71
    G. armeniaca, 71, 112*
    G. grossa, 71, 74*
    G. horichiana, 71, 112*
    G. maculata, 75
    G. quinquenervis, 75
Good, 160
Goodyera,
    G. repens, 79
Gorytes, 132, 133
    G. mystaceus, 132*
Gramineae, 144
Grammatophyllum,
    G. speciosum, 43, 70, 156, 158
Grammoptera, 124
granular pollen, 16, 104, 119
gregarious flowering, 156
guidance 13, 25, 102
gullet-type, 12, 146, 151
Gymnadenia,
    G. conopsea, 84, 169
    G. albida, 87, 160
gynostemium, 15

Habenaria, 5, 11, 84
    H. dialata, 85
    H. drageana, 85
    H. galpini, 85
    H. hyperborea, 85
    H. grandiflora, 85
    H. leucostachys, 85
    H. leucophaea, 85
    H. polyphylla, 25, 85
    H. polyphyodontha, 85
    H. psycodes, 85
    H. obtusata, 122
    H. tetrapetala, 85
habitat disturbance, 167, 171
Hadenia, 84
Haemaria, 16
    H. discolor, 89*

Halictidae, 36, 40
Halictus, 3, 37, 38, 39
    H. languinosus, 25, 40, 138
    H. subinclinans, 50
Hartwegia, 96, 102
hawk moths, 29, 83
Heliconia, 117*
Hemiteles, 36
Heriades, 36, 39
Herminium, 125
    H. monorchis, 37, 124
Hesperiidae, 87, 89
heteranthy, 156
Hexisia, 96
Himantoglossum,
    H. hircinum, 38
    H. longibracteatum, 39
hinge, 67
Hippotion,
    H. celeris, 85
Holothrix, 86
honeybee, (see Apis)
hummingbirds, 91, 171
Huntleya,
    H. meleagris, 47*
hybridization, 84, 165, 166
hygronasty, 158
Hymenoptera, 35
hypochile, 13, 73

Ichneumon flies, 36, 37, 38, 122, 134
incompatibility, 124, 159, 166, 170
intoxication, 40, 49, 120, 138
introgression, 164, 167
Isochilus,
    I. carnosiflorus, 95
isolation, 170

Kegeliella,
    K. atropilosa, 69
kettle-type, 119, 154
Kullenberg, 26, 42, 78, 133
labellum, 4, 7, 10

Laelia, 27, 94
    L. anceps, 28*
    L. harpophylla, 28*
    L. muelleri, 95
lantern-type, 102, 107, 161
leap-frog speciation, 164
Leochilus, 38
Lepidoptera, 29, 83
lesion-effects, 159
Leptura, 124
Leucania, 90
Leucorchis,
    L. albida, 87
Limodorum,
    L. abortivum, 39

lip (see labellum)
Liparis,
   L. caespitosa, 127
Lissochilus, 42, 78, 123
Lissopimpla,
   L. semipunctata, 38, 134, 135*
Listera, 15, 22
   L. cordata, 122
   L. liliefolia, 122
   L. ovata, 37*, 124, 154
longevity, 156
loose pollen, 16, 104, 119
Lycaste, 51
   L. ciliata, 82
   L. gigantea, 82, 100
   L. denningiana, 82*
Lycoria, 109*, 119

Macodes, 10, 89
Macrodactylus, 19, 24
Macroglossa, 83, 84
Malpighia, 141*, 142
Masdevallia, 108
   M. coccinea, 109
   M. erythrochaete, 108
   M. fractiflexa, 109, 117*
   M. muscosa, 109
   M. rosea, 94*, 95
maze-relation, 147, 160
Maxillaria, 23, 95
   M. divaricata, 24
   M. flavo-viride, 24
   M. fletcheriana, 31
   M. fulgens, 96
   M. furstenbergae, 77, 115*
   M. grandiflora, 23, 46*, 47
   M. lepidota, 122
   M. reichenheimiana, 77
   M. rufescens, 23, 25
   M. sanderiana, 23, 47, 55*
   M. veriferum, 24
Megachile, 40, 78
Megachilidae, 7, 36
Megaclinium, 108, 156
Meliphagidae, 92
Melipona, 36, 76
   M. beecheii, 76
   M. eburnea, 77, 115*
   M. flavipennis, 81, 117*
melittophily, 29
Meneris, 83
mentum, 22
microclimate, 166, 167
micro-species, 164
Mierycilium,
   M. gemma, 96
Miltonia,
   M. endresii, 81, 116*

M. vexellaria, 81
M. phalaenopsis, 81
M. roezlii, 81
mimicry, 129
Monomeria, 119
monophily, 32
Monosepalum, 108
monotropic insects, 31
Mormodes, 9, 17
   M. atropurpurea, 66
   M. buccinator, 61*, 66*
   M. cartonii, 66
   M. flavidum, 66
   M. ignea, 66
   M. lineatum, 65*, 66
   M. powellii, 66
   M. uncia, 66
Mormolyca, 137
mosquito, 39, 122
moths, 29, 83
motile labellum, 100, 106, 109, 120, 122
mycotrophy, 149
myophily, 30, 101
Myrmechis, 127

nectar, 21
nectar-guide, 13, 92
Nectariniidae, 92
nectary, 4, 22, 77
Nelsson, 12, 145
Nemestrinids, 89
Neottia, 15
Neottiae, 16
Nephelaphyllum, 87
Neuwiedia, 11*
Nigritella, 12, 90
Noctuidae, 29, 83
nocturnal bees, 81
non-resupination, 9, 12, 63, 64, 90, 106, 120
nototriby, 7, 11, 12, 84
Notylia
   N. barkeri, 22
   N. buchtenii, 57*
   N. bicolor, 155
   N. xyphorius, 48*, 155*
number of ovules, 149, 166

Oberonia, 108
Odontoglossum,
   O. flavescens, 100
   O. grande, 24, 41, 55*, 141
   O. kegeljani, 24, 75, 80*
   O. mystacinum, 100
   O. retusum, 96, 99
Ocrateus, 95
odor, 25
odor guide, 25
odor regulation, 63, 159
Odyneros, 40

oil-secretion, 104
oligophily, 32
oligolectic bees, 22, 32
oligotropic bees, 31
Oncidium, 16, 18, 124, 140, 142, 156
    O. abortivum, 156
    O. glossomystax, 125, 126*, 168
    O. heteranthum, 156
    O. hyphaematicum, 24, 41, 140
    O. longicornu, 24
    O. macranthum, 24, 116*
    O. ochmatochilum, 41, 141
    O. onustum, 43*
    O. ostlundianum, 125
    O. papilio, 164
    O. planilabre, 24, 41, 190, 118*
    O. pulvinatum, 24
    O. pusillum, 164, 167, 168*
    O. pumilio, 164, 167, 168*
    O. stipitatum, 141
one-day orchids, 157
opening-time, 158
Ophrys, 130, 131
    O. apifera, 125*, 132, 133
    O. arachnitiformis, 133
    O. atlantica, 133
    O. bombylifera, 133
    O. fuciflora, 133
    O. fusca, 134
    O. insectifera, 132*, 133
    O. lutea, 132*
    O. murbeckii, 134, 169
    O. muscifera, 133
    O. scolopax, 133
    O. speculum, 132*, 133
    O. tenthredinifera, 132*, 133*
Orchis, 90, 125
    (see Leucorchis, Anacamptis, Traunsteinera,
      Dactylorchis, Gymnadenia)
    O. latifolia, 22, 79, 80, 122, 169, 170
    O. laxiflora, 170
    O. maculata, 37, 78, 79, 80, 122
    O. mascula, 17, 79
    O. militaris, 40
    O. morio, 78, 79, 169
    O. praetermissa, 79
    O. purpurea, 40
    O. spectabilis, 79
    O. tridentatus, 79
    O. ustulata, 90, 169
Ornithocephalus, 41
    O. avicula, 55*
ornithophily, 30, 91
oscillator, 102
Osmia, 36, 39
Osmophore, 25, 102

ovary, 4, 159
ovule-retardation, 159
ovules, 4, 159
Pachdynerus, 38
Pangonia, 89
Pantrope insignis, 95
Paphinia
    P. clausula, 69*
Paphiopedilum, 40, 103*, 159
    P. barbatum, 104
    P. fairreanum, 104
    P. insigne, 104
    P. purpuratum, 104
    P. villosum, 104
Papilio, 89
    P. polyxenes, 117*
Paracolletes, 25, 40, 138
Paragymnomma, 136*
parallelism, 108, 109, 122, 156, 160, 161
Paratetrapedia,
    P. testacea, 55*
parrot-colors, 93
pedicel (see stipe), 16
Peristeria
    P. elata, 68, 129
    P. pendula, 62*, 68
Pescatorea, 51
    P. wallisii, 57*
Phajus, 22
    P. tankervilliae, 42, 124
Phalaenopsis,
    P. amabilis, 25, 42
    P. violacca, 159
Phalenophily, 29, 83
photonasty, 158
Phragmopedium, 40, 103*, 159
    P. caudatum, 104, 125
    P. grande, 104
    P. lindeni, 125, 127*
    P. longifolium, 40, 104, 105*
phylogenetic lines, 151
physiology, 19, 52, 63, 145, 149, 157,
    158, 161
Physosiphon, 154
plan behind flowers, 160, 165
Platanthera, 84
    P. bifolia, 85
    P. blumei, 85
    P. chlorantha, 85
    P. ciliaris, 85
    P. fimbriata, 85
    P. leucostachys, 85
Platyclinus,
    P. longifolia, 124
Plecopterid, 36
Pleione, 43
Pleisconeura, 89

Pleurothallis, 108, 119
   P. cardiothallus, 119
   P. eumecocaulon, 119
   P. monocardia, 109*, 119
   P. ornata, 119
   P. redmondii, 22
   P. ruscifolia, 119
   P. schiedei, 109*, 119
   P. xanthochlora, 119
Plocoglottis,
   P. foetida, 121
   P. porphyrophylla, 121
Plusia, 80, 84
pollen-deposition, 17
pollen-imitation, 22, 132
pollinarium bending, 17, 64, 154
pollinator spectrum, 128, 146
pollination stimulus, 158
pollination-unit, 151
pollinium, 5, 16
Polycycnis,
   P. gratiosa, 62*, 69
polyploidy, 168
Pohl, 73, 106
Polyrrhiza,
   P. lindeni, 142*, 144
Polystachya, 22
   P. luteola, 23
   P. lineata, 23
polytropic bees, 31
Porpax,
   P. meirax, 144
Porphyroglottis,
   P. maxwelliae, 139
Porsch, 64, 100
post-pollination changes, 159
Prasophyllum, 126
   P. archeri, 121
   P. dispectans, 121
   P. gracile, 121
   P. morrisii, 121
   P. mulleri, 121
   P. nigricans, 121
   P. odoratum, 123
primitivity, 41
progression, 147
Prosopis, 36
protandry (flowers) 36, 52, 67
protandry (bees) 133, 140
pseudoantagonism, 140
pseudocopulation, 131
pseudonectaries, 79, 130, 131
pseudopollen, 22
pseudoparasitism, 142
Psychodidae, 119
psychophily, 29, 27
Pterostemma, 47

Pterostylis, 16, 109*, 119, 120*, 126
   P. mutica, 119
   P. trullifolia, 119
Ptiloglossa, 36, 81
   P. ducalis, 116*

rachis-flattening, 108, 156
reception (of pollen) 15, 17
repellant (to visits), 34
Restrepia, 119
   R. xanthopthalma, 108*
resupination, 4, 7, 153
reticulate relations, 147, 160
Renanthera,
   R. lowii, 156
Rhizanthella, 126
Rodriguezia,
   R. secunda, 92*, 95
rostellum, 5, 15, 124

Saccolabium, 96
sapromyophily, 30, 101
Satyrium, 8, 10, 12, 86, 152
   S. odorum, 86
   S. pumilum, 122, 156
   S. saxicolum, 122
saw flies, 35, 36, 37
Scaphosepalum, 119
Scaphyglottis, 22
Schlimia,
   S. trifida, 51*, 69
Schomburgkia, 126
   S. crispa, 77
   S. lyonsii, 44
   S. splendida, 44
Scoliidae, 38, 133, 142
seed dispersal, 149, 167
seed retardation, 159
Selenipedium, 40
   S. palmifolium, 104
self-incompatibility, 154
self-pollination,
   (see autogamy), 75, 80, 124
self-pollination toxicity, 159
sensitive anthers, 51, 66
sensitive labellum, 109, 120, 121, 122
Serapias, 39*
   S. cordigera, 39, 169
   S. neglecta, 169
sex determination, 52
sexuality, 146
shapes of flowers, 151
Sievekingia
   S. fimbriata, 69
   S. jenmannii, 68*
   S. suavis, 68
skippers, 87
slide-flower, 70, 75, 106, 153

Sobralia, 5, 22, 43, 47, 50, 156
    S. amabilis, 95, 97*
    S. decora, 82
    S. macrantha, 50
    S. rosea, 50, 81
    S. violacea, 45*, 50*, 81, 156
    S. aff. weberbaueriana, 43, 55*
social bees, 31, 32, 76
solitary bees, 31, 35, 38, 132
Sophronitis, 96
Spathoglottis,
    S. plicata, 22
Spathiphyllum, 50*
speciation, 157, 163
Sphecidae, 35, 132
Sphingidae, 12, 83, 87
Sphingophily, 12, 29, 83
Sphinx, 85
spider-orchids, 86
Spiranthes, 5, 16
    S. aestivalis, 87
    S. autumnalis, 78, 154
    S. gracilis, 78
    S. romanzoffiana, 78
    S. speciosa, 96, 99*
    S. standleyi, 96
spur, 22, 79, 84, 88, 153
Stanhopea, 67, 69, 75, 100, 164
    S. annulata, 69
    S. candida, 70, 111*
    S. cirrhata, 69
    S. connata, 70, 111*
    S. costaricensis, 70
    S. ecornuta, 69
    S. florida, 70, 72*
    S. gibbosa, 70, 71*
    S. grandiflora, 70
    S. graveolens, 169
    S. jenishiana, 70
    S. lewisae, 169
    S. oculata, 71
    S. pulla, 69
    S. reichenbachiana, 71
    S. saccata, 71, 73*
    S. tigrina, 70, 111*
    S. tricornis, 70, 111*
    S. wardii, 71
    S. warscewicziana, 71, 74*
Stanhopeinae, 25, 52, 67
stelidium, 18
Stelis, 22, 108, 158
    S. aemula, 108*, 109
Stellilabium, 135
    S. microglossum, 138*
Stenoptera,
    S. pilifera, 96
sterility, 144
sternotriby, 11, 36, 152

stigma, 5, 18
stigmatic fluid, 6, 18, 124
stipe, 6
Strangalia, 123
sugar birds, 92
sun birds, 92
swan orchid, 64
sympetaly, 119, 153, 154
Symphoglossum, 96
    S. sanguineum, 99*
synchrony (with bees), 134
synchronous flowering, 156
syndrome, 28
synsepalum, 119
Syrphidae, 101, 104, 122
Syrphus, 40, 105*, 122
system of taxa, 175

Tabanidae, 89
tabula infrastigmatica, 18
Tachinidae, 122, 136
tails, 102, 104, 106, 108, 120
taxonomic groups, 170, 175
Telipogon, 135, 137*
Tenthredinae, 35, 37
Terebranthes, 35
Thelymitra, 11, 16, 18, 126, 158
    T. javanica, 126
thermonasty, 158
Thrixspermum, 156, 157
Thygater, 41
Tipula, 122
torsion, 12
toxicity of pollen, 159
trap flowers, 23, 102, 120
Traunsteinera
    T. globosa, 90, 155
triandrous form, 125
Trichocentrum,
    T. tigrinum, 48*
Trichoceros, 135
    T. antennifera, 130*, 135*
Trichoglossidae, 92
Trichopilia, 51
Trielis,
    T. ciliata, 132*, 133
Trigona, 36, 77, 139
    T. amalthea, 77, 115*
    T. droryana, 78, 139*
    T. nebulata, 78
    T. nigrior, 77
    T. testacea, 77
Trigonidium, 137
    T. obtusum, 77*, 137, 139*
Trogoderma, 121, 123
trumpet shape, 87
tubate flowers, 92, 152, 153
tubercle, 67

unisexuality, 52
Urbanus, 89

Vanda, 22, 42, 159
   V. *hookeriana*, 42
   V. *teres*, 42
Vandopsis, 24, 43
   V. *lowii*, 156
Vanilla, 23, 77, 125
Vespa, 37
Vespidae, 35
Vespoidea, 35
viscidium, 5, 6, 15, 84
viscin, 15
Vogel, 41, 50, 94, 102, 139, 151, 160

wasps, 33, 36, 122, 132, 133
wax secretion, 24
windows, 102, 107
window orchids, 109, 161

Xanthopan,
   X. *morgani*, 84, 165
Xylobium, 77
   X. *latilabrum*, 115*
Xylocopa, 34, 39, 41
   X. *fimbriata*, 44
   X. *frontalis*, 43*
   X. *lachnea*, 44
   X. *latipes*, 42
   X. *micans*, 40, 43
   X. *tabaniformis*, 43, 44*
   X. *transitoria*, 43*
   X. *tricuspidifera*, 43
   X. *viridis*, 43

Zingiberaceae, 10, 12, 143
Zygaena, 84, 90
Zygopetalum, 24, 75